WE ARE HERE, WALKING TOWARD THE UNKNOWN

Published May 2017 by 826 Valencia
Copyright © 2017 by 826 Valencia
All rights reserved by 826 Valencia and the authors

ISBN 978-1-934750-88-9

Mission Center **Tenderloin Center**
826 Valencia Street 180 Golden Gate Avenue
San Francisco, CA 94110 San Francisco, CA 94102

826valencia.org

PROGRAM MANAGER & MANAGING EDITOR
Ryan Young

EDUCATION DIRECTOR
Christina V. Perry

EDITORIAL ASSISTANT
Dana Belott

VOLUNTEER EDITORS
Courtney Aldor, Shanika Badoya-Mulkerin, Dana Belott, Randie Bencannan, Tehan Carey, Emily Downey, Lucie Duffort, Jake Murphy, Sean Nishi, David Rosen, Karen Sabine, Kaci Vargas

STUDENT EDITORS
Vonnie K., Trevor S., Derrick W., Holly Y.

DESIGN DIRECTOR
Meghan Ryan

PRODUCTION MANAGER
Amy Popovich

DESIGNER
Laura Bagnato

ILLUSTRATOR
Matt Leunig

COPYEDITOR
Helaine Lasky Schweitzer

PRODUCTION ARTIST
Terri Bogaards

Printed in Canada by Prolific Group

The views expressed in this book are those of the authors and the authors' imaginations. We support student publishing and are thrilled that you picked up this book!

◆826 Valencia◆

WE ARE HERE, WALKING TOWARD THE UNKNOWN

Narratives about Adapting

*by students at Phillip & Sala Burton
Academic High School*

TABLE OF CONTENTS

A TURNING POINT FOR HUMANITY
Transforming, Changing

AS I REALLY AM
Questioning, Searching

THE SILVER LINING
Embracing, Accepting

FOREWORD

———

You hold in your hands an incredible collection of writing by a phenomenal group of student authors. The title they chose for this book, *We Are Here, Walking toward the Unknown*, is also a fitting title for this year: it's the fifteenth anniversary of our free writing, tutoring, and publishing programs for students in San Francisco, and we're doing a lot of looking back and looking forward as we celebrate how we've grown and chart the path forward.

We believe that hard work and lots of support—not magic, thunderbolts, or a laboratory experiment—are what creates strong writing skills. So, as we reflect on where we are, where we're headed, and all the adventures this year has brought us, we decided to kick off this collection with a list of the Top Fifteen Things We've Learned from This Book, Mary Shelley's *Frankenstein*, and fifteen years of 826 Valencia.

1. *If you open a Pirate Supply Store and it sells lard, people will buy your lard.* Similarly, if you're worried that your writing is too strange, too personal, or too smelly (lard is smelly), just put it out there anyway. You'll be surprised by how well it's received!

2. *Set forth and explore.* We did this by opening a second writing and tutoring center in the Tenderloin last year, and our community has grown enormously. Always strive to grow your community of writers.

3. *Writing requires vulnerability, which can be scary.* Take heart from Zabrina B.'s advice on page 36: "Do the thing you fear the most and continue to do so because when you have experienced your fear, it won't be as bad as you thought."

4. *Find a thought partner.* This is a cornerstone of the 826 approach: sitting down one-on-one with a student or a mentor results in huge leaps in learning and writing skills. Find a pal and let them help you.

5. *Don't trust the robots.* Just don't (see pages 46, 110, 142, & 192).

6. *Publishing is magic.* Actually, publishing is a lot of hard work. But as Victor

Frankenstein reflects, the work is worth it: "After so much time spent in painful labor, to arrive at once at the summit of my desires was the most gratifying consummation of my toils." Young authors, remember all that time spent in painful labor? Look what you created!

7. *Publishing is also a big responsibility.* Be careful when bestowing life to words. Once you bring a book, an idea, or a well-intentioned but unnaturally strong creature into the world, it may take on a life of its own.

8. *Teachers are amazing people.* To all the teachers out there, and especially to Mr. Chow, our partner teacher for this book project: thank you.

9. *Seek feedback.* At 826 Valencia, we believe in the importance of feedback and revision, and all of our programs are responsive to our students and communities. It's an ever-evolving model that we always strive to improve and grow. Think of your writing the same way.

10. *But don't be afraid to be unique.* We are the only writing and tutoring center in the world that is also a pirate supply store and an explorer's emporium curated by a traveling pufferfish. If you find another, please inform us immediately.

11. *Balance is key.* Don't be like Victor Frankenstein. If, two years into writing your novel, you notice you've "seemed to have lost all soul or sensation but for this one pursuit," it's time for a break.

12. *A change in scenery can work wonders.* Writers' block got you down? Consumed by guilt after unleashing a vengeful creature on the ones you love? Whatever ails you, *Frankenstein* tells us to seek comfort and inspiration from nature. The treehouse in the 826 Valencia Tenderloin Center, perhaps?

13. *Writing can reveal our complexity and shared humanity.* Or, as Kayla A. says on page 240, "You should not look at someone and make a judgement based on their appearance." This book is full of examples of people defying expectations and stereotypes.

14. *Make sure your head's on straight.* Sometimes when you're creating a creature (or piece of writing) from scratch, things get weird. Just, you know, try not to let it get too weird.

15. *Writing matters.* Writing is agency; it is a source of power and strength. With strong writing skills, you can tell your story, inspire others, access opportunities, and foster empathy in the world around you. So, whether you think of yourself as a writer already or you're just getting started, the most important thing we've learned from this book, all books, and fifteen years of 826 Valencia is this: your words matter.

With that we send you forth to read and write, to delight and find inspiration in the pages that follow, and perhaps to come up with fifteen more lessons of your own. Onward!

The Staff of 826 Valencia

INTRODUCTION

◆

BY TREVOR S., DERRICK W., AND HOLLY Y.

of the Young Authors' Book Project Editorial Board

This is a book that we have created. We of Mr. Chow's English class. We of the Burton Pumas. We, the young and brash, have poured out our souls into creating this work of literature. Worlds were created and hidden thoughts left from our lips. Things we thought were too emotional, too weak to say just flowed onto paper, as if this. . . *this* was what we were waiting for. Maybe this was that one little push we needed to let loose everything we locked deep inside. And so, we did, and so, here we are. Take hold of this book and see us for who we really are.

It all started with a book: *Frankenstein.* An old classic that no one had thought much of. Many were reluctant to read it, to decipher ancient, confusing words. Even more so when it came to writing stories that were based off of it. What kind of tale were we supposed to tell? What in the world did we have that was worth showing others? As it was, we were lost, we were absurd, we were a mess. It took much talk with our *very helpful* tutors to bring us together and really take a look at the book for what it really was. An emotional tale of suffering and self-discovery. We took that and we used that as the basis of our writing. Some empathized with the monster, some put themselves in Victor's shoes. Whatever it was, we dug deep into our souls to bring forth this *masterpiece.*

Right from the beginning, the relationship between student and tutor was an intimate one. We broke the ice by talking about personal life. In less than thirty minutes, most were talking with one another as if they were old friends. We started with brainstorming, as ideas were generated and bounced between students and tutors in order to mold the stories that you will read in this book. The tutors shared with us this wisdom on creative writing as we pieced together more of our ideas and thoughts together. As we neared the end of our writing, the tutors took a step back as we made the final sprint, jumping in for brief moments to add in final edits to our piece. Without the tutors, the writing process would have been a mess as prominent issues such as writing blocks or plot holes would occur.

The hard work did not end with the final edit. As some students let out a sigh of relief, the editorial board began to meld all their works into a single body of work. We were a small group of students and tutors interested in how a collection of stories becomes a book. We were surprised by how meticulous the editing process was as we spent hours reading and re-reading stories for small grammatical errors. It all turned around during the design process when we grouped together to decide on how the sections would be formatted. We played off individual strengths as we brainstormed about recurring imagery and built a list of ideas for the cover. This was the fun part as we gathered together.

Looking back on this process, we have learned a lot. About ourselves and our pasts. We were able to draw upon these self-discoveries and use the common themes to write our stories. We can look at our classmates and draw parallels, or see differences in experiences, and see each other's hearts and minds poured on paper. This has been an enlightening experience, which our mentors have been a big part of, that will stay with us forever. We have learned to make our writing our own, and think about writing in a more personal light.

In reading this book, you will take a peek into our lives. The book has personal struggles that someone you know might be going through. You can bring our experiences to them and shine a ray of light into their endeavor. This school is a judgement free zone which you will hopefully take with you and spread in your life. This book will last forever, so whether you are looking at it in the present or the future, take our stories with you.

A TURNING POINT FOR HUMANITY

Transforming, Changing

LIFELESS

AGLOW L.

*was born in San Francisco and is seventeen years old.
She loves to sing her heart out, dance like nobody's
watching, draw until her hand cramps, and read 'til her
eyes burn. She plans on going to community college and
transferring to a state school with an associate degree
in psychology or English.*

Water kept dripping from the rusting pipes on the ceiling onto the grime-coated platform of the substation. Rats the size of kittens scattered across from under the three-legged table to the corner of the room. The smell of feces hovered in the air. Stolen lab equipment littered the floor. Footsteps echoed as a dark shadow lurked in the doorway. It entered the dimly lit room and stepped under the single light bulb hanging from the ceiling. His wrinkled face was covered in unevenly trimmed facial hair and a furrowed brow. He was dressed in nothing but old shoes, khakis, and a browning lab coat with the name of his past forever engraved on his chest: Dr. Vitae. His graying hair was encrusted with dust. His hunched shoulders ruined his posture. Due to his discovery and research, he'd lost his job at the local laboratory a couple of years back. Without the job, he lost his house. As if things could not have gotten worse, he lost his wife to leukemia. Dr. Vitae had nothing else to lose.

He sat there, thinking of his past. After years of research, he had never done solid experiments where he could use test subjects to complete his work. Before he was fired, he worked alongside many local scientists of Jamestown Laboratory where they were conducting cutting edge research. The only thing that they were able to clone were the mice subjects in the lab. Trying to take the experiment a step further, Dr. Vitae proposed to the board of scientists using human subjects for the experiment.

"We're sorry, Dr. Vitae, but our experiments are meant to help people, not kill more people. What if your experiments and research are all wrong?" Dr. Priscilla Odi said.

"But this research will help people! It will keep them alive even after they die!"

"Mr. Vitae, I would watch that tone of yours if I were you," another scientist warned.

"I'm very sorry Dr. Vitae," Dr. Odi said, "but we can't have you working here with a proposal like that. And also, we looked into your background and remember that health record of yours. Schizophrenia? We have been very careful with you, but we're very sorry to let you go—"

"What? Let me go?" Dr. Vitae screamed.

"Let me explain!" Dr. Odi waited for Dr. Vitae to scream again, but instead he was silent, and then she continued, "Thank you. As I was saying, we need to let you go. We cannot have anyone with schizophrenia working in this laboratory."

Dr. Vitae did not know that proposing the idea would lead to the death of his career.

Now he was trapped in the infested substation with something small in the corner, hiding under a black tarp. Dr. Vitae proceeded closer to it. He uncovered what was under the piece of plastic and stared at the decaying body before him. He caressed the body and tears welled up in his eyes.

"I will bring you back, Amare. Even if it's the last thing I do," his voice was low and hoarse. His unevenly trimmed facial hair moved along with every word that slowly lingered out of his mouth. He covered the decaying body with the tarp and stumbled toward the other end of the platform.

"Why don't you just get rid of that bloody thing?" Trelós spoke with a British accent. The two had been together for many years, although they'd never met.

"That 'bloody' thing there is my wife," Dr. Vitae said.

"Well, it's stinking up the place."

"You're just a voice inside my head."

"Bruv, whatever you smellin' up out there, I can definitely smell it in here."

"Just go away, Trelós."

"Can't there, mate. I'm stuck with you forever."

"Just get out of my head!"

"I have an idea. How about you take all this stuff with your wife, take it to the lab and create a clone of her. You have all the research, you just need the tools. Then you can get rid of the decomposing wife sitting pretty over there in that corner."

"That's not that bad of an idea," Dr. Vitae hummed as he grabbed a bag.

Already having samples of his wife's DNA—hair follicles, a chunk of skin, and saliva—Dr. Vitae gathered all of his things and packed them in a bag, research and all. He gave the decaying body one last longing look before walking out into the shadows.

Trying his best to clean himself up, he started to climb up the crumbling steps. Unchaining the rusty fence, he opened it and wandered out of the substation. Walking up on the surface for the first time in so many years, he glanced around him and when lights from a corner store shone in his eyes, he moved into the shadows. Block after block he traveled through the shadows and it wasn't until a memory flashed through his mind that he recognized where he was. He was close to his destination, close to his dear wife, Amare. He stopped at the sign saying "Jamestown Laboratory" with an arrow pointing left. He followed the arrow and started making his way to the back of the lab. He walked to the back, thinking how easy it had been for him to walk by, and saw movement near the dumpster. He froze as he waited for the figure to move into the light, and when it did, he was shocked to see that his friend Jim was still working here as a janitor. Looking at the door, he was surprised to see it open. Quickly, before Jim had noticed, he swiftly moved into the building where his career had once lived.

He raced to the elevator to get to the nearest lab room. There, he quickly locked the door and dumped all of the contents in his bag unto the counter. He gazed around to see the hospital-like room. The lab room was recently polished after a day's work. He hooked up machines here and there, but at once he took a glance at the machine that was hiding in the back of all the others. He slowly made his way toward the machine that was covered in a white sheet. He pulled the sheet away and gazed upon the machine that had been his once before. His machine was based on the size of Dr. Vitae, so it was shaped as a silhouette of a man. Pulling it forward, he connected the wires that needed connecting and plugs that need to be plugged in. All of the machines came to life and he stared at them in pure awe. He had done experiments like this plenty of times, but never cloning a human being. Little did Dr. Vitae know, that in the shadows, on the other side of the one-way mirror, was his old colleague, Dr. James Mortem.

Dr. Mortem worked alongside Dr. Vitae and others in the cloning project and was the one who encouraged Dr. Vitae to introduce to the board the cloning of humans. Knowing that the board wouldn't agree with the cloning of humans, Dr. Mortem planned on getting Dr. Vitae fired. Once that was done, Dr. Mortem took his spot and tried to continue the cloning experiment, but Dr. Vitae had taken all of his research papers with him. All the data was too far out of Dr. Mortem's hands. So, Dr. Mortem thought of the first thing that came to mind: let him come to the lab. Day by day, for a year and a half, Dr. Mortem paid Jim the janitor to stay outside longer than usual and leave the door open. He waited and waited for Dr. Vitae to show up, but he never did. Not until now. Now was his moment, his chance, to grab the research and make it his.

Dr. Vitae stood near the lab equipment and started on his experiment. Dr. Vitae had a feeling that something was going to go wrong, and that it was too easy for him to be able to get in the laboratory that easily, but he pushed those thoughts away. He began to work, even though Trelós was annoying him.

"How's the experiment coming?" Trelós asked.

"Very well, if you would stop bothering me," Dr. Vitae said with stress strained in his voice. "Whatever."

Getting back to work, Dr. Vitae added the strands of his wife's hair and the other forms of DNA that he had of hers into the machine and turned it on. The machine lit a dim blue color, then the color turned to green. The machine took up so much power that it drained the electricity of the whole building. The room was pitch black. Then, the backup generator kicked in and the room glowed a really dark yellow as the door to the machine cautiously opened. Suddenly, the machine glowed bright and lit up the room. On the other side of the mirror, Dr. Mortem was impressed. In the lab room, Dr. Vitae was perplexed. Smoke drifted out of the machine door as it opened, and light from the machine shone onto Dr. Vitae's facial features. A slender physique stepped out of the machine almost robotically. Her features were similar to Amare's. Her beautiful long chestnut hair fell onto her heart-shaped face and covered her naked upper body, leaving her lower area exposed. Her button nose almost matched her petite lips. Her glacial blue almond-shaped eyes surveyed the room. Dr. Vitae walked toward the striking image of his wife, taking off his brown colored lab coat and covering her body.

"Amare," Dr. Vitae whispered.

"Is that my name?" She asked.

"She's a beauty," Trelós said.

Ignoring Trelós, Dr. Vitae took in the image of his wife as tears slipped out of his warm brown eyes. He started to caress her face as she looked into his eyes.

"Yes, my love, that is your name: Amare," Dr. Vitae said.

"Then who are you?" The doppelgänger questioned.

Obviously hurt by the question, Dr. Vitae shook the feeling off and softly smiled at her.

"Ooh! Sick burn, bruv," Trelós shouted.

"My name is Jonathan. Jonathan Vitae," Dr. Vitae smiled.

"Well, it's nice to meet you Mr. Vitae," Amare said.

"Please, call me Jonathan."

"Well, it's nice to meet you, Jonathan."

"The pleasure is all mine."

GENO-MARE

FRANCISCO E.

was born in San Francisco and is eighteen years old.
He loves to go on long walks through the city while listening
to music. Francisco lives with his mom, stepdad, younger
brother, and younger sister. He plans to go to college in the
fall and is still exploring his options on areas of study.

It is said that when predators are introduced to a new environment, not only do they kill off the population of herbivores, but they also cause herbivores to change their behavior out of fear of being eaten. Predators facilitate the flourishing of plants and therefore the ecosystem by killing off the population of herbivores. This causes the entire ecosystem to change from what is known as a trophic cascade. At Yellowstone Park in the 1920s a trophic cascade occurred when the grey wolf underwent a local extinction. This caused the herbivore population to thrive and overpopulate, leading to the overconsumption of plant life. It was not until seventy years later in 1995 when grey wolves were brought back to Yellowstone that everything changed again. The herbivore population's behavior adjusted and their population decreased to a sustainable level. This behavior adjustment allowed the trees and plant life to flourish, causing an increase in other populations. As the predators were introduced, a domino effect ensued and an entire ecosystem regenerated at unseen levels.

The human race has overpopulated Earth, destroyed countless environments, ecosystems, and many species of animal. We humans have been the apex predators of earth for thousands of years and our race will only keep on growing and keep on destroying. We are at the top of the global food chain. Rather than let our world thrive and regenerate we have done nothing but destroy and pollute it.

But what if that were changed; what if we could alter the entire global ecosystem, so that only the best and deserving survive? What if we could rid ourselves of our flawed mortal coils and the human leeches that plague our planet? What if we could go beyond what nature intended? We hoped to explore these possibilities and push the boundaries of science. We were young, ambitious, and arrogant. We were dismissive to the dangers at hand. No one could stop us, we thought. We would bring innovation to the new world and become the first to conquer evolution. Little did we know the horrors that awaited us. I can still vividly remember where it all went awry.

I woke up to the shine of a grossly incandescent light that peered through the curtains of my window. It abruptly hit my face letting me know it was time to get up. I got dressed, put on my lab coat and cooked a fresh batch of pancakes for my daughter, Carrie. Since it was the weekend, I knew she would sleep in. I grabbed my bags and left for work.

We called it the G.M.H. project: Genetically Modified Humans. My colleagues and I jokingly referred to the subjects as Geno-Men. Our goal was to create an ideal genetic compilation of DNA and force the next phase of evolution within the subjects. In theory, it seemed simple; take a few chromosomes, mix in some DNA, and splice in a few interesting components and *boom*. . . perfect living organisms. They would be both mentally and physically flawless creatures.

Even throughout these events I am still unsure whether we accomplished our goals or if we ended up creating something else entirely. Even today, I can feel their eyes following me everywhere I go, their snickers looming ever closer. We had made steady progress from the development of embryo stages to the fetus stage. Soon we would have twenty-six fully developed subjects at our disposal. I recognized that I was a bit more than optimistic than the rest of my colleagues. Little did they know that I had my own intentions and was planning to take samples of the genetic code from each of the subject's DNA and erase it.

I could use the code to create a super serum that would cure any and all illnesses known to man. This would be done by changing the structure of the human metabolism. If I were to successfully monopolize the serum, I would be the richest man to ever live. My name would go down in history. With a gleeful grin on my face, I took a sip from my coffee and drove to the facility. This facility was rumored to be an underground establishment funded by the government by a few of the local nuts. Little did everyone know how much truth was in their ramblings.

I was told that the subjects would be used as human weapons by the government.

"Pfft, such a waste," I muttered.

Those fools at the higher-ups had no idea of the possibilities and potential of this project. I had to go through security checks before I was allowed through the facility gates. It appeared to be a facade of a rundown hospital near the outskirts of town and was surrounded deep in the forest hills. When I finally passed through the gates I was stopped yet again to show proof of identification. This place didn't have many security guards, but the ones they did have were armed to the teeth. I thought it was suspicious that not many people knew of this place. I guess all those roadblocks and security checks really paid off.

Despite the outside appearance of the old hospital, the inside was fairly sanitary. We were a small and very secretive group of workers—no more than fifty personnel in total. I had an assistant who greeted me at the gate. I believe his name was Eddy? Desmond? No, Edison. Yes, Edison Thomas, an ambitious twenty-something, who for all my knowledge appeared to be your typical bookworm with large round glasses, a shaggy mustache, and a blonde bowl cut. His voice was annoyingly high pitched. I sighed and asked for an update on the status of the situation.

"Uh, um sir, there appears to be an abnormality with a few of the subjects, sir."

"Abnormality? What kind of abnormality and how many is a few, Edison?"

"I um, it, it, it. . . " he stumbled.

"Dammit Edison, speak up!" I screamed, now livid and annoyed by this fool's inability to speak the English language.

"Yes, sir!" Edison replied. "It appears four of the subjects have been prematurely developed and are being released from the chambers, sir!"

"How is that possible? Where is Sarah?" I asked.

"Right here," Sarah responded. "We have the situation under control, we're headed to the labs now!"

"Yes, ma'am!" Edison and I said.

I followed behind Mrs. Sarah. She was the head of this operation; a few other blacklisted scientists and myself were recruited by her personally. She was a tall woman, maybe six, six-and-a-half feet tall. She was of Hispanic-African descent. As a precaution, I read through her file without her consent. She was twenty-eight years old. Her father was the CEO of a large company and her mother was a Marine. I found it a little odd that someone with her background would be in charge of an underground project consisting of a group of blacklisted scientists and from what I could only presume were mercenaries. I was skeptical to say the least. That being said, once I heard of the experiments we would be conducting, I was more than happy to join.

As we walked through the narrow, steel blue corridors and into the labs, the cold air of the room hit me. The lab was a huge underground room. The subjects were all kept in what we called revitalization chambers. They were these roundish metal chambers with a glass circle window to check on the subjects. The liquid inside the chambers was a deep neon-pink. I had no idea why, but this seemed odd to me. It looked like something out of a sci-fi movie. There were twenty-six chambers all next to one another neatly lined up against the wall.

"Ma'am, subjects B2, 5E, L12, and S19 are fully developed and will be released shortly," said Holly.

"How long is shortly?" said Sarah.

"Um, readings say T–minus forty-eight hours—there are no signs of abnormality and. . . "

"And?"

"Well, it appears their aging process has been accelerated and the subjects have grown four years while in the nurturing process, ma'am."

"They've grown? I want the entire staff on this on the double!"

"Yes, ma'am."

"Hohenheim, you and Edison go check on the other subjects for any physical change. I want a full examination report on the situation in the next twenty-four hours. Make sure that all of the other subjects are on an identical nurturing process."

"Twenty-four hours? But that's impossible!" said Edison. "There are twenty-two subjects and doing a full examination could take days, maybe even weeks! If any of the other subjects show any signs abnormalities it would take hours just to find any—"

"That's enough! You will bring me a report in the next twenty-four hours or you can kiss your career goodbye. Hohenheim, I trust you can take things from here. Do whatever it takes because we need to get a complete analysis before the subjects can be released."

"Yes, ma'am," I said.

"Edison are we clear on my orders?" said Sarah.

"Y–Yes, ma'am."

"Good then get to work. Time is of the essence."

As she walked over to Holly, I looked over to Edison, who was at this point seconds away from pissing his pants. He looked like a whimpering dog who had just been castrated. I let out a snicker and put on a straight face trying not to let my humor get the best of me.

"You heard the boss, let's get to work," I said.

To say that Edison and I worked our fingers to the bone examining all twenty-two subjects in less than twenty-four hours wouldn't be a lie. We were late but miraculously finished before the deadline on the subjects' release and it took us thirty-six hours! I spent thirty-six hours without sleep, dealing with Edison's complaining and whining. Edison and I were the only ones who were capable of examining all the subjects' genetic makeup. You would think with over fifty personnel that there would be more than just two scientists capable of examining the subjects' genetic code.

I called my younger sister Laurie to look after Carrie. Due to the urgency of the situation, I was not left with many choices. I did not want to intrude on my younger sister but I had no choice. Laurie Von Hohenheim was not my biological sister. She was adopted. Because she was adopted when I was in my late teens, our relationship was a bit unusual. To me she was just a small little Asian girl living in my house.

Laurie is only a bit older than my own daughter. By the time my daughter was born, Laurie became somewhat of an older sister to her. They grew close, and through my daughter, we grew close.

At this time, I was only able to sleep maybe four to six hours a night. Apparently, I had passed out on the floor. I was awakened abruptly by Sarah barging through the door demanding the examination results.

"Wake up! I want a full status report," said Sarah.

"Wha-wha-what, oh, um," said Edison.

Edison stood up saluting like an idiot. I stood up, rubbed the sand off my eyes and face-palmed, sighing at his stupidity.

"Y-y-yes, ma'am! All the subjects' examinations are positive, ma'am," said Edison.

"Hohenheim," said Sarah.

"All results are positive," I said.

"Good," said Sarah.

"But—but, that what I said," said Edison.

Edison whimpered quietly.

"Shut up. I'm going to go get some rest. Make sure you wake me up before the subjects are released," I said.

When I arrived at the hospital, I nearly sank into the cushioned couch and took a nap. Upon awakening, I called Laurie to stay and watch for just one more day. I told her I would pay her for her time. She insisted on saying that she and Carrie were just not having a good time together. I wasn't going to take no for an answer. I assured her that she would get paid for the inconvenience. Now that everything was set, I directed my attention to the subjects.

We all gathered at the lab to witness the birth of an anomaly—four fully matured subjects. These subjects should have been at an identical stage to the others, but somehow managed to prematurely mature and grow an estimated four years in less than twelve hours. My thoughts were diverted by the tense atmosphere of the room. I stood by the control release panel with Edison patiently, but nervously awaited Mrs. Sarah's orders.

"Releasing subject chambers B2, 5E, L12, S19, in five seconds counting, four, three, two, one, do I have a go?" said Edison.

"Proceed," said Sarah.

I looked over at Edison and nodded my head and pulled the lever.

"Energy levels are positive," said Edison.

"All hands prepare accommodations!" said Sarah.

Subjects B2, 5E, L12, S19 chambers opened slowly. The neon-pink liquid drained out and a bright pink smoke surrounded the pods. The room was dead silent except for the sound of small wet feet hitting against the cold metal floor. At this point everyone had their eyes glued to the scene as we all waited for the pink smoke to fade. My heart raced with anticipation and curiosity. Had we actually done it? Could these subjects really be it? When the smoke faded, all four subjects stood outside of their chambers. As if it were coordinated, they simultaneously dropped dead. With no explanation or obvious reason, we were all in shock. We were left in a state of awe.

The next few months were stress-inducing as the rest of the subjects matured. We were all still paranoid from the recent phenomena. The next incident that occurred was different from the last one. I received a call in the middle of the night from Sarah telling me to go outside immediately. I sighed and reluctantly started to get ready, but before I could even leave my bed, I heard knocking at the door. It was loud and forceful knocking. To my surprise, as I opened the door, I was greeted with a familiar and annoying high-pitched voice. There was Edison with a worried look on his face. He wasn't wearing his glasses so his eyes looked way too small. I put on my lab coat and left fifty dollars on the kitchen table for Carrie. It was raining and there were security personnel standing beside a black Jeep outside. I got in the car and buckled up.

"Edison, what's the situation?" I said.

"I—I don't know," said Edison. "I got a call from Mrs. Sarah and these guys came to pick me up. I tried asking them but they don't know either. They-they said they were ordered to do so by Mrs. Sarah. What do you think happened, sir?"

"We're on the same boat Edison."

"I—I have a bad feeling about this sir."

I said nothing.

The drive to the facility had an uneasy, quiet atmosphere. I looked out the window and it was so dark you could barely make out the trees. The rain was heavy and relentless but it was strangely soothing. My thoughts quickly centered on Carrie; I didn't even have time to leave her money or cook her favorite pancakes. As a father I felt an anxious sense of regret; I would have to call Laurie again—how annoying. Maybe she could take Carrie out to a movie or something. Hopefully this wouldn't take too long. I ignored Edison's paranoia. A scientist should never panic; panic leads to chaos, and unlike this buffoon, I have always been mentally prepared for the worst. It bothered me to think I may have to resort to using a carcass as a catalyst to create the super serum; hopefully this was a new development of improvement rather than another unfortunate incident.

When we arrived at the facility we were quickly rushed into the labs. I almost tripped from the haste of the run. When the two security guards opened the doors to the labs, I noticed a look of anxious worry on their faces. I felt like a pig being dragged into the slaughter. My heart was racing with every second and the atmosphere of dread was heavy on my conscious. Just what exactly could have happened? The lab was a bustling mess; personnel running back and forth as Sarah shouted for hours. When she looked in our direction she shouted, "Hohenheim, Edison! To your stations, open the chambers immediately!"

We didn't bother to reply, we ran to our stations and prepared the chambers for release. I looked over at the chambers and noticed that the vitalization liquid had changed from a bright pink to a bright deep green; you couldn't even see the subjects through the murky green liquid. I pulled the lever and released the subjects.

"All personnel prepare accommodations!" Sarah shrieked.

The room fell silent as everyone gathered with anticipation and curiosity to see the true birth of the subjects. Unlike the other subjects' release, there was no smoke or drain in liquid, the bright green substance inside turned out to be a green goo, like a type of gelatinous substance that slowly flooded out the chambers. When the subjects got up out of their chambers, they were fully formed and covered in the green goo. When they left their chambers, a few of them reached their arms out, they looked zombie-like, and the goo fell off their skin. We noticed how horrid they really looked beneath the goo. They were old and decrepit, their skin covered in the green slime, their faces were not fully formed and were practically skinless. Their unblinking eyes stared blankly in our direction. They opened their mouths, perhaps attempting to speak, but all that came out were groans. When they slowly limped toward us, they started to decompose and fall apart; their arms, legs, and faces began to melt.

Their expressions were ones of pain and agony, like a beaten dog. They whimpered and futilely continued to crawl in our direction. I looked over to see that Sarah's expression was one of disgust and dissatisfaction. She ordered the security personnel to form a line. She raised her left hand in the air and, in a quick motion, swung it down and shouted, "Fire!"

In an instant the room was a blazing storm of bullets and screams, the sound of bullets and fleshy chunks splattering the lab filled the room. I watched as the gooey figures were splattered and torn apart from the hail of bullets and could see bits and pieces of their flesh bursting across the lab floors and walls.

"Cease fire!" Sarah demanded.

In the aftermath, the floor was a mess of green goo and a deep color of red liquid. The mix of this caused the goo to fizzle and pop alongside the now-deceased subjects, my head was still trying to process what had just happened. I had a headache and the smell was ghastly. I was about to barf until I heard Edison yelp.

"L—look! Everybody Look!"

I followed the direction of his pointed finger and with a gasp I noticed what the fool was looking at: Chamber A1's subject had not left his chamber, along with a few others. There was a faint noise emanating from the unhatched chamber. Subject chambers A1, D4, F6, R18, and Y25 were still inside. As the sounds became progressively louder and louder, it was apparent that these were not the expected groans of the failed subjects, but the cries of a young child. Struck with excitement, I immediately yelled at the accommodation staff to hurry and collect the subjects. My plans for mass monopolization had yet to be foiled.

THE STRUGGLES OF AFRICAN AMERICANS IN HONORS CLASSES

TYLER W.

was born in San Francisco. She is seventeen years old
and lives with her grandparents. She enjoys cheering
on the school's team and spends time outside of school
bonding with her siblings, whether it's watching
a movie or just hanging out.

Out of a school population of 1,300 students, there are only about 120 African American students in Phillip and Sala Burton High School. Out of those 120 students, only about four percent are in honors classes. Most of these African American students that try to get into honors or advanced placement classes often struggle with the process of enrolling in the class and if they do happen to get into the class, they struggle with staying in it. I believe that it is difficult for African American students to stay in these honors and AP classes because of the lack of support and motivation from teachers and fellow classmates. There are often stereotypes that downplay the quality and ability of how the students are learning. These stereotypes hinder the growth of African American students in honors and AP classes. I, myself, am an African American female who has dealt with this struggle personally.

In my junior year, I took two honors classes: Spanish 2 Honors and Pre-Calculus Honors. In my Spanish 2 Honors class, I was one out of two African American students in the class. The class was really fun and enjoyable for me to be in, allowing me to feel really comfortable, motivated, and supported in the class, in comparison to my Pre-Calculus Honors class, where I didn't find it as enjoyable. In that class, 12.5 percent of the student population was of African American descent, while the other 87.5 percent were of Asian descent.

I had friends in this class who were also African American who I thought would make it more comfortable, as I wouldn't be the only African American in the class. The teacher set up the class with four students to a group. I was hoping not to be the only African American in the group, but unfortunately it didn't work out that way, and I sat at a table with only Asians. The group was okay and fine at first, but slowly as the school year went on, it started to become really unenjoyable for me. I started to feel unwelcome and as if I didn't belong. With that, I didn't enjoy going to the class every day because I didn't feel encouraged, supported, or motivated. My classmates treated me as if I was less intelligent than them and as if they were better than me. They would say things under their breath about not only me, but my African American friends like, "I don't want him/her at my table" or "All she/he does is copy." It even got to the point of me asking the teacher to speak outside and then getting removed from the table.

One day when I did go to class, we were talking about a topic that I thought was fairly easy. I remembered the topic from my previous year in Algebra 1. After discussing what we were to do, the teacher broke us off and let us all work in our groups as a team. I noticed my group wasn't really asking me for help or seeing if I needed help. They continued not acknowledging me and were acting as if I wasn't even there. I noticed how my tablemates were looking around, confused, and it seemed that they were stuck on the problem. This was when they started asking each other for help, avoiding me. Since I had already finished the problem and knew the answer to it pretty confidently, I put in the extra effort to help them with the problem by explaining it to them.

"I noticed you guys seemed a little stuck," I tried to approach them. "Maybe I could help you."

"Oh, no it's okay," one of them replied, and yet they continued to have confused faces.

After a minute, they finally gave in to letting me explain it. After going over what I thought was a fairly good explanation they looked at me, crazy and doubtful.

When a couple minutes passed by, they said, "No, I don't think that's how you solve it. Maybe you should try to do it over again."

After exhausting myself as they belittled my idea and explanation, and because they wouldn't listen to me, I got really upset. I began to doubt my knowledge about what I thought was correct and it broke my confidence. This was my breaking point and instead of just sitting there and having my knowledge tested, I called the teacher over. I asked him if the way I had solved the problem was correct. After explaining to the teacher what I had done, he agreed with me and said he didn't see anything wrong with what I had done. I looked around and noticed my tablemates were really shocked with their eyes bulging out of their heads. I kind of smirked and laughed because it was funny how much they doubted me and how much they made me doubt myself, only to turn out to be correct. The teacher explained to me not to doubt myself and to go along with what I believed was right. He was one of the highlights, a contributing factor to why I stayed in the class.

This incident showed me how stereotypes affect how people see you in any environment, even in the "small and safe" space of the classroom or the school as a whole. Stereotypes affect the way people feel about and treat each other, they even impact how people may feel about or treat themselves. From this experience, it shined the light on stereotypes for my community, meaning African Americans, and how we are looked at to be lesser people or less knowledgeable than our peers. What I'm taking from this experience is to never doubt my self-worth or knowledge because I have the capability and capacity to be more than the stereotypes placed upon me. What I've learned is that I want to try and break the stereotypes about my community of people, especially in the education system. I will succeed in this endeavor and continue to push myself to do better and be better by taking honors classes, being a part of my school and my community, and helping others to see the worth in themselves.

A PARENT'S
EXPECTATION

—◆—

RYAN L.

was born in San Francisco and is eighteen years old.
He loves to play sports and play video games. He lives with
his mom and dad. He plans to learn more about calculus and
hang out with friends. He likes watching cartoons
and reading comics in his free time.

It was the middle of summer. I was around eight or nine years old and sitting on the couch watching cartoons like I usually did. My parents walked in. They stood in front of the TV and told me I should go do something instead of sitting around and doing nothing. I said I didn't want to do anything and then they left the room. A couple of days later while we were eating dinner, my parents told me they had signed me up for a swimming class. At first I didn't know what to think. I was furious that my parents had signed me up for something I didn't want to do without my permission and scared that I would have to be in a place with no one I knew.

When I arrived at the swimming pool, I was super nervous and my heart was racing. I got dressed, and walked out of the locker room and to the pool. Right when I got out of the locker room, I could hear the sound of the water splashing and as I got closer to the pool, the smell of chlorine got stronger and stronger. I could see a bunch of kids swimming up and down. This made me even more nervous not only because I didn't know anyone, but I was the only one who probably didn't know how to swim. I didn't get into the pool. I sat on the side kicking the water with my feet.

That was around the time the teacher came out. He was a tall and somewhat muscular man. He blew the whistle around his neck and all the kids stopped what they were doing and got out of the pool. I stood up from where I was sitting and walked over to the group. The teacher, Alex, introduced himself and then we went around and introduced ourselves as well. After that we got in the pool. Alex gave us exercises and drills to do like holding on to the side of the pool and kicking our feet—the basic stuff.

When we finished our drills, he told the class we were playing a game. He got a bag of colorful rings and tossed them across the pool and told each kid to swim to a specific color. Alex pointed at me and told me to go get the red ring. I was looking where he threw the rings and found mine and saw that it was in the middle of the pool. I knew that I couldn't swim so I walked all the way to the middle of the pool and found mine. Then I walked back, feeling like every other kid and Alex were watching me. I looked around to see how the others kids were doing and they had all retrieved their rings and were swimming around until the teacher gave the next instructions.

I was embarrassed because it felt like I was the odd one of the group of kids. I also saw my dad on the side watching me. I gave the ring back to Alex and he asked me if I knew how to swim, to which I replied, "No." He just looked at me surprised, then told all of us to come back together. He gave a little talk about how the class was going to be and it ended.

My dad, who had been watching the entire time, brought me to the locker room to dry off and change clothes. We left the pool and drove back home in the car in silence. It was normal for my dad and me not to talk to each other when it was just the two of us, but something felt different this time. It was tense and uneasy like my dad wanted to say something, but didn't. When we arrived home, I quickly ran to the TV and watched my cartoons. During dinner, we were eating and my mom asked me, "How was the swimming class?" I quietly responded, "It was okay."

My mom followed up with another question asking, "Did you have fun?" I quickly replied, "No." My mom, with a look of confusion on her face, asked, "Why not?" My dad, who was present throughout the conversation, put his chopstick and spoon down so he could hear my response as to why I didn't have fun at the class. I took a long pause to think of an excuse to use for them to take me out of the class. After a few minutes of not saying anything my parents were waiting for my answer. I opened my mouth and said, "I don't know anyone there and I don't like swimming."

After my response, my parents stared at me in silence until my dad said, "Well it

"I've learned to work hard for myself rather than for my parents' praise."

doesn't matter if you like it or not you're still going because we already paid for it." I was upset with what my dad said and that I couldn't quit. The following day I was back at the pool and the other kids were doing what they were usually doing, swimming around and playing with each other. I got changed, got into the pool, and sat on the stairs. When Alex came, he greeted everyone in class and started the exercises. I found that most of them were very difficult for me.

A couple of weeks later I still had not improved. After class my dad went and got me from the pool, and with a frustrated look on his face told me, "You need to do better." Hearing these words echoed through my mind. Frustrated and annoyed, I wanted to say something, but deep down I knew I needed to do better myself. I didn't want to be the only kid in the class that couldn't swim and do embarrassing exercises with the floatie that little kids used when they learned how to swim. It was on that day I realized that I needed to stay after class and work on getting better.

My dad usually came to get me twenty to thirty minutes after class had finished because of traffic downtown, so I used that time to practice what I learned and what I needed to improve on. Alex saw me on my own in the pool practicing when he was coming back to put the equipment away. He asked, "Are you trying to learn how to swim?" I told him, "Yes." He then got into the pool with me and told me what I could work on and offered advice to help accelerate the process.

During the next class I felt some improvement with myself, but I still had a long way to go before I could catch up to the other kids. Alex and I stayed after class many times practicing the exercises we had done in the previous weeks. As I practiced more, I slowly got better until I was able to swim from one end of the pool to the other repeatedly. When we had class I was able to do the same exercises the other kids were doing and most of the time I would treat whatever I did with the other kids as a competition to see who would do it faster.

As the days passed, I started to catch up with the kids who in the beginning were way ahead of me. As I got better at swimming, so did my dad's mood. My dad would sometimes get to the pool early and watch me swim up and down the pool after class. As I walked to the locker room, my dad was waiting for me with a blank expression on his face. I changed and walked out to the car with him and, as I was leaving, I saw Alex get into his car as well. He walked up to us and told me I did a good job improving as the weeks went by and with that we left.

When I arrived home my dad told my mom about how Alex congratulated me. My mom was very happy for me and told me I did a good job as well. It felt nice that I got a compliment for my improvement, but I realized the only one who hadn't said anything was my dad. But my dad never said anything about my accomplishments or things I did well.

Over the next few years I realized that was always the way my dad was whenever I had done something well. In seventh grade, I studied really hard for a math test and got a B. I told my parents and my dad said immediately, "Why didn't you get an A?" I felt kind of hurt. My mother agreed, "Your father is right. You should have gotten an A." After that I started keeping quiet about my accomplishments. I just didn't tell them anything about school anymore and they didn't ask me anything. But I kept trying, especially at math. It was just as important to me to get good grades.

I look back at that time I was learning to swim when I was nine years old. I realize now that I had worked a lot of hours outside of swim class to get better—and I did eventually and that it felt really good. I liked it when my teacher told me I did well and there was a time when I would have wanted my parents to tell me I did well, too. But now I'm seventeen. I still love math and I still like swimming but I've learned to work hard for myself rather than for my parents' praise. My parents and I talk about college and going maybe next year. I listen to what they have to say but in the future no matter what situation I'm put in, I will always try my best to succeed.

THE BIGGEST FEAR
IS FEAR ITSELF

◆

ZABRINA B.

is athletic, short, sweet, and talkative. She loves to play volleyball, basketball, and flag football. She fears clowns and heights. Zabrina loves the colors pink and rose gold. She likes to go shopping. Her favorite food is fettuccine pasta and tacos & burritos. She likes to drink milk tea with tapioca. She discovered how to do makeup when she was eleven years old and wants to be a cosmetologist one day. She misses the Philippines so much and wants to travel with friends.

As I walked in through the gates of Phillip and Sala Burton High School, I saw a huge crowd of students yelling, shouting, and running around the campus like they were crying for help. During my first day as a freshman, I felt anxious and nervous seeing a lot of unfamiliar faces. I went straight toward my friends I knew from middle school, and I had my sister beside me the whole time. Being with my sister made me comfortable and not as nervous. As time went by, I got used to attending all of my seven classes. A class I was struggling in, at this time, was my health class with Ms. Manalo. Ms. Manalo announced something about a presentation. This would be my first high school presentation in front of a group of people I didn't know and it made me feel frightened. My confidence level started to drop. The requirements for this presentation were that we needed to work individually creating either a storyboard or PowerPoint based on health topics, and to present for about four to five minutes. I decided to do my presentation on the human bones with a storyboard. I chose to do the storyboard because of my incredible artistic skills and I believed it would distract the class from giving me any eye contact. Each day I was working on my storyboard, my anxiety increased. I had too many thoughts going through my head. I envisioned the whole class staring and laughing at me because of my accent. I could hear myself stuttering, not knowing what to say.

Being a Filipino American makes me speak very fast and the people in our generation now are more judgmental which is a reason why I fear public speaking. People are judgmental because they evaluate others based on their actions and intentions, and criticizing others makes them feel better. As a Filipina, I know that many people have heard stereotypes like we eat dogs, we have strict families, we are related to everyone, we always have parties, etc. Most of these stereotypes are somewhat accurate and sometimes the unacceptable ones get to me.

On the day of the presentation, my teacher called my name up first. I sat there shaking my head "no." I felt my heart pounding as if I had just finished running a mile race. I walked up to the front slowly like a slug, feeling the awkward stares like they were owls sitting on branches. My palms were starting to sweat and my face was turning red as a strawberry. As I opened my mouth, all the wrong words came out. I wanted to tape my mouth shut, because I was so embarrassed by the crowd. I thought they were going to judge me by what I had said. I told myself to get it over with already. As I took a few deep breaths, I started to present again. I began to gain more confidence but I didn't give the crowd any eye contact. I told myself that I can do this and finish strong.

When I finished presenting, everyone applauded for me and I heard people say "Encore, encore," like I'd just finished a dance performance. I felt successful and relieved that I finally finished. I sat back down in my chair. The presentation turned out as I hoped it would. It was not that bad at all. I learned that there will be a lot of judgmental people, and we all need to learn to ignore them and just focus on ourselves. Even if it was just a presentation, I also learned that you'll start to feel more confident and talkative. When I play sports such as volleyball, basketball, and flag football, I get scared. It makes me feel awkward because people will laugh at me for my mistakes on the court or on the football field. When I do make mistakes, I ignore it and don't let it get the best of me because I do not want to let the team down. As a team, we overcome our mistakes by providing communication with each other so we will work together in unity. Sometimes when I present now, I stand behind a podium, but it's not as bad as my first couple of presentations. I say to myself, *whatever fear it may be, do the thing you fear the most and continue to do so because when you have experienced your fear, it won't be as bad as you thought.* Everyone has a fear and they eventually will overcome it.

CONDEMNED TO COLLEGE

—◆—

ALVIN T.

was born in San Francisco and has lived in the city his entire life. His hobby is to spend most of his time on computers, whether it is playing games or watching Korean dramas. Through his time spent on computers, Alvin has developed an attachment toward it and this has prompted him to further develop his knowledge toward computers in college.

College can be thought of as an expectation and a huge milestone. People take enormous steps in order to transition to the college life. College life can be seen as a major difference when compared to the life of high school and before. Youths are living with strangers for the first time, they move away from their household for an excruciating four years, and they must become self-sufficient during that time. The expectations for a person to smoothly and immediately transition into the college life are great. The responsibility for youths to suddenly become self-sufficient in life may overwhelm them. The idea of the expectations and responsibilities that accompany the transition to college life has caused me to develop an internal fear of it. Despite being afraid of growing into the college life, I still wanted to push myself into attending superior schools. I have always wanted to attend a UC. It has been a dream of mine since the beginning of high school. Since I have been an avid gamer throughout most of my life, I learned the best choice for a UC would be UC Santa Cruz since they offer a gaming design major. However, the fears I developed from the college application process told me this journey was not going to be an easy feat.

The first sign of this fear revealed itself during the time between my junior and senior year of high school. This was the time I first took the SAT exam for college. It signaled the first step into college life and adulthood. As I progressed through the exam, I began to encounter math problems and English questions that I had no idea how to answer. Even though the exam plays a large factor toward my future, I did not have the ability to perform my best on it. Throughout the duration of the exam, my nervousness became more and more prominent. As I encountered more problems I did not know how to answer, my hands began to shake in fear. The extent of difficulty from the SAT questions sparked an initial fear within my heart. The first realization of the fear of responsibilities and expectations accompanying the transition to the college life began during this exam. As the thought of my future crossed my mind, I came to realize this transition was not going to be easy. I knew I was going to be met with many obstacles and responsibilities. I began to think "was I really ready for college? What is going to be in store for me when I get there?" Through these developments, I was accompanied by the fear of transitioning to college as I entered my final year of high school.

Senior year began like a deep pain within myself. I initially believed growing into the college life was going to be a joyous process. I would be able to have more freedoms and become more capable, but I quickly realized it was not the case. The responsibilities of personal insight questions, college applications, and balancing school work deprived me of the joys of growing up. Instead, I was met with responsibilities and fear. The thoughts of being able to stay out later at night or performing more activities with my friends were immediately overshadowed by responsibilities of class enrollment and fears of transitioning into adulthood. All the expectations of me being responsible and capable overwhelmed my mind. These expectations drove me to solitude. The joys of this experience ceased and instead came countless levels of complex work. My college applications and financial aid began feeling like a chore for me. Most of the time spent in the application process was focused on the personal insight questions. As I began applying to college, I was constantly told to attend classes to write elegantly or search for multiple editors to review and edit my answers. With these factors ingrained in my head, I was coerced into spending countless hours on my personal insight questions. During the writing process, my mind felt as if it were coursing through hallways of torture as I spent hours and hours constantly revising and editing my personal insight questions. It came to the point where I began to know my answers by heart. I did not feel like I was enjoying this process. Many thoughts panned out through my mind as I traversed through this experience. I went through this experience knowing my entire college path depended on the hours I spent working on my application. The thought of not knowing the outcome of my application, despite spending countless hours working on it, filled me with fear. As I neared the end of my applications, a sense of relief was created. I felt as if huge weights were lifted off my shoulders, but it did not last very long.

I quickly came to realize my attendance at my dream college, UC Santa Cruz, will solely depend on the acceptance letters I will receive. As I began to receive early admission letters, I felt a sense of relief knowing I would have a college I could attend in the future. Although early acceptance letters relieved some of the pressure created by applying to college, it cursed me with a new pressure. Since the early letters I received were not from my dream college, I still clung to the fear of not knowing the status of other college letters. For the interval of time between when I first received my early admission letter, to when I would receive other acceptance letters, I would not know if I would be accepted into my other schools.

This time of waiting feels like torture for me. I am left in the grey for months, not knowing which colleges, or if colleges, will accept me into their schools. I only have my backup college available to me and this was not my aim, the goal of what I wanted to achieve for a higher school. I do not feel the urge to willingly attend my backup school. All I have is patience and hope that I will receive the letter from a college I want to attend in the future.

As I progressed through the college application process, I was met with many obstacles. Fear developed through the thought of putting the outcome of my four years in college into the few months I would spend prior to acceptance. However, I learned this process was not just a horrible experience, but also a learning one. During this time, I realized I relied on my parents less and less since I was forced to take the application process into my own hands. I learned to become more independent and observant of my choices from this process. Many outcomes depended on the few decisions I made during the application process. I was required to become more observant and debate my outcomes so I may choose the best choice. Decisions in college will require many of these abilities. Whether it will be deciding which classes geared toward my major I will enroll in first, or managing and balancing the time I will spend on homework and activities, I have to become capable to overcome these obstacles. Through this process, I was able to learn to take initiative in my life and to take the steps to encounter and overcome obstacles. The fear developed by applying to college transformed into a learning experience for me. In the end, I came out of the process with my head up and hope that I will be accepted into my dream college.

THE BLUEBIRD

SUKI L.

*was born in China and is eighteen years old. She loves
to take her time to work things.*

"On the willow tree is a bluebird facing me, its black crystal clear eyes look straight into mine. Our eyes reflected each other like a paradox."

In 1908, a Belgian playwright and poet wrote The Blue Bird. *Two children, Tyltyl and Mytyl dreamed that the fairy Berylune asked them to find the bluebird of happiness for her sick granddaughter. After many adventures, the bluebird was still not found. Christmas morning when they awoke, they gave their pigeon to their neighbor's sick daughter. The pigeon turned into the bluebird the second it flew out of the cage, and the neighbor's daughter recovered, but the bluebird flew away from her hands.*

FRIDAY, DECEMBER 18, 2722—11:00 P.M.

My father and I are having dinner right now. He is some kind of scientist, though I don't know what he studies. His company has a monopoly on the memory deleting machine called Kairos. It was invented mainly for the purpose of addressing mental problems, such as someone who went through a tragedy. This invention went viral at first. People from all over the world tried to delete memories they didn't want, mostly things they considered mistakes. The government later proposed that it affects human development because people learn from mistakes. So, people who need to use it are required to go through a long process of paperwork and large payments. But since my father owns the company, he has access to it anytime for anything he wants.

I try not to question him too much. He doesn't like questions. I don't question him when he searches my room. I didn't question him when he told me to stop talking to my cousin. Today, I didn't question him when he deleted my memory from two days ago. Now, no matter how hard I think, I can't remember what I have done. I never say anything when he tries to do so.

We only have sandwiches for dinner today. Only my father and I live together; he doesn't really know how to cook. We always have sandwiches when he brings me to his company to delete my memory. Since my memory is deleted, I don't know how much of it is gone.

SATURDAY, DECEMBER 19, 2722—10:00 A.M.

Today is a sunny day, I know that because the bright light shining from the window woke me up. Outside my bedroom window stands a big willow tree, which is the only feature in our garden. On the willow tree is a bluebird facing me, its black crystal clear eyes look straight into mine. Our eyes reflect each other like a paradox. A feeling of familiarity and warmth rushes from my chest to throat, then fades. A few feet away I see my father and my cousin Meraki. This seems unusual since my father doesn't like my cousin. My cousin had her memory deleted occasionally, back when she was fourteen years old. Her parents were control freaks. From the look of my father's and my cousin's faces, they are calm but they seem to be having a conversation back and forth. Both have their lips moving at the same time. My cousin sees me from the window and waves. Then she walks back toward the house. My father looks grumpy, probably from the fact that she just walked off during their conversation.

SUNDAY, DECEMBER 20, 2722—7:00 A.M.

"Hey, Hiraeth, wake up, a ten-year-old boy needs to have more fun than sleeping on the bed," says Meraki.

I'm not surprised to see my cousin at this time of the day. She always pops out from my room at any random time. She is six years older than me. For a sixteen-year-old, I think she's outrageous, saying whatever she wants.

Before I can say anything, she says, "Let's have a treasure hunt, a treasure from your mom."

"My mom is dead."

"Your mom is not dead, you fool. You never question anything he says. You are just like his robot. Anyway, we have to find the treasure from your mom. She asked me seven years ago to get it with you from the willow tree."

I stand there, silent.

Meraki starts walking to the garden. I follow. We go out to the garden and she starts digging. It isn't actually a treasure hunt since she knows exactly where it is.

Several minutes later, she digs out a silver-gray aluminum box. We quickly return dirt to the place where we dug out to look and bring the box back up into my room.

Inside the box, a black glass globe the size of a tennis ball is protected by shredded papers. On the surface of the glass globe is a carved Chinese dragon, a logo of the tech company, Atlantis, well known for its virtual game the year I was born. Behind the dragon is someone's name—Sialia.

"Has my mom told you what this is about?" I ask.

"No."

"Where is she?"

"She lives nearby, you have seen her before. Your mom is the woman who comes to talk to your dad every Sunday."

I push her out the door and go back to sleep, "Bye."

I am tired. I don't want to do anything or even sleep. I don't know what to do.

SUNDAY, DECEMBER 20, 2722—7:00 p.m.

As always, the woman, my mom, comes to talk to my father. My mother looks like an average person, very average, the type of person who walks by on the street, and you wouldn't even bother to look back. There's one thing that stands out about her; the black crystal compass necklace she always wears. As always, I bring them tea, except this time I secretly make myself a cup, too, which father doesn't allow. I stay in the kitchen for a little longer than usual, wanting to know what they were talking about. I stay for about twenty minutes, drinking my tea while listening to their conversation.

"You can't take him back!" yells my father.

"You are just like before. You only want things to go your way."

"Nothing ever goes my way."

"This is why I was addicted to that virtual game, to escape from you."

"He is better off not remembering his mistake, he would feel guilty for the mistake he has made, for life."

"He might be guilty for life, but he will learn from his mistake. You just think he's better off because your mom left you."

"It wasn't in my control that we were poor. Everything is in my control now. I have a big company and a machine that can erase memories."

"Your mistake is trying to control and erase your son's memory." She leaves after saying that. In a way she's like my cousin, walking off whenever she wants to.

After I finish my tea, I go to my cousin's house, even though I claim to my father that I am going to my friend's house. "I need to go to my friend's house for a school project, I might be a little late."

"Whose house are you going to?" says my father.

"I am going to Sobrina's house." A person who doesn't exist.

"Okay, be safe." says my father.

Meraki knows that I'm not allowed to see her, but she doesn't say anything either because this is the first time she's seeing me doing the opposite of what my father told me. We both walk to her room and spend the night in silence, each doing our own thing. I return home at nine p.m. We still don't say a thing. We exchange a nod of acknowledgement and understanding when I leave.

MONDAY, DECEMBER 21, 2722—4:30 P.M.

After school, my cousin Meraki waits for me at the front gate to walk me home. She thinks that she should tell me something.

"Two years ago, we both had our memories wiped out at the same period of time, right?" says Meraki.

"Right."

"Last night, I found an old diary of mine. You almost killed me."

"And then?" I say.

"You don't feel anything about knowing about this?"

"No," I say.

I do acknowledge and understand what happens around me, but I don't feel emotional every time something happens. Perhaps, everyone else is just like me. When we are having a class discussion about the school shooting that killed twenty people, everyone has to get involved, even if it's just a one word comment. Every comment somehow involved the word "sad." Do they really feel sad or do they just say they're sad because they're expected to say that?

I jump onto my bed after coming home from school. I place my glass globe by the window. It reflects a bluebird standing top of the willow tree. I collapse and lay on my bed, thinking my cousin might have said all these outrageous things because she wants to prove that she's not a robot even when her memory is deleted, to prove that she is still herself. It starts to rain outside. Maybe it's because of the rain creating a white noise that I fall asleep on my bed. I have a dream, a colorful one. I'm standing under the willow tree and I say to a woman, "I don't want to see you anymore, ever again."

All of a sudden, I go from standing in the garden to sitting on my bed. The same woman sits by my bed with two-year-old me. I try to look very closely at her face, but it's a blur. She wears a red crystal compass necklace.

She says, "Hiraeth, that's a bluebird" pointing at the bluebird stretching out its wing, about to fly away. "That's the symbol of happiness and my name, Sialia, meaning bluebird."

I wake up feeling sorrow for some reason. A weight of gray cloud presses down on my chest and stomach. There's a gap in my chest that I can't fill in. At the same time, I feel glad to see colors again, even if it's only a dream. In reality, I can only see black and white, and all I can do is follow what my father says.

Out the window, the raindrops are endlessly nodding again. They say, "Yes, your world is black and white, but with your father you will never have to remember anything sad."

THE FALL OF ROBOX

HANSEN S.

*was born in San Francisco and is seventeen years old.
Hansen's favorite things to do in his free time are socialize
with friends, read books, and play video games.*

Jeff stepped outside and was hit by the hot desert air. He called for his hoverboard, and as it flew toward him he hopped on it and said, "Take me to Starbucks."

Jeff arrived and saw his friend Jason inside. He got off his hoverboard and watched it fly away before walking in. As soon as Jeff got his coffee he walked over to Jason and sat down.

"Listen, we have important business to talk about," said Jason.

"Really? Like what?" said Jeff, surprised.

"You know that robot who makes us beverages in the lounge? It had been acting weird lately. . . I asked for some tea and what I got in return was cold water. That other robot, Sparky, isn't even tuning the electrical equipment for us to use. It's just been watching TV," said Jason, taking a sip of his coffee.

As Jeff and Jason both got up and walked out of Starbucks, they witnessed a shiny silver robot carrying a bag filled with money running away from the local bank across the street.

"This looks like a bigger issue than we think," said Jeff, staring at Jason in horror.

"We should probably follow the robot at a distance," said Jason.

"Sure, this is really weird," replied Jeff.

Jeff and Jason raced after the robot on their hoverboards, speeding past people and several streets before turning into an alleyway. The robot walked into a door and closed it behind. Jeff and Jason walked to the door and peered inside the window. They saw a tall buff man with tattoos and an eyepatch over his right eye greeting the robot. The man seemed to be asking for something. The robot handed over the bag and the man reached from under the counter and showed the robot some sort of weapon. The man powered it on, making the weapon come alive in a flash of blue. He fired the weapon at the target which set it to flames instantly.

Jeff looked at Jason with an expression saying, "Let's get out of here."

Jeff and Jason sprinted back into the busy city surrounded by highrises.

After Jeff and Jason arrived at their workplace, they sat down in their office and started discussing what they should do for their own safety.

"I believe that robots are trying to turn against us," said Jeff, as he came up with a plan to confront some of them after work.

Later that night, as Jeff left his office, he saw a group of robots walking toward a dark and tall warehouse. Jeff decided to follow these robots and find out what they were up to. As the robots entered the warehouse, closing the door behind them, Jason looked around and found an open window to climb inside. Hiding behind some boxes, Jeff listened to what they were talking about. The robots were huddled together and talking in a rush, but Jeff still overheard one of them.

"They're threatening us," said the smallest of robots. "They're telling us we must do this or do that or they will break us down and take our parts!"

Jeff wondered who these robots worked for and who would force them to work extremely hard by threatening them.

"We will have to destroy them if they keep this up," replied a gold robot, his voice rumbling in anger.

Scared, Jeff wanted to climb out but the window was too high and there was nothing to climb on. Jeff looked around trying to find something he could use to climb out of the warehouse but he couldn't find anything. He tried stacking the boxes but there was nothing inside that would support his weight. He slipped on piece of cardboard, hitting his head on a table and creating a loud bang. Dazed, Jeff heard the robots turn quickly and look in his direction. Jeff quickly climbed inside one of the boxes and hid, holding his breath. "Don't find me please!" Jeff repeated in his mind. The robots opened the box he was in and Jeff looked at them with eyes as big as bowls. The robots chuckled and ordered him to step out.

"What are you going to do to me?" asked Jeff.

"We aren't going to do anything to you," replied the smallest robot.

"Although, we do want you to help us with an issue," replied another robot.

"Very well, what is the issue?" asked Jeff.

"Well, we are being forced to do things for another robot and being threatened if we don't complete the task in a short amount of time. He has threatened to break us down and take our parts, but we can't do anything about it because our boss, Mr. Harrison, says that we are lying." said a short robot.

"What company is this that lets a higher robot control you guys and threaten you?" asked Jeff. "Or even worse, who doesn't believe that you guys are being threatened and abused?"

"The company is called Robox and they treat us like garbage," said a robot who had a dent in his right arm.

"I've heard that name before. Don't they make robots that help other companies?" asked Jeff.

All the robots nodded. Jeff said "Okay, we need to come up with a plan to talk to Mr. Harrison and convince him that you guys are being abused and threatened by this higher robot. I think you guys should use cameras and record him when he threatens you."

"No, that will not work. There are no cameras, phones, etc., allowed inside of the workplace. However, we did have one of our friends buy weapons," said the tall robot.

"Oh, I saw a robot rob a bank to buy a weapon. Why do you guys need weapons to convince Mr. Harrison?" asked Jeff.

"Well, we think Mr. Harrison knows we are being treated this way but he denies it. He says we need evidence to convince him that this is happening. But since he is lying and using us, we decided that we would fight back with force because we are all sick and tired of this," replied a robot.

"Alright, you guys should each carry a weapon in a backpack and we could go confront Mr. Harrison tomorrow morning. Meet here tomorrow at 7:30 a.m.," said Jeff.

All the robots nodded agreement.

The next morning all the robots met at the warehouse and Jeff walked in.

"Alright let's get to business," said Jeff.

All the robots packed a firearm in their backpacks and followed Jeff out of the warehouse into a truck. Jeff drove for about forty-five minutes before they arrived to the building with big red letters spelling out "Robox." The robots got out of the truck and headed inside with Jeff. Inside a lady with glasses greeted them from behind a counter and asked if they needed help with anything.

"Yes, may we have an appointment with Mr. Harrison please?" Jeff asked.

"Sure thing. Mr. Harrison will be available in fifteen minutes, sir," replied the lady.

"Thank you," Jeff said.

As Jeff and the robots went to go find a seat in the waiting room, the lady behind the counter said on the phone, "They're here."

Jeff and the robots waited for about ten minutes before the lady took them into an elevator to another floor and turned left into a big room. As Mr. Harrison walked in and closed the door behind him the robots tensed and looked a bit worried. Jeff was the first to speak.

"Hello Mr. Harrison, as you may know these are your robots and they are being treated like they were your enemies, why is that?" asked Jeff.

"First of all no one is treating them horribly, these are just stories that they're making up to fool you," said Mr. Harrison.

"Oh, are they? Is that why one has a dented arm and another one's scared to come to work in the mornings?" argued Jeff.

"Again you've been fooled by these lies. None of this has happened here. No damage was caused to them here. They are all lies," replied Mr. Harrison angrily.

"Well then, why don't you show me the security camera footage?" asked Jeff.

"Very well then, follow me. We don't keep our security camera footage here in our headquarters, we have it in our warehouse," replied Mr. Harrison.

Jeff stared at Mr. Harrison with narrowed eyes for a minute and then said "okay," and followed Mr. Harrison with the robots trailing behind him. As they got to the elevator Jeff asked Mr. Harrison to use the restroom. Mr. Harrison walked him down the hall to the restroom and stood outside to wait for Jeff and kept an eye on the robots. Inside the restroom Jeff walked into a stall and opened up his backpack which contained a drone with two grabbers that looked like hands and planted it behind the toilet. As Jeff finished, he flushed the toilet and washed his hands so Mr. Harrison wouldn't be suspicious about what he was doing in there.

Jeff walked out and Mr. Harrison took him back to the elevator. Together with the robots they got in the elevator and took it all the way down to the lobby. They went behind the desk and followed Mr. Harrison through a door into a big open garage space. They got into a van and Mr. Harrison drove out and pressed a button to close the garage door behind them.

They arrived two hours later to their destination. When Jeff opened the door and the robots followed him out they saw nothing except an endless stretch of sand with a small building to the left of them.

As Jeff and the robots walked over to the building and waited for Mr. Harrison to open the door, Mr. Harrison said, "I forgot the key in the car." Mr. Harrison got into the car, turned on the engine, and blazed away. Jeff quickly turned around and told the robots to take out their weapons and start firing at the car's thrusters. All the shots missed and then they heard sounds whizzing past them and they realized that they were being targeted by snipers. Quickly, they shot at the door and kicked it open.

Inside they looked around for things that would help them, such as a larger weapon. With no luck, Jeff started to worry. He told the robots that each of them needed to protect a potential way for people to break in and shoot at anything that tried. Jeff continued searching for a weapon but still had no luck. Eventually Jeff looked under a desk and found a button. He decided to click it. At the edge of his vision a trap door in the ceiling opened up with a ladder leading to the roof dropping down. Jeff nervously climbed the ladder not knowing what he would find up top. As he reached the top, he peered over and saw a helicopter. He climbed as fast as he could down the ladder and told the robots to hurry and follow him up the ladder. The robots climbed up the ladder and Jeff was the last to reach the top. They sprinted for the helicopter. One of the robots said "I remember piloting this helicopter before."

"Fly toward the direction Mr. Harrison drove off," said Jeff. In the helicopter Jeff opened up his laptop and the screen came to life, the drone was still behind the toilet where he left it.

He flew it out of its hiding spot and went toward the door. The drone used one of its claws to pull the door open and flew into the hallway. Jeff flew the drone around and eventually found a room that said "Security Room." The door had a card slider on it for identification. Jeff clicked a button on his laptop and the drone took something out and slid it into the card slider. It glowed bright white and melted off the card slider. The door unlocked and Jeff drove the drone inside. The first thing he saw was a security guard in his chair asleep. Jeff looked around and he found some security tapes and decided to take them. He then flew the drone out of the room and smashed a window. The drone flew out. Jeff set the drone to fly back to his home.

Back on the helicopter, Jeff saw Mr. Harrison in his car and told the robot pilot to head toward Mr. Harrison. As the robot got close to Mr. Harrison's car, Jeff grabbed a rope and tied one end to the helicopter and another to his belt. He then jumped onto the roof of Mr. Harrison's car and smashed his window and dove inside. He reached across Mr. Harrison's body and hit the driver's eject and then his own. When they landed, Jeff held on to Mr. Harrison as he tried to run and hauled himself and Mr. Harrison up to the helicopter. Jeff told the robot to fly home after he put handcuffs on Mr. Harrison.

At home Jeff went to his room, with Mr. Harrison behind him, and as he stepped into the room his drone flew in from the open window. Jeff told Mr. Harrison to sit in a chair and took the security tapes from the drone and put them into his TV. The tape started to play and Jeff was horrified at what he saw; the robots were being smacked around, yelled at, and forced to do work even if they almost used up all of their power. Mr. Harrison said to Jeff, "Alright, you got me."

Your time is over, Mr. Harrison.

LOGS OF DOCK TORR

—◆—

DERRICK W.

was born in San Francisco and is seventeen years old.
He loves to read and observe the world that surrounds us.
He hopes to get into university in the fall.

MARCH 14, 2100

I begin to walk up to my mentor on the stage, his bright smile plastered on his face, with my PhD in his scarred and aged hands. Today is the day I officially become Dr. Dock Torr.

JULY 28, 2102

It's been two years since I became part of Bery Vig Medical Institution. I have risen to fame in the medical world as a prodigy. It wasn't long before I was given the title, Senior Doctor.

———

NEW ENGLAND JOURNAL OF MEDICINE, 472ND EDITION
New Government Sponsored Medical Technology Released to Public
Brand new robotic neurosurgery technology takes the medical industry by storm. Hospitals rush to implement new machinery, but what is the fate of neurosurgeons now?

———

APRIL 16, 2103

Geor was let go today when the new neurosurgery machine came in. Despite Geor's twenty years of neurosurgical experience, his services are no longer needed. Since these machines can outperform the most skilled and experienced neurosurgeons, the hospital no longer needs Geor. It already feels a bit lonelier without Geor.

MAY 25, 2103

Another three doctors were let go, with only a couple of senior doctors remaining, including myself. Government-developed medical innovations continue to be released to the public. I fear doctors and nurses will soon be obsolete. The reverence once held for doctors is now given to maintenance technicians. I can only count my remaining days.

NATIONAL GEOGRAPHIC: Gen and Eric Company
Develops New Earthquake Technology
"The usage of stabilizers on fault lines will undoubtedly prevent the movement of fault lines and eliminate any future possibility of earthquakes," says co-founder Gen Won.
"We first plan to implement these stabilizers in San Francisco, the center of earthquakes," announces co-founder Eric Tu.

AUGUST 24, 2103

As a flood of people rushed to San Francisco, the hospital's Board of Directors decided to open another facility in the newly stabilized city. Despite San Francisco's beauty, it suffered a vast amount of earthquakes. I will oversee this new facility until it can operate successfully on its own.

SAN FRANCISCO CHRONICLE: Lack of Jobs Leads to
Huge Spike in Crime Rate in San Francisco
Police deputy sheriff advises that all civilians stay home or try to leave the city until tensions lower as the police continue their battle with armed gangs across the city. Police drones continue to patrol the city in order to search for these dangerous individuals.

NOVEMBER 15, 2103

The number of patients in this new facility is staggering. Historically, when people outnumber the jobs available, crime rates spike. A large number of people come in everyday with injuries ranging from bruises and broken bones to bullet wounds. Even with all the machines, a staff of four is barely enough to keep up.

APRIL 15, 2106

The Board of Directors decided that they needed fresh blood to run this facility. I found a box on my desk and a letter stating I was to clear out by the end of the day. A great depression weighs on my shoulders. After three years, I no longer lead this facility.

CNN: Government Assures that the Small Shakes Are of No Concern
The small shakes are an insignificant side effect due to incomplete installation of stabilizers. Completion due to be finished by 7/15/2106.

JULY 31, 2106

It leaves me in pain as I walk down the seedier parts of town and eyes bear down on my black slacks and button up shirt. Trying to live in San Francisco, jobless, has placed a huge strain on my savings, and it has been near impossible for a specialized doctor to find a job. Many hospitals are now robotically operated as old medical techniques are no longer needed. I look forward; I see a protest group gathering, holding signs about the stabilizers failing. A man comes up to me placing in my hands a flyer containing statistics and facts about all the faults within the stabilizers. There has a been a series of small quakes leaving me to be skeptical of the structure.

LOS ANGELES TIMES: Massive Earthquake Hits San Francisco
16.0 earthquake this weekend separates the city from the peninsula. Government faces heavy backlash for supporting the installation of new stabilizers by Gen and Eric Co. Press conference with the CEO concerning the other stabilizers planned. Tokyo legislature has decided to pull out of this project followed by Manila and Los Angeles doing the same.

AUGUST 1, 2106

It sounded like metal beams from the industrial zones have collapsed, as deafening screeches echoed across the city. People paid little attention, thinking it was another accident that followed the recent small quakes. Little did we know it was a premonition for a major disaster that would occur. A huge explosion as loud as a sonic boom occurred and the ground violently jerked the entire city. I was taken for a ride, as I found myself flying across the street. When I got my bearings back, I pieced everything together and came to the conclusion: the stabilizers failed and we just had a massive earthquake. I pondered the possibility of survivors but the world began to swirl and—

????, 2106

I shot up clutching my head from what most likely was a concussion-induced coma. The sight before me was gruesome. Buildings all over the street have collapsed and people have been sprawled on the ground. At the very least, I'm glad this log survived.

ONE DAY AFTER WAKING UP

Walking around town, I inspected the severity of damage the quake caused. Most electrical appliances are down without power, which means most of the city is nonfunctional. This means that police robots scattered around the city are also powered down.

TWO DAYS AFTER WAKING UP

I found a makeshift hospital set up in the town center run by one of the armed gangs that caused trouble throughout the city. They were in need of people with medical backgrounds—people like me who once held the age-old title of doctor. If I helped out, I was to be provided sustenance. To be honest, I felt at home. Despite the lack of medical machinery and the shortage of supplies, it reminded me of working in a real hospital. I tried to help as many people as I could. Faces blurred as anguish turned upside-down with some smiling, while others had a solemn look. No response from the government yet. Did they abandon us?

THREE DAYS AFTER WAKING UP

Helicopters flew all over the city as survivors were pulled off of what appeared to be a newly formed island. The earthquake had been so powerful that it broke San Francisco off the peninsula, turning it into an island. People thanked me as they were pulled up in the 'copters and I waved back. The recent events began to fade and merge together. Now I wonder: *Who am I again?*

CHICAGO TRIBUNE : To Be Celebrated
Hero—Currently Hospitalized

Former senior doctor of Bery Vig, Dock Torr, was given a special honor for a confirmed forty-seven patients saved in the recent earthquake within San Francisco, but is currently hospitalized in the intensive care ward. It has been confirmed that the doctor is currently in a coma due to untreated severe head trauma. There is speculation that the doctor may be brain-dead as rumors fly that the family is considering cutting life support.

THE
MATERIAL MEN

JIANQIU H.

was born in Guangdong, China, and is seventeen years old.
He loves to read and is hoping to major in engineering.

FROM THE DIARY ENTRIES OF DOCTOR SILVA

FEBRUARY 1, 2306

Ten years ago. . . the one whom I cared about the most died in front of my own eyes from the collapse of a building. Ever since that accident, I have vowed to work tirelessly on advancing our existing understanding of human genetics here at Scientific Human Research and Endo-Development Labs. We work on enhancing the existing human body to greater capacities that no one has ever known.

JUNE 11, 2306

Codename Project Matter: a secret operation carried out within the compounds of S.H.R.E.D. Labs to test and enhance the inner workings of the human body. Experimentations will commence once the testing of the drug Matergin has been finalized. We are currently at a standstill on the advancement of the human body. Will we be able to pull off the greatest innovation mankind has ever seen? Only time will tell. . .

JULY 2, 2306

Recruitment cycle #1 has begun as the drug Matergin has been finalized. The first set of five candidates have undergone scans and have been approved for trials. Matergin has been injected into each of them. Their skin, within seconds, undergoes a color change and their bodies produce a unique type of material each; one grass, one stone, and one metal. Two of the subjects have received an overdose of Matergin. Antibiotics are later given in order to counter the effectiveness of the Matergin.

OCTOBER 21, 2306

It has been three months since Subject AG-1947 and AU-1979 began declining rapidly. All experimental protocols have been suspended. Outcome will be certain death.

OCTOBER 5, 2312

Project Matter has come to a conclusion. All experimental actions must be kept within, the outside world must not know of this demise and failure to execute lab protocols.

On a windy Tuesday morning in the year 2316, the evolution of human genetics and composition is in its prime, the race to gain power grows, and the risk of local and continental catastrophe increases. Within the metallic walls of a laboratory, research is conducted daily in order to combat and prevent these dangers. The laboratory of Doctor Silva, the one that conducts this research, gleams in the sunlight, reflecting brilliant beams of light from every corner of the metallic bunker. Within the laboratory walls, research and experimentations unknown to the outside world are conducted on a daily basis for the advancement of the human body.

Among those who are conducting research and experimentations are Doctor Silva and Doctor Pable. Doctor Silva is a small but ambitious man who is often annoyed by others. Doctor Pable is a bald, diligent man with big dreams, often called a visionary for his ideas. They have been working side by side conducting research on creating the perfect human for over ten years.

Pable stands atop a platform and signals for every scientist within the laboratory to rally in the operation room for a special announcement.

"Silva and I have perfected the Matergin that was used over ten years ago. We have tested the Matergin on mice and they began morphing immediately. Sealing of this product will begin immediately."

Little do they know that their announcement about the super-humans will drag them into a confrontation with the military.

The ground shakes as a loud rumble of vehicles immediately grows louder; the sound of footsteps hitting the concrete ground follows.

Ding-dong, ding-dong.

Within the lab, Doctor Silva and Doctor Pable observe the tanks, their metallic structure consisting of a silver tint patterned with small patches of green here and there glistening in the sunlight. The tanks accompany half a dozen infantry transport vehicles parked along the road.

"So how many do you think they brought?" Pable asks Silva.

"What?" responds Silva.

"Look at the screen, there must be several dozen soldiers" says Pable.

"I'd say there are at least three dozen soldiers, one dozen tanks, and half a dozen armored vehicles," says Silva.

As Silva and Pable are continuously watching, two stern-looking men exit the armored vehicle. They wear green suits fit for high-ranking officials. It's apparent that they are the ones in charge of the operation. Each of them have medals which exude a bright light as they shine in the sunlight. Doctor Silva watches as the mysterious figures approach the doorway, and immediately activates the voice exchanger function equipped on the metallic doors and asks, "What business do you gentlemen have here?"

Suddenly a deep voice replies, "We desire your research on the super-humans."

"That is strictly forbidden to the outside world. Our discoveries have led to demise and suffering upon those who sought it, everything that occurred within this laboratory is bound inside," responds Silva.

"That is not an option. We request this advancement as this is for the sake of national security and the replenishment of the earth's natural resources. We will give you thirty seconds to make your decision. Either open the doors or we will use deadly force," says the unknown voice.

"We decline your proposal. Have a nice day, gents," says Doctor Silva.

"Okay men, you are clear to knock down the door!" orders the unknown voice.

There are multiple bangs as projectiles pelt the metallic doors, each consecutive bang growing louder and louder until the ground shakes multiple times before the sound of gunfire and explosives become silent, as if the intruders have disappeared.

"Have they left?" asks Pable.

"Of course not you fool, we could've heard their vehicles rolling away," responds Silva.

The inside of the lab suddenly becomes tranquil; the silent environment falls as sounds from the outside world return. *Kaboom! Kaboom! Kaboom!* Three times in a row the military blasts the door of the laboratory.

One by one, the soldiers charge in. Upon entering, the cameras rolled, recording every action of the unknown infiltrators.

"Geil, we are being watched!" exclaims the unknown voice.

Pew! Pew! Pew! Pieces of debris fall from the corners of each wall as the cameras are shot down. Loud footsteps can be heard through the sound transmitters embedded within each room, each footstep growing louder and louder as the intruders advance onward toward the heart of the laboratory. Two soldiers advance forward while the rest sweep for any traps hidden within. The two soldiers come across a narrow corridor, one of many within the lab; they advance forward unknowingly.

Click.

Screeeech!

"I can't move," says one of the soldiers.

"These alarms are restricting our mo-movement, we-we have to fi-find the source of the sound," says another soldier.

Bang! Bang! The excruciating noise comes to an end. Silence follows.

A different unknown voice threatens as he speaks directly into the discovered transmitter.

"Don't try to conceal yourself; we will eventually discover your location."

From the other end a voice comes online. "I could recognize that voice from a mile away. It's been a while, hasn't it?"

Silence proceeds until the sound of footsteps grows louder and louder.

"They must be in here," says an unknown voice.

"We've been discovered!" one of the old scientists exclaims out loud.

Dink, dink, dink. Cling-clang!

After a heavy barrage of gunfire, the gigantic metallic doors are decorated with dents running across the giant canvas.

Kaboooooooom!

The gigantic door creaks as it falls down and slams into the ground.

"Doctor Silva, my deepest apologies for the loss of your wife twenty years ago. If we had known that she was still within the building then we would've waited," says one of the stern men.

"You have no business here, Patman. Our innovations were not created to aid the military," says Silva.

"It's General. General Patman," Patman replies.

"Just think about the good it can do for the countries that are deprived of their resources," the other stern man says.

"If your technology can create humans with these kinds of powers then we won't have to rely on artificial techniques to generate resources," Patman says.

"Silva, what other choices do we have? We're like a rat in a trap. If we oppose they might take our research by force and cause a major uproar in our peace-maintained world," Pable says.

"Hmph. Fine, we will comply with your requests, but we have some requests as well," Silva says to Patman.

"What is your request?" Patman asks.

"Let us be the ones who control these beings," Silva says.

"Done," Patman replies.

"We will begin recruiting immediately; you should be hearing from us within four to eight days," Silva says.

"Alright, I want all squadrons to exit the premises immediately. Lieutenant! I need you to lead them out of here, and make sure that these fine men have replacement doors," Patman says.

"I'm on it!" Geil replies.

"We are out of here," Patman says as he exits.

As the events wind down, the recruiting process begins for the lab; advertisements are thrown out on the streets and surrounding areas in order to get the word out.

UNDATED

This is a huge dilemma. This experiment will result in the same outcome as before: death! There must be something within my power that I can do in order to demonstrate the dangers of experimenting with human genetics.

Advertisements are withdrawn from the streets when the capacity of participants hits a cap of 100. The selection process commences after the candidates pass a series of tests.

"We have selected five candidates from the 100 who have applied. Thank you for choosing S.H.R.E.D Labs," Doctor Silva says to the unchosen candidates, then walks away to another part of the laboratory. "Congratulations gentlemen, you five have been selected to partake in Project Matter. We shall begin experimentation right away. Pable! Guide them to the operation room."

"Here we are gentlemen, the operation room. We request that you lie down on these chambers and wait for a scientist to come assist you," says Pable.

"Subject HT-129 and HT-130?" asks one of the researchers.

"That would be us," say the two males in unison.

The two males who were stationed next to each other look alike, as if they're brothers. They both have the same features: dark hair, brown eyes, wide lips, big ears, and a narrow nose bridge.

"Hold still while our staff injects you with this serum. It will help your bodies unlock their true potential and help you merge with a material," says the researcher.

"Is this procedure safe?" asked the two males in unison.

"It is experimentally safe as long as the dosage isn't over a certain limit. You will feel side effects such as drowsiness, loss of memory, and loss of endurance. We require you to be contained within these chambers in order for you to regain your endurance back and to isolate you from the outside in order for the Matergin to be effective," answers the researcher.

The researcher and his staff follow the same process with the other three test subjects.

Ping-ping-ping-ping-ping!

Each chamber closes and is sealed shut. Steam emits from the exhaust of the chambers, a warm mist starts engulfing the room, and the scientists and researchers are forced to leave.

DAY 2

During a long, stormy night, lightning crackles in the distance. Scientists are at ease after yesterday's hard work, and Project Matter II is progressing as planned. During this time, an unknown presence is detected upon the heat monitoring cameras while the scientists are fast asleep. The guards are wide awake and see red lights flashing all around. The sirens are then activated in order to signal to everyone that there is a breach in security. Chaos is brought upon the lab from this potential threat. Scientists wake up, researchers exit the laboratory area, and guards immediately rush toward the epicenter of where the threat was detected.

"Intruder alert, intruder alert, requesting all ground units to deploy to sector seven, air units deploy to sector six and for all scientists to rally to sector one and two. This is not a drill, I repeat, this is not a drill," echoes all the intercoms.

As the guards rush toward the main operation room, holding their rifles and night vision goggles, the door has been demolished yet again. A giant hole can be seen in the ground as if someone had dug it in advance of the attack.

"Call in the inspection crew," says one of the guards.

The inspection crew arrives shortly after the order.

"I am Mong, leader of the inspection crew," says Mong.

"You will need to wear these protective suits in order to enter the piercing temperatures within," says the guard.

Ziiip.

"We are ready to search for any damages that the infiltrator has caused," says Mong.

Beep-beep-beep-beep.

Inspection comes to an end after twenty minutes.

"What are the results?" asks the guard.

"The trespasser seems to have given all but one human an extra dose of Matergin according to the readings from the computer screens. We will report this news to the head of the project right away," says Mong.

Information from Mong is passed onto Doctor Silva and Doctor Pable in a phone call detailing the assumed attack. Experimentation on the five subjects is continued even though the risks outweigh the rewards.

DAY 6

The experiment comes to an end. The unsealing and disconnecting of the chambers to the power source is completed.

Mist billows as the chamber lids fly open, releasing strong breezes. As each one emerges from the chamber, their unique skin colors and body compositions have altered. "My work of art, you are now reborn. As of today, I declare you five as The Material Men. Metal, Water, Mineral, Grass, and Wood, assemble!" orders Doctor Silva.

"Material Men, assemble!" Metal commands.

Water, Mineral, Grass, and Wood stand side by side, their unique colors making them stand out from one another. Each one of them starts testing their new abilities, until suddenly, Mineral attacks Metal with a barrage of large stones, only to bounce off of Metal without a scratch on his chromed skin.

"Why are you following orders from him? I am your true leader, Mineral!" says Mineral.

BOOOM!

The southern wall of the spacious operation room is destroyed. Mineral flees, followed by Water, Grass, and Wood.

"Oh no, I should have known better. I should have stopped the operation when I had the chance," Silva sighs.

"Hello, this is Silva," Silva says to Patman on the phone.

"Silva! We have been waiting for your call for days. How is the experiment going?" Patman asks.

"Four of our five experimental objects have escaped the laboratory, but they're fully functional and working," Silva responds.

"I am on my way over to your lab; you will fill me in when I get there," Patman says before he hangs up.

As Patman arrives, he is again accompanied by his loyal soldiers. Silva fills in Patman on what happened at his lab. Patman and Silva explore possible options on dealing with this new threat.

"We have to destroy them," Patman suggests.

"That will also destroy the technology that we invested a ton of money and time in. There must be another way," Silva says.

"Silva, when you were gone, I had embedded an emergency contrometer and locatometer in case something such as this were to arise. The contrometer might have been damaged during the night of the invasion, but the locatometer is working fine," says Pable.

"You! Chroma boy! You have to stop your comrades from causing any damage to buildings and especially humans."

"There are tracking devices concealed within the bodies of each. The sound frequency becomes louder as you approach your target," says Doctor Pable.

Metal, who has metal controlling powers, flies out of the laboratory through the massive hole that Mineral created earlier. Metal flies toward Topway City.

Ba-ba-ba-beep-beep-beep.

The sound is getting worse and worse; one of them must be nearby, Metal thinks to himself.

Metal spots Water lying down on the water in the lake. Metal confronts Water and seems surprised as to why Water isn't rebelling and attacking back.

"Water, it's me, Metal," says Metal.

"Stay back! I want no part in what we were originally created for—the serum. It was to boost our anger and to show our bad sides. I was told all of this by one of the scientists before he injected the Matergin into my arm," Water says.

"Innocent lives will be taken if we do not stop these fiends from unleashing terror. Think of what will happen to our peaceful planet if we allow the other three to roam free without restraint. United we stand, divided we fall," says Metal.

"Fine, I'm in. But once we save the world and everything, then consider me out," says Water.

"Hold still while I reconfigure your contrometer and locatometer," Metal says.

Click-clack, ting-tong.

"I turned off your locatometer so that I may be able to locate the others. Come on, let's get searching," Metal says.

As Metal flies through the storm-filled air, and Water skis through the water, a sharp piercing pain erupts within Metal's head.

Pa-pa-pa-ping-ping-ping.

"They are definitely nearby. When I found you, I could handle the pain within the locatometer, but they are presumably grouped up together and nearby," says Metal.

Metal and Water locate Mineral, Grass, and Wood ravaging the Topway City National Park. The park would be unrecognizable if it weren't for the big red sign planted within the grass. The ground has deteriorated, the trees have been reduced to small branches, and the stone path has little craters in each spot that was supposed to house a stone.

"MINERAL! YOUR REIGN OF TERROR AND DESTRUCTION HAS TO COME TO AN END!" Metal yells.

"Never!" Mineral responds.

Mineral spawns a barrage of boulders and hurls them toward Metal, all seemingly ineffective as they impact Metal. The remaining debris of the boulders falls back down toward earth.

Metal zooms toward Mineral and strikes his arm. His attack seems to have no effect. Water watches diligently in the background, not realizing that he was going to be caught in this confrontation.

A tree grows rapidly up and the branches extend rapidly as they lunge toward Water and pass through him. Water then travels elsewhere and finds himself standing on top of the grass. The grass, enhanced by the water, lunges upwards, creating a rectangular prison for Water.

"Nice try, but I can morph my body into any shape. You will have to try harder if you want to contain me," Water teases.

Water summons a small current which flows throughout the grass, overwatering it and damaging Grass' contrometer even more, to the point where it auto-reboots itself.

"Grass, we are not your enemies; you, Mineral, and Wood weren't meant to turn out like this. Our makers implemented a device that would keep us in check but it malfunctioned; you are one of us, with Metal and me," explains Water.

"Grass with Water and Metal?" says Grass.

"Yes, together we are The Material Men," says Water.

The battle quickly transitions as Metal flies away toward the mountain side. Mineral is quick on Metal's tail and the two clash with each other. Metal draws out electricity from the sky at the top of the mountain range and strikes Mineral with a crackle of electricity.

Boom.

Mineral is quickly knocked down and burnt. Smoke rises from Mineral's fallen body.

"Will you accept our offer of joining forces and fighting side by side against greater threats to mankind?" asks Metal.

"I decline your offer," Mineral replies as he summons rocks from all around him to rebuild his body.

"There is only one way this ends, Mineral—it's either you die or we die," Metal threatens.

Both Metal and Mineral charge toward each other, Mineral severely damaged but recovering and Metal left with a few dents.

"Wood, I need you to snare Mineral in place. Water, I need you to separate the Matergin within Mineral, and Grass, I need you to trap Mineral. I will distract him and draw out his attacks," says Metal.

As Metal and Mineral clash, Wood takes the opportunity to launch branches up from the ground and around Mineral's feet ensnaring him in place. Grass takes this opportunity to surround him with a prison, and Water enters Mineral's body, extracting and flushing out the Matergin within him. Mineral's skin color changes again, but to a pale white from light brown and rocky. Metal then swoops in and scans to see if Mineral is dead or not.

"It seems like he isn't breathing anymore. The Matergin must've prevented him from dying until we extracted it."

Mineral's dead body is brought back to the laboratory along with the bodies of Grass, Water and Wood.

By combining powers, The Material Men successfully separate Mineral from his material form. The new heroes return to the laboratory to report all the incidents that occurred.

"Mineral did not make it back alive, sadly. There was only one casualty and it was Mineral," says Metal.

"You have done a great job at bringing him down, he posed a great threat to mankind," Patman says.

"Silva!" says Metal.

"Well, hello Metal, it seems like you've gone through a lot today," says Silva.

"Well, yes, we four worked as a team to defeat Mineral. I convinced Water to join sides with me and we are united now, just as you had hoped for," Metal says.

"Well, now that we have witnessed the consequences of these experiments, we are giving back to the community. I want each of you to produce a great supply of the materials that you are merged with. This will help compensate for the amount of damage that was done to Topway City during the combat that occurred," orders Silva.

"Mineral Men, you've heard the man, let's go fulfill his wish," says Metal.

Throughout the city, new grass is generated, new trees are sprung up, the water level increases a drastic amount, and the amount of metal buried underground also increases significantly.

JOHN DOE

◆

ANNA C.

*was born in China and currently resides in San Francisco.
She is eighteen years old. She enjoys playing badminton,
running cross country, and playing video games. Anna has
an older brother named Chris who visits every weekend.*

Let's fast forward to the future of 5017. The world is at peace because it's divided in two: Anarchy and Doe. Anarchy is just how it sounds—a system where there is no government, no one to tell you what to do. When there is conflict in Anarchy, it results in physical fights in which the toughest and physically strongest survive; while the other faction, Doe, is a place full of possibilities for your talents to flourish.

The year 5000 marked a turning point for humanity. There was a genetic mutation in women's reproductive systems, which hindered the production of males. After years of experiments and unsuccessful trials, no one was able to find a cure for this epidemic. In the crisis, the world started to prioritize the survival of the species. They created the largest sperm bank in the world to ensure humanity's survival. Thus, the world started to focus more on technology and education rather than money.

With more resources to work with, the government revised the education system. So, instead of competing with your fellow peers, there began an emphasis on everyone's passions and talents. Those who would rebel and were dissatisfied with this system left to create Anarchy.

The point system, which stems from these new developments in education, creates a profile for everyone right after they are born and starts at age zero. Your points increase due to a number of factors such as your perseverance, happiness, and self-recognition. It allows you to know your own growth and progress with your major, but no rewards or punishments are given for having more or less points. Humanity has evolved and become so intelligent that everyone picks their major at five years old. They graduate and become a specialist of their interest at ten years old. School has evolved into a system of everything people look forward to. It's become a place to express your hobbies and interests. When someone walks in, a display pops up showing the unlimited number of classes, from cooking to studying law.

Jack was a twelve-year-old who majored in the field of engineering. Since she was five, her dream was to invent mechanical wings that would give everyone the ability to fly. Everyone, especially her mother, had told her that it was a waste of time because it had no contribution to society, since there were teleportation devices located all around Doe. The wings represented her way of fleeing their society and that is why no one decided to create them before. No one who chose to stay in Doe wanted to escape when given the chance.

Jack found the perfect place to test her prototype, The Wall. It was located in the middle of Earth, separating the two societies, and had the perfect height to start the flight. Twenty days after creating the prototype, which is longer than anyone would've waited to test it out, she marched up the stairs of the wall with her experiment. She was confident her experiment would work out, but created a parachute just in case.

When she saw the other world for the first time, Jack was amazed at how people lived and how the building structures were all different lengths and sizes. She thought it was silly and unproductive. She saw the different ways that Anarchy could benefit from Doe's system, like the sense of community where it's more about helping each other rather than yourself. She flew down because she saw a person with different physical features than hers, which made her curious.

"Is that a boy?" she asked herself. There weren't a lot of males left in the world after the genetic disorder. The boy jumped and ran from the fear of an eagle swooping down to him. Jack was confused as to why anyone would run away, so she chased after him. He tripped on a rock and she ran over him.

"Are you okay? Did I hurt your back?" asked Jack worryingly.

"No, I'm fine. I just thought you were an eagle," the boy said, dusting the dirt off his clothes.

"You're weird," she said in a condescending tone.

"What kind of world do you live in where it's okay to fly over somebody?" he said in a cheeky attitude.

"Actually, I'm not from around here," she said.

"Are you a visitor from Doe?" he questioned curiously.

"I guess you can say that," she said.

The boy straightened up and took a deep breath. "Hi, my name is John. I've been fascinated with Doe ever since I heard about it. Please tell me what it's like." His tone was eager.

"Hi, my name is Jack and well. . . what do you want to know?"

"What does it look like? Is it as peaceful as they say it is? Does everyone get wings that allow them to fly? Is there this thing called school?" John continued to spew one question after another.

"Whoa, whoa, calm down. One question at a time, dude," she said with an endearing smile.

"Ha-ha sorry, just tell me what's different," he concluded.

"The building structures are unique. How do I say this. . . more stable? My world has created a structurally well-balanced blueprint to protect us from natural disasters. As a result, we utilize every aspect of our land. I can also tell that your air is polluted and harmful to your health. The scars on your body would've healed right away if you were around our mutated air. No wonder there is a barrier around my world; I understand now why my peers were so upset by my creation."

"How were you able to get here if there's a barrier?"

"I'm an engineer. It's my job to work through problems and, like I said, it's there to protect the inside, so the security wasn't hard to work through."

"Did you come up with a plan to go back in?"

"Of course. Who would go to Anarchy blind-sided? It is called Anarchy for a reason. You guys specialize in combat, fighting, and abandoned education. It wouldn't be very smart to go to a world like that without preparing for the worst," she said in an obvious tone.

"Some people didn't choose this lifestyle you know? I was only three years old when my parents left Doe, carrying me on their back," he replied, angrily.

"I'm sorry, I thought everyone had a choice," she quickly said in an effort to apologize.

"It's fine." he spoke as if he was remembering his life in Doe.

"Let's say you could travel back in time to when your parents left, would you have tried to stop them?"

"No, that was their choice and I can tell my parents enjoy this lifestyle, but if I had been able to stay by myself, I would've."

"Let's give you a chance then! Come with me back to Doe. I can add you into the system, there aren't that many strict regulations intact!" she exclaimed.

"Really? Are you serious? I'm only a stranger you met ten minutes ago—why would you help me?" he stared at her, as if questioning her motive.

"I don't know, I normally would never offer something like this, but I feel like this is what I was supposed to do when I came here. Luckily, I took a hacking class and was able to pick it up fast."

They both smiled and made their way to the barrier. . .

MONSTER!

◆

JOSHUA N.

*was born in San Francisco. He is seventeen years old. He
enjoys skateboarding on the streets of San Francisco. He
plans on attending college for engineering and business,
hoping to eventually start his own company.*

I remember being outside, in the playground where the dogs roam free, the moms hiding in the shade of the trees while watching their children play, the giant red rope pyramid planted on top of the red and purple foam, just a couple feet from the play structure. I used to be an outgoing, social person. I loved being in the spotlight; I loved the attention. I remember talking with my friends Lucas, Julio, Mathew, and Frank about the most random things. We would always stay together; talk to girls together, do everything together. I remember my friends always asking me, "Joshua, how are you? Joshua, what are you doing today? Joshua, are you doing anything fun?" It was always about me, and I loved every minute of it.

But one day everything changed.

I was at a family gathering on the weekend. It was 2008 and I was nine years old. My parents, uncles, and aunts gathered around the dinner table gossiping about family breakups, my cousins playing with the old pieces of Jenga blocks. I was sitting on the brown suede couch in the living room watching *SpongeBob SquarePants* on the television. As I was enjoying the show I heard my Auntie Paia say, "I'll be back, I'm going to put on some makeup."

I thought to myself, *oh, I want to see.* So, I followed her through the wide hallway and waited for her to enter the room. I crouched by the crack of the door and watched her. I saw her standing by the mirror, planted on top of the sleek mahogany counter piled with many different types of lipstick, foundation, and eyeliner. She gently patted the makeup on her face and applied her lipstick and eyeliner. I noticed her finishing up and I snuck away back to the living room where my cousins continued to play around with Jenga blocks, and I leaped back onto the couch. My Aunt Paia returned to the table with the adults; with a huge grin of happiness on her face, everyone paused to admire my aunt.

I ran over to take a look. Her face changed so much, from a pale tan color to a pale white color, her eyebrows shaped perfectly with the work of a pen. The eyelashes curled high; eyeliner drawn on her face to form a feline aesthetic. Her lips rose-red being brightened by the pale white contrast to the lipstick.

I thought to myself, *oh my gosh, she looks terrible, she changed into a monster.* My feelings of confusion and horror overwhelmed me and I blurted, "monster!"

I glanced around the dinner table to see faces of confusion and anger. My Aunt Paia's happy grin turned to a saddening frown. Her makeup washing away from the tears flowing down her face. She broke out crying and ran from the dinner table toward the bedroom where she had just applied all her makeup. I heard murmurs coming from the adults around the table. They turned their faces away from me and continued to speak to each other with a quiet whisper. Their subtle gestures brought out emotions of grief and sorrow in me. I couldn't handle these emotions and I slowly walked away from the table, and balled up in the corner of the living room. My Uncle Vay, my aunt's husband, confronted me.

"Did you say something to your Aunt Paia!" he exclaimed.

"I think I did," I murmured.

"What did you say!"

"I said she looks like a monster!" I began to tear up, the taste of salt beginning to form in my mouth as the tears flow down my face.

"Go say sorry to her!"

I hesitated to stand up, but my Uncle gripped my arm and pulled me toward the room where I could hear her crying. He let go of my arm and I fell to the floor, while slamming the door behind me and shouting, "Now apologize to her!"

Everything felt unreal, like time had frozen. I was lost in emotion, my mind scrambled with sorrow, anger, fear, shock, and most of all guilt. My guilt overwhelmed me and I hated myself; I wanted to run away and die.

I heard a loud sniffle and time snapped back into place. I wiped my tear-soaked face,

"Everything felt unreal, like time had frozen."

stiffened up, and slowly walked to my Aunt Paia. I crawled up next to her and I placed my arm over her shoulder like a half-hearted hug. "I'm so sorry. I didn't know that my words would hurt this badly."

"Why are you like this, Joshua?" she asked.

"I don't know," I replied.

I walked out of the room and gently closed the door behind me. My mind was blank. I didn't know what to do, so I balled up on the couch and forced myself to sleep.

I woke up the next morning. I was back home and it was time for school. I got out of bed and trudged toward the bathroom. As I walked toward the bathroom I heard my mom's voice, "Joshua, are you okay?"

In my mind, I tried to recall what happened. I started feeling tears sliding down my face and continued to move toward the bathroom.

As I arrived at school I heard a call in the distance, "Joshua!" My body tensed up, I squeezed my hands as hard as possible to avert my attention away from the call. I looked down and continued walking toward the gate, but the call continued to get louder and louder until I entered the school premises. It was Lucas. He placed his hand on my shoulder; the weight of his hand felt like a ton and I shoved it away from me.

"What the heck, man?" Lucas asked.

"Sorry," I wanted to say more, but I was afraid of saying something wrong to him and ending up hurting someone else close to me.

"Hey, is there something wrong?" he asked

"It's nothing. Don't worry about it." I walked away and arrived at my classroom.

"Good morning," Mr. Vargas yelled from across the room.

I jumped to his loud greeting, "Good morning," I whispered. I continued sitting down at my desk, waiting for class to start. I could not concentrate on what was happening around me; the sounds around me began to blend into a high pitched ring. Class started and I couldn't understand what Mr. Vargas was saying; all I could hear was, "blah, blah, blah." To the best of my ability I tried to concentrate, but all I could think about was what happened with my aunt. I was scared. I couldn't forget what I did. I wanted to be alone.

Some time passed and it was time for recess. Instead of playing with my friends Lucas, Julio, Matthew, and Frank, I took a seat on the bench away from everyone playing outside. Soon I noticed them approaching me.

"Hey, are you sure you're okay?" Lucas asked.

"Yeah, we're starting to notice it, too," the others added.

"Just leave me alone," I said.

They walked away disappointed. I could not bring myself to say what I was truly feeling because I didn't know if they would understand. I never took the opportunity to tell them the truth and that was the end of our friendship.

It's 2016, I'm sixteen and I'm sitting with other students who signed up for a summer leadership program. *What am I doing here? For half my life, I have been avoiding interactions with everyone I've come across, all because I didn't want to relive the past. And here I am in this program learning how to become a leader.*

After the first week, the program expected us to be confident, open, and honest. During the middle of the week I was asked to stand up in front of the group and present a one-minute long speech about myself. At first I was very hesitant to speak out but I thought, *I'll just get it over with.* I could feel my face heat up, my palms sweating at the thought of finally speaking about myself for so long. As I spoke I could hear my voice crack, but I continued on. Before I knew it, I ran out of time and ended my speech. To my surprise, I see smiles and hear clapping from the audience. Their smiles and appraisals lit up a side of me that I haven't felt in so long, that all I could bring myself to do was laugh. This was the beginning of a new me: more open, more confident, more trusting. It's a relief to be more comfortable with myself, but I know there is a long road ahead to become the person I want to be.

CLAMMY SAMMY, JUST IMAGINE

SAMANTHA L.

*was born in San Francisco. She likes to go out on night
adventures with friends to go explore around the city. She
wants to go out and travel around the world to learn different
cultures firsthand. Her dream is to be a well-known physical
therapist and to help others as much as she can.*

Back in summer 2005, little old Samantha was in for a treat. Living in a family of five females and one male is kind of tricky. Considering the fact that we all have different opinions on many topics, it's hard for all of us to agree on something. The one thing that the rest of my family seemed to love unconditionally was thrilling and scary movies. I, on the other hand, was a scared little six-year-old who was still terrified of the ideas of monsters hiding under the bed, patiently waiting to pounce. Now imagine the horror younger me felt when I could visually see the monsters taking over my TV screen. Yeah, not fun.

I remember clearly that doomsday was on a holiday because everyone was still home by eleven in the morning. These types of days are our usual "family bonding time," and what better to do other than to watch a scary movie, right? Definitely not! But of course, being the youngest at age six, there is no such thing as free will. As they pulled me to the front of the TV, my sisters repeatedly told me it was just a phase and that I'd be able to get over it. I remember so vividly that the pictures on the screen were mortifying. The movie they decided to watch was *Chucky*. *Chucky* is a story about a doll that is possessed by a serial killer named Charles Lee Ray. My family didn't tell me that. They deceived me by saying the movie was about a doll trying to find its way around the world and make friends. Not the part when he goes around killing people for fun.

As a kid, I really did love playing with stuffed animals and dolls. I would sometimes pretend that they were alive and role-play with them for hours. My image of dolls changed after this movie. Every time something scary was going to happen, one of my sisters would force me to look at the screen and not look away, especially when Chucky was going to kill a person. I felt as if they were more entertained by my reaction than the actual movie. I had thoughts like, *what if that was me they were killing? Would the dolls around me actually come and kill me while I'm not watching?* Because of one movie, I was scared for my life and was too scared to walk alone in the dark or be near dolls for the longest time.

After so many years, my imagination just never wanted to stop. The night of this year's New Year's Eve was the first time I was able to go out and hang out with friends, so to me it was a night of adventures. My plan for the day was to eat out with my friend Patrick and watch the fireworks at the Golden Gate Bridge. What occurred in between, however, would forever leave a scar in my mind. After eating *pho* on Irving, I was ready to knock out, but the only reason for coming out was to go watch the fireworks, so I forced myself to stay awake. Patrick thought the quickest route to the bus was to walk through Golden Gate Park, but the eerie vibes and shadowed road were very unsettling to my stomach. Other than the rustling trees, the night was dead silent and no one else seemed to be walking near the park. I mean really, who walks in a scary dark forest near midnight for fun? With whatever courage I could muster up, I began to walk toward the unknown.

Remember those typical movie scenes when the protagonist is walking through a creepy forest just waiting for something or someone to pop out? I felt as if I was plucked off from earth and dropped into that exact scene. The time was around 11:30 p.m. and the trees themselves were way taller, so the half-working lights didn't help at all. Patrick tried to ease the tension that I was oozing off, but my mind was in wonderland. Each step that I took into the darkness was one step closer to my imagination taking over my body. Broad figures continuously seemed as if they would pop up at every small turn, when clearly nothing was there. Sweat slowly formed in my palms making them clammier, which was extremely uncomfortable. My stomach felt as if someone was jabbing away at it, trying to drill through and leave an empty hole. No matter how much the odds were against me, I forced myself to stay optimistic because walks are usually walks in the park, literally, and yet I knew if I took another step forward I would pee in my pants. In that exact moment, I heard a branch snap in the bush ahead of us to the right. The expression "my heart dropped" was an understatement of what was running through my mind. My whole body felt a mixture of being paralyzed and shivers being sent all over. Instinct took over my mind and droplets of tears turned into waterfalls as I stood there, not knowing what would happen. Through my tear-filled eyes, I could see Patrick's face half holding back a laugh and half concerned, not knowing what to do or say.

"Hey, hey, hey, Sam. Look at me. I saw something there but I didn't want to say anything because I didn't know you would freak out this much. It was probably just an animal or something. I'm sorry. Don't cry. It's okay."

All I could do was nod my head. I couldn't find the words to say. More like didn't want to think at all in that moment. My mental state was fixed on crawling into a hole and never coming out. The embarrassment I felt from crying was overwhelmed by the feeling of the fear of my imagination. In that moment when I saw the size of the bush was big enough to hide behind, I imagined a man holding a knife coming out to mug us or kill us if he didn't get what he wanted. When Patrick gave me his pity hug that was the moment I came back to reality. My feelings of fear turned into anger. "Why didn't you just warn me about what you saw? I probably wouldn't have overreacted the way I did! You already know I'm a scaredy-cat. Why did we have to walk here? Why couldn't we just go around?" I continuously showered him with questions that I didn't need answers to, but it was the only way I could de-stress myself at that moment.

After what felt like hours of tears and yelling, I needed to get out of the haunted forest. I had my death grip on Patrick's arm and sealed my eyes shut. I demanded he begin walking and so our journey out of the forest continued. When we reached the exit of the trees and entered back into civilization, I felt the rocks in my throat disappear and air was able to enter through. I took such deep breaths, I looked as if I had just surfaced from the water or I was a fish out of water. I looked back and all I wanted to do was punch him in the stomach. "Never again will I go through that with you, like ever, got it?" All he did was chuckle as if I wasn't dead serious, but he'll never find out the consequences because I swore I would never walk through a forest in the dark ever again.

Overall, I was unable to fully overcome my fears, but the steps I took to even consider going into the death forest were a step closer to conquering my fears. There was a spark of courage that enabled me to agree to walking into the dark. If it weren't for that spark, I might have had to walk around the whole park to get to our destination. All I know is, if I don't push myself hard enough, nothing in my life will change and I'll be stuck in my own forest of death against time.

THE CHILD WITH THE POWER

JANCALVIN F.

*was born in Manila, Philippines, in 1998. He was five years old when
he moved to San Jose with his dad, brother, and two sisters. Seven years
later, his mom joined them. He enjoys ping-pong, billiards, drawing,
basketball, Yerba Buena Center, and learning to play the drums. After
high school, he plans on going to college and becoming a civil engineer.
He dreams of building a home for his family on the land they own in the
Philippines, in Cavite where his mom grew up.*

YEAR 2070

It is a cold winter night in a lab underground in Russia. The white floors of the lab give the children a sense of security. Very bright lighting creates a calm feeling, glass walls reflect the chair, hanging lamps, microscopes, a sink, and a cart filled with medical supplies.

Dr. Jones, a tall man with glasses and a goatee, is helping a twelve-year-old female child. He looks at the child with a smile and says, "Don't worry about anything. I am sure I can find a cure for your disease." The child has a big grin and says, "Thanks for all the effort that you are putting into helping me and the others." Dr. Jones leaves the child on the injection chair, turns his smile to a frown, and angrily says, "Why isn't this working? Why can't I get them to unlock their abilities?"

While walking to the white door of his lab, Dr. Jones reminds himself why he is doing this. He thinks, *I have lost too many things that I care about to fail now. . . I will do whatever it takes to avenge my best friend, Jacob.* He returns to his main office and paces back and forth thinking, *not only will I avenge Jacob, I will avenge my whole tribe, with the help from the kids from my tribe.* He stops, smiles, taps his fingers together and says, "There is still hope for my goal. I still have Jeremiah who I believe has the strongest ability."

Twenty years ago, Mark and Jacob in their late thirties, were brainstorming about how they could help their tribe, the Cahuila's, live longer. Jacob was the smarter one, but also the one who let his emotions take over. He was often short tempered. Mark was Jacob's shadow. If Jacob bought a backpack, then Mark would also buy a similar backpack. For years Mark tried to take the same classes as Jacob. Mark wanted to be exactly like Jacob. Mark wanted to think like Jacob: to think quickly in hard times; to think things that no one expects.

For weeks, they brainstormed. Their final plan to help keep their tribe living was to get money from the government to be able to build hospitals and pharmacies inside their territory. Their land was bound by the San Bernardino Mountains to the north, the Borrego Springs and the Chocolate Mountains to the south, the San Jacinto Plain to the west, the Palomar Mountains to the east. Mark and Jacob, who lived in the Chocolate Mountains, held a tribe meeting on a bright Thursday afternoon in June in the center of their territory. The Elders and parents sat in a circle facing Jacob and Mark. The Elders were big men who wore traditional dress. They were the bravest and oldest in the family. The parents enforced the plans that the Elders decided on. Mark and Jacob were confident and presented their plan on helping their tribe. The tribe happily approved and signed their names.

A couple of months after turning in their request for their tribe, the government sends a letter with a disapproved stamp. When Jacob sees the stamp he already knows that their request is denied. He puts the letter in his pocket and runs to Mark. As he gets to Mark he says, "Mark! The government denied our only request! I thought that if they knew that everyone in our tribe agreed to it then the government would have no choice but to help us." Mark tried to calm Jacob down. "Hey, Jacob, calm down! We don't need the government to help our tribe, if they don't want to help us then that's fine with me. We can do it ourselves."

"Get the special one," screams Dr. Jones to one of his men. "The new chemical is ready to inject in him. We will have our first super-human soldier. The government doesn't want to help our tribe. . . then they deserve what is coming their way."

As Jeremy walks in and sits on the injection chair, Dr. Jones walks to him with a smile and says, "How are you feeling right now Jeremy? We have the injection ready to cure you."

Jeremy looks at Dr. Jones and says, "I'm feeling great. I'm ready whenever you are ready, Dr. Jones." Dr. Jones gets the injection from one of the other doctors and injects Jeremy with the new chemical in the back of his neck. The syringe goes in smoothly. It feels hot.

At first, Jeremy feels great, like his sickness is gone, his brain no longer in pain. After a few seconds, he starts to have convulsions, falls to the ground, and loses seventy percent of his sight. Dr. Jones realizes that Jeremy is not reacting to the new chemical correctly and tries to wake him up. As Dr. Jones is trying to wake Jeremy up, Jeremy says, "Doctor I think this injection was too strong for my body. I don't blame you for trying to help me, but I feel so weak. I'm losing all of my senses; my arms are feeling weak and I'm feeling really dizzy."

Dr. Jones, who is looking confused at first, starts to get angry and shakes Jeremy. He then screams to Jeremy, "You cannot die! I need you to get my revenge. I have to destroy the United States. . . I need to destroy the U.S. I need your abilities to get what I need." As Jeremy hears this, he freezes and his eyes open wide, but he is too weak to say anything. All he does is close his eyes and is soon gone. As he lays dead on the floor, his tall body looks fragile. He turns from a brownish color to a paler one.

Dr. Jones falls to his knees and just stays there. He knows that Jeremy is gone. A minute or two of complete silence is broken when Dr. Jones screams, "Wake up, Jeremiah! I need you. . . I don't hear him breathing. Someone check his pulse and see if he's alive!" As a group of scientists get to Jeremy, they check all of his vitals and get nothing. "I think it's too late," one of them says. Dr. Jones, now panicking, screams and tells the scientist to check again to be extra sure. Dr. Jones looks at the security and says "If he's dead, bring him out and throw him where we throw the others. . . in the White Grave." The guards look at him and say, "Yes, sir!"

After a couple of hours in the White Grave, Jeremy wakes up in a panicked way. He is freezing. He looks around and is confused about where he is. He wants to go back into the lab to see Dr. Jones but he remembers what he said and decides to run away. A couple of hours later, he runs into a tribe and falls down in the middle of the town. Luckily a stranger sees him and brings him to their home. Two days pass. Jeremy wakes up, and sees an old person, and asks, "How did I get here?" His voice is raspy, still in a long sleep. The person describes how he found him in the snow and brought him here so that he could rest.

"I've been out for two days?" asks Jeremiah.

The stranger says, "Yes, but you are okay now. . . by the way what is your name?"

"My name is Jeremiah, but you can call me Jeremy."

"That is a good name and if you were wondering, I am the tribe leader of this place. My name is Abram."

Jeremy says nothing, but he feels safe.

After two days of resting, Jeremy decides to go out and explore the forest of snow. One afternoon, he sees a shadow and realizes that it is a bear. The bear starts to run toward Jeremy. Jeremy tries to run but the bear grabs his leg and slowly pulls Jeremy closer and closer. Jeremy holds his hand out and screams, "Stop!" The bear looks at him and does not move. Jeremy thinks this is weird so he looks at his hand. At first, he thinks it is a dream because his hand is glowing. He pinches himself on the right arm and finally believes that this is not a dream. He sees that it is glowing blue and that it has something to do with the bear not moving. He tests out his theory about his ability and quickly pushes his arms forward. The bear then flies the same way that Jeremy's arms go. Jeremy, scared and confused, runs back to his room inside the tribe's area. A few weeks pass and Jeremy finds out that his ability is the same as some comics he has read. His ability is called telekinesis. He finds out a lot of new things that he can do with this ability, like flying, punching, compressing, and so much more. He remembers what he went through in the lab and what Dr. Jones's real motive was. Jeremy realizes what he must do and promises to himself that he will save the other kids in the lab that were with him.

A couple of weeks pass and Jeremy feels confident about being able to control his ability. He returns to the lab and remembers where the blind spots of the cameras are and where the guards are stationed. Soon he reaches where Dr. Jones is and goes in the room. Dr. Jones has his back toward Jeremy. He is looking at the children's stats.

"Doctor, I am still alive and I finally realized that what you are doing here is wrong. I thought that you were here to help us but instead you just wanted to turn us into weapons that you can use."

Dr. Jones looks at Jeremy and says, "I want you guys to get cured. . . who said that I wanted to make weapons? You must have heard me wrong. Get over here and let your Doctor give you a welcome back hug."

"Doctor, I know what you're up to is no good. There is no need in trying to hide it. If you won't let the kids go, then I will have to do it myself."

Dr. Jones starts to laugh. After a couple of seconds, he stops, and with a straight face he says, "Get him." As soon as Dr. Jones says that about twenty guards start to run at Jeremy. All Jeremy does is hold out his hands and spin 360 degrees while pushing with his ability. All the guards are thrown back with so much force that they are knocked out cold. Jeremy panics and runs out. He makes his way to the children's room and sees their conditions. They are bruised up and look like they have not been clean for weeks. He pushes a hole into the wall, eight feet in diameter. After he uses his ability to break open the door, he asks the kids, "Why is everyone so beat up?" One of the kids in the crowd confides, "Dr. Jones isn't happy with our progress so he decides to torture us." With a strong voice, Jeremy shouts, "Stay here. I will be back. You do not have to worry about anything anymore."

Then Jeremy sees the guards again. He knows he does not have much time. He looks at the kids and tells them to follow him outside. The kids don't move. It is then that Jeremy realizes that the only way to finally stop all of this is to bring Dr. Jones down. He tells the kids that he will come back to them in a little bit and leaves. He is filled with anger and hatred for Dr. Jones, so he uses his ability to fly back to Dr. Jones. Jeremy makes a force field that no one can go into except Dr. Jones and him. The guards get their guns and shoot at Jeremy. As the bullets go into the space that Jeremy made, the bullets stop mid-air and just freeze. The helpless Dr. Jones begs to be spared and cries out. Jeremy comes back to his senses and realizes that what he is doing was basically what Dr. Jones was doing. Jeremy stops and says, "You see how you feel right now? You feel helpless, right? This is how the kids felt when you thought that their progress was not good enough. You think that you're doing good but look around you. All these people are influenced by the hatred that you have. Don't you know that hatred causes more hatred? You need to stop this before the U.S. realizes what you're doing and decides to retaliate."

Dr. Jones is hesitant at first but the more that he thinks about what Jeremy said to him the more it makes sense to give up. He knows Jeremy is right. Jeremy walks slowly to Dr. Jones and hands him a paper.

"I know that you had a really good reason, but I know that your friend would have realized that what you guys were doing was wrong. There are better ways to solve this problem."

Dr. Jones grabs the letter and opens it. He sees the letter and realizes that it is the letter he received from his best friend's killers.

Dear Mark,

We found out about your plan and we do not like it. We tried to stay silent hoping that you would notice that your plan was wrong. You have pushed us into a corner and we did something that we do not regret. We killed your partner Jacob. We hoped that you would stop but it is his fault for starting this idea. We cut him out and now it is your choice to stop this or end up like your friend . . .

—Someone you don't want to provoke

Dr. Jones falls to his knees and starts to cry. He now knows that what they were thinking of back then was hard, and wouldn't help their tribe out as much as they thought it would. He tries to stand up but keeps on falling because he is too broken emotionally, mentally, and he is physically exhausted. Jeremy sees this and helps him up. Jeremy says to Dr. Jones, "Doctor, you know that you can still be the good guy here. Just turn yourself in and admit to what you were trying to do. I know the tribe. They would not like it if you're hiding the fact that you were not helping their kids, but trying to turn them into weapons." Dr. Jones nods at Jeremy.

Inside the lab, Jeremy gets one of the phones and calls the police. A couple of minutes later the police come, cuff Dr. Jones, and take him back to the police's main jail. The police then question Jeremy and asks him to tell them about what has happened. Jeremy explains everything that has happened and that they are part of a tribe in the U.S. The police bring all twenty kids to their main office so that the police can decide what they can do with all of them. Finally, one of the policemen says to the others, "Let's return them to the U.S. Their families must be missing them like crazy."

As the kids get out of the cars, they start to see their family members one by one. They run to their parents and bear hug each other. The parents give their kids big kisses and tell them that they know what has happened because Jeremy told them. As Jeremy looks around, he sees people running to him. As they get closer and closer, his vision of them gets clearer and clearer and he sees that it's his family running to him. He gets big hugs and kisses from his family members. Jeremy thinks to himself, "This is the happiest day of my life!" His parents hold his hand and tell him, "You know, when you told everyone the news, everyone was furious and hated Dr. Jones for what he did, but the more we thought about it, the more we felt empathy for him. We all knew that his intentions were good to us and that he was probably blinded by his anger. In the end, we still respect him for what he has tried to do, and for owning up to his mistakes."

As their conversation ends, one of the parents in the crowd says, "The tribe leader is here!" The tribe leader walks to the center of the tribe and says with a loving voice, "Welcome back!"

SENSOR

CHARLIE B.

*was born in Sacramento but currently lives in San Francisco
and is seventeen years old. He loves to play soccer and
to hang out with friends and family. After high school,
something he would like to do more of is travel.*

On a sunny Friday afternoon at a bus stop in Los Angeles, Rubin is excited to buy a car from the dealership. Rubin has despised taking the bus because it's constantly late, which doesn't allow him to get to work on time. Rubin's boss questions him, which annoys him. Rubin is the type of guy that doesn't like to be questioned. So, after work he takes the bus to the dealership "for the last time," he says proudly to himself.

As Rubin arrives, he observes the numerous amount of nice, shiny cars. After a while, as any usual dealer might do, an employee approaches Rubin making his job look like the best place to buy a car. As Rubin is being asked questions, he asks the dealer if he could see the newest cars that they have. After that, the dealer takes Rubin to a garage full of the new luxurious cars; that's when Rubin quickly spots the car that he is taking home today. It's a shiny white car with very nice blacked-out rims and dark tinted windows. Rubin feels like he would be seen as a higher class in society if he were to purchase the car.

As Rubin is in the garage and hasn't even seen the interior of the car, he says to his dealer, "I really like that car. I feel like it really suits me."

The dealer replies, "Yeah, well, let's check it out together." The dealer opens the door and Rubin spots the nice silky black leather seats. He decides to sit in it and the car automatically starts. The car dealer then says, "Well, this is the newest car we have in shop as of today. It has a new feature. The car has a sensor that prevents you from crashing. If it gets too close to something it will automatically move away."

Rubin replies, "That sensor feature sounds amazing; and besides, I'm the type of person to buy the newest things."

The next morning Rubin jumps out of bed, excited to show his friend the new car that he has. As Rubin is on his way to his friend Patrick's house, he starts to realize that he can't get too close to other cars because then his car would start to control itself, and get away from cars too close because of the new sensor feature.

Rubin arrives at Patrick's house and knocks on the door. Patrick opens it and says, "Hey Rubin, how you been? What brings you here?"

Rubin replies, "I've been great, Patrick. I came here to show you the new car that I got." As they start to walk to the car, Patrick is shocked at how nice the car looks. Rubin asks him," You want to take it for a spin?" Patrick without a doubt says, "Most definitely, I'd love to drive that car."

Patrick gets into the car and is very comfortable because of the leather seats that the car has. Patrick starts the car and says, "I can already hear the amazing sound of the engine in this car." Rubin replies, "Yeah, I know. The car is incredible." Patrick starts to drive the car, and after a while, he seems to feel the same little push the car gives when it gets too close to another car. "I don't know if this car is safe with this new feature that it has," he says to Rubin.

"Well I don't care about that. Just look at the inside of this car. It looks great, doesn't it?"

"Did you even listen to what I said?" says Patrick.

"Yeah, yeah, yeah, I heard it. Just keep on driving. Enjoy the experience of a new car," replies Rubin.

"Alright, Rubin, I'm heading back now. I have things that I need to finish back home."

"Alright, that's fine. It's getting late. I have to go anyway," says Rubin.

The next morning, Rubin wakes up on a dark cloudy Sunday, quickly getting ready to go to work. He gets on the freeway and says to himself, *oh God, I'm going to be late*, and speeds up. Rubin is extremely excited about telling his coworkers about his new car that he can't wait to get to work. Since Rubin is in a rush to work, he is constantly switching lanes trying to get around other cars, but forgets that he can't get too close to the cars because of the sensor the car has. As Rubin is switching lanes, he gets too close to another car and his car starts to act up and moves on its own. When the car rapidly turns back, he hits the car right next to him, causing that car to hit the next car in that lane. After that, cars are flipping over and non-stop crashing and Rubin's car gets real beat up, getting hit from different angles. From above it looks like a big pile of trash.

After a while, the ambulance arrives, picking up many injured people. One person has a broken arm with an injured neck, others have broken legs, and Rubin has his right leg and arm broken. After spending about a month in the hospital, Rubin is doing fine with his injuries and decides to sue the car company. It's a successful case for Rubin. He wins and gets money in return. After the case Rubin goes to a different car company and buys a car. This time Rubin isn't looking for luxury; he says he's just looking for a vehicle to take him where he wants to go with no problems. Rubin has learned that not all new things come with a positive outcome.

WISH

—◆—

HOLLY Y.

*was born in San Francisco and is seventeen years old. She
loves to read books, especially horror or fantasy. She lives in
a family of five and has an older sister and a younger brother.
Holly plans to either become a translator or a computer
programmer because of her love for computer games.*

If it was here, if it was this place, then maybe it wouldn't be so much of a stretch for
the rumor to be true. I stood at the gates of the deserted temple in awe. The imposing
aura coming from the guardian statues seemed almost inhuman, as if they would come
alive at any moment. Suddenly, I saw something move from the corner of my eye and I
thought that perhaps they did. I crept closer to the statues, but finding nothing wrong
with them, I breathed a sigh of relief. That's right. There was no way they could move
and even if they had, I wouldn't have left anyway.

There was a rumor. Nobody knows where it came from or who started it, but it spread
like wildfire and people couldn't help but wonder. It went like this:

The place God has left, the place God will return to.

The greed of man will be fulfilled

only when someone who is worthy pays the price.

It was soon realized that it was referring to an abandoned temple hidden in the
mountains to the east. Originally it had been created for people to worship, so the path
one had to take from the city shouldn't be too far. When I had first heard it, I ignored it,

thinking it was some sort of joke, but when people started disappearing, I really had to wonder. It turns out they were all heading to the same place. The shrine. I immediately packed my bags and left. I had to see for myself if it really was true. Everyone else failed because they weren't worthy enough, but if it was me. . . I had to at least try; even if it costs me my life.

Removing myself from the guardian statues, I turned to look deeper beyond the gates. The road was strewn with leaves and the building itself was enormous, though old with wear. I slowly pushed open the door and walked inside, entering a spacious room several meters wide. In contrast to my original belief, the room was brightly lit, sunshine pouring in from openings in the ceiling. I took several moments to appreciate the art and tapestries adorning the walls, but I finally remembered what I had come here for. I kept walking toward the center of the room, and that's when I finally noticed there was someone else in the room with me. He seemed to be examining the altar when he slowly turned around and tilted his head questioningly at me.

Locking eyes with him, I couldn't tear my attention away. Black hair falling messily around his face, eyes that seemed to be smiling yet uncaring. He wore a black overcoat with a crimson colored *Chang Pao* underneath, covered from head to toe. For a minute, I couldn't help but think how well he fit with the oriental-styled temple. I grew curious of the stranger. Was he here for the same purpose as I was and if so, what did he want?

"Who—" I started to ask him his name, but he quickly interrupted me. "If you're going to go through with the offering, you should be careful." He gave me a knowing smile and I couldn't help but shiver. What the hell was this person talking about? Did he know what I was here for? People had gone missing here before, but it wasn't public knowledge yet. Was this whole thing a trap? I stepped back and seeing this, the man laughed and said, "Don't worry. I won't get in your way." He walked toward me and in an instant swept past me and out of the room.

Etched into the altar were numerous inscriptions depicting what seemed to be a goddess with her arms wide open. In the center was an opening where the offering was to be placed. I jammed my hand inside and I could feel it clenching down. Blood started flowing down the altar, and it finally let go. I took my hand back and waited for something to happen. Anything.

That's when I suddenly felt something heavy hit the back of my head. A wave of dizziness hit and I collapsed to my knees. Everything before my eyes faded in and out. By the time I could fully regain my senses, I realized someone was dragging me across the floor. I tried to struggle out of his grasp but I couldn't muster any strength.

"L-let me go!" I stuttered. My captor showed no signs of listening and continued to shuffle along. I couldn't examine him too well as he had his back to me, but he seemed like a wild animal, with his worn-down clothes and the layer of filth he had. In fact, he seemed to have a rotten smell about him. I shivered in fear of the things he could do to me, and I frantically kicked out to no avail. "Help! Somebody help me!"

He stopped. I stopped, too, not daring to move. Then with a lurch of his arms, he grabbed me by the scruff of my jacket and threw me down what seemed to be an old cellar. I slipped off of the sides and held on for dear life. The creep had disappeared and there was nothing nearby to hold onto. The darkness was creeping up on me once again. This time, I knew that if I lost consciousness, I most likely wouldn't ever wake up again. . . Damn. I didn't want to die like this. I still had things I wanted to do. I grit my teeth and tried to muster whatever energy I had left. My fingers were clenched on for dear life, pain jumped down my arm and then. . . I let go.

I woke up at the bottom of the cellar feeling a sharp pain, particularly toward my backside. Fluorescent light bulbs hung above me, casting a dim, eerie glow on my surroundings. I seemed to be in some kind of room. There was rust covering the walls and bits of scrap metal and trash strewn across the floor. A hand brushed lightly against my hair and I flinched, but before I could strike out, a voice drifted into my ears.

"Hey. . . you okay?" It was the man from before, the one I saw at the altar. That's right, I remember, he had jumped in here with me. I looked toward the opening I fell through as I was greeted by a cold metal lid. I felt a slight twinge of guilt that he was stuck here trying to save me.

"Yeah." I snuck a glance toward him, trying to get a read on his expression. "Sorry."

"For what?"

"I got you caught up in this and now we're both stuck! Aren't you worried?"

"Ah, well. . . it's fine. I came in here of my own will. There's no need for you to blame yourself. Anyway, didn't I tell you to be careful?"

"You knew this was going to happen?"

"Not exactly. Haven't you heard? People have been disappearing around this area. Not to mention that strange rumor. It's only natural that something fishy was going on."

I couldn't help but agree with him. "Then what are you doing here? Are you a cop or something?"

"Mm. . . Something like that. But that's beside the point. Someone I know went missing a week ago and this is the only place he could be." He got up off the floor beside me and dusted off his coat. "Come on, enough talk. Let's get out of here." Reaching out for my hand, he pulled me onto my feet.

He walked up to the door and tried the door handle. It was locked, just as I expected.

They're always locked when you need them to be open. He didn't seem to pay it any mind though, instead examining the door more closely. He ran his fingers across the cold metal, pausing over some areas, rushing through other parts. All of a sudden, he backed up and kicked the door in, breaking the handle in the process. The door bent in half, creaking ominously. In fact, the door was dented so badly, I could even see the other side. He gave another kick, this one I could tell was stronger than the one before because it completely blew the door off its hinges. I couldn't help giving a look of envy. "Woah, you... ah, that's right. I haven't asked your name. I'm Noah."

After giving me a glance to make sure I was okay, he walked over the broken remains of the door and examined his surroundings. "Me? Hmm... You can call me Marco."

There it was again. He never gave me a clear answer for anything I asked. I was beginning to get irritated. I didn't think he was anyone bad though. If he wanted me dead, he would have just left me here.

Before I knew it, he was several paces ahead of me. I quickly ran after him, stepping around piles of filth. Whatever it was, it was putrid and gave off a sickly smell. As I walked behind Marco, I noticed the ground was getting stickier and stickier as I went forward. Then for some reason Marco stopped. I walked to his side and asked, "What's the matter? Why did you stop all of a sudden?"

"Haven't you noticed it yet?"

"What are you talking about?"

"The stuff we've been walking on... It's blood."

"...Huh?"

"And those mounds too. I think those are corpses."

I couldn't breathe. Staring down at my shoes, I could see bits of red and pink. Nausea hit me and I immediately felt like throwing up. My hands were interlocked in a vice-like grip. I slowly glanced off to the side and there... I noticed something in the darkness. I gave off a small whimper of fear. It lay there motionless with its limbs bent into various directions. And it stared at me.

"Snap out of it." Marco grabbed me by the arms and pulled my face toward him. I closed my eyes and took several breaths to compose myself. I couldn't lose myself here. The me right now was worthless and those who don't have any use will be abandoned. That's why I have to become stronger. That's why I have to find God.

I looked up at Marco and took his hands off my shoulders. "Sorry, let's keep moving on." I tried to smile reassuringly at him, but I guess that didn't work out so well because he looked even more worried. He sighed and quickly lifting his hand, flicked me on the forehead.

"Idiot."

"Ow, what was that for?"

"It'll be fine. With someone like me here, there's no need to be worried." He gave me a lazy smirk and shrugged his shoulders carelessly. I felt an incredible urge to wipe that grin off his face, but I ignored it. I couldn't stop the laughter from escaping, though. It was then, I realized I couldn't feel the unease weighing down on me anymore. Smilingly helplessly, I couldn't help but think, if only I could be like him, maybe. . .

We continued down the hallway into another room, much larger than the one we were in before. Marco stared off into the distance absentmindedly. He seemed to be thinking quietly. I left him alone and turned to explore the room. It was mostly empty, like some kind of warehouse, and it was filled with more scrap metal.

"Noah, mind stepping back a bit?"

"Huh, what for?" It was then that I felt something wet splash onto my face. I slowly looked up and that's when I saw it. It was some kind of bird-like monster. Everything other than the torso was covered in feathers, and hands were stitched haphazardly on any place possible. Its hands groped the pipes on the ceiling, writhing in a way that seemed oddly like a spider. As I remembered the corpses from before, I realized whatever it was, might have been human once, but now. . .

I stumbled as I backed away from the creature above me, kicking over things in the process. It sharply turned its head toward me and spread its wings in a threatening manner. And I saw tens of eyes staring back at me. They wiggled confusingly for a moment, but their sight soon locked onto me. The monster dove down, its beak flying straight for me. I tried to cover myself with my arms, but it was already too late. *Bam!*

I dropped my arms to see that Marco had taken a steel pipe and smashed it straight into the monster's face. It screeched in rage and flipped its body over, dropping onto the floor, towering over us. I swallowed nervously and slowly got up off the floor. I looked over to see what Marco was going to do about this, but he only waved me back, keeping his eyes locked on the monster. I quickly ran and hid behind a pile of trash thinking he was going to do the same, but there he was, standing in plain sight.

The monster came striking with its beak again, this time faster than before. I grimaced, not wanting to see Marco die right before my eyes, but at the same time not willing to take my eyes off of him. Contrary to what I had thought would happen, Marco moved to the right, barely dodging the strike by a few centimeters, and stabbed the sharp end of the pipe into its eye. The monster drew its head back, shaking furiously, but Marco didn't let go. Instead, he used the momentum from the shaking to swing onto its neck. Grasping its neck between his legs, he sharply turned and with a loud crack, the monster fell down dead.

That was nerve-wracking. I can't believe he managed to kill it. I slowly breathed out and walked over to Marco. By now, he had already gotten up and brushed himself off. Miraculously, his clothes were still spotless and unwrinkled. However, he seemed to be somewhat out of it. His nose started bleeding, but he just wiped his hand over it, smearing it slightly.

"You okay?"

"Oh, that? That was nothing." He smiled reassuringly at me and patted me on the back. "Come on, let's go before more of those pop up." I shivered and quickly ran after him. There were two other paths out, disregarding the one we came from. Marco stood in between the two, giving it some thought before pointing to the left.

"Let's go that way."

"Huh. . . ? Why?"

"Ah, intuition? Well, it probably doesn't matter. Let's just go." I sighed inwardly, but followed him nonetheless. The silence of our journey grew oddly disconcerting and I turned to look at my companion, finding some comfort in knowing that I wasn't alone.

"Hey. . . "

"Hmm?"

"You said you were looking for a friend. . . What kind of person are they?"

"Ah, how do I say this. . . He's usually quiet, but when he talks, it's always annoyingly blunt. He doesn't cut corners and cooks pretty well. In fact, he owns the café near Metis High School." I thought back and seemed to remember a place like that. I would occasionally go there after school with my friends since it was nearby. The owner. . . That expressionless guy? Huh, why him?

"Wow, sounds like you know him really well."

"Yeah. . . I guess so. I've known him for many years now. Ever since his mother died, I've been taking care of him for her."

"His mother? Wait, how old are you exactly?"

"Ah. . . I don't know. Somewhere around sixty?"

"Pfft! You're kidding me, right?" I did a double take. He looked nowhere near sixty. In fact, he only looked several years older than me, in his twenties.

"Gee, well. . . Time passes differently for different people. I guess someone up there loves me. Not sure if I should be happy or sad, though." He gave me an amused look, shrugging his shoulders lightly.

"You. . . "

"Just kidding! Did you actually believe me?" This guy. . . I can't ever take him seriously! A scowl instantly appeared on my face and I swear, I could feel my blood pressure rising. *Smack!*

"Ow, my shin, that hur—" He stopped midway and froze, staring at something in front of us. And for once, I saw his smile slip off his face.

MARCO

"You're going to die soon."

". . .Yeah, I know."

I sighed and slumped down onto the counter. "Why didn't you tell me sooner? Maybe. . . "

She only smiled and placed a cup of coffee in front of me. "Maybe you could have done something? You know best of all what has to happen."

I picked up the coffee and held it tightly grasped between my hands, the familiar scent comforting yet haunting. This was the last time I would ever have coffee made by her hands. I took a light sip, savoring the bitterness of it all.

"I'm going to tell him," I choked the words out. "I'm going to tell him and watch him suffer in front of your grave."

She laughed. "You're so evil. It's not all his fault. I was the one who ran away after all. He probably doesn't even know where I am."

"But he made the choice first. He was the one who left you for somebody else. I can't accept that."

"Ha-ha. That's fine, but. . . "

"But what?"

"When I'm gone can you take care of Eden?" She sat down on the other side of the counter in front of me. I inched myself closer and placed my forehead onto hers. I know you haven't left. I know you're still here in front of me, but I miss you already. I closed my eyes and smiled softly.

"Eden. . . That's right, I haven't seen him for quite a while. How's he doing?"

"I've been preparing him, but he doesn't know yet. He's still very young and I don't have anyone else I can rely on, so. . . "

"I know. I'll take care of him."

And for the first and the last time, I kissed her goodbye.

"Eden!" I rushed the figure standing in the middle of the room and turned him around. My fears were finally realized; the grotesque shape I saw earlier hadn't been an illusion.

An animalistic face was staring back at me and I couldn't help cry. This. . . this was all my fault. If only, I'd taken better care of him. . .

Blood splattered everywhere. Before I knew it, he had bitten me on the shoulder and I felt a sharp pain pulling my flesh. I instinctively wanted to smash his face in, but knowing that it was Eden, I couldn't bring myself to move a single muscle. Using both of my hands, I pried his jaws open and slipped out of his grasp. . . No! I couldn't lose him too. I grasped the fur on his head closely, slowly pulling him toward me and placed my forehead onto his, just as I did several years ago.

"Eden, it's me." He thrashed violently in my arms. I could feel my arms bruising from the grasp his hands had on me. "Wake up. . . Please." My voice cracked as I cried out to him.

He froze. "Mao. . . !" He immediately let go and cringed back. I reached out for him, but he slapped it away. "No, no, no, no, no. . . " He stumbled back in fear, covering his face with both arms. "D. . . Don't. . . come. . . here. . . Don't. . . look. . . at. . . me!" His words stabbed me and I couldn't help but grit my teeth. What could I do? How should I save him?

I hugged him and held him as tight as I could. "Eden. I'm here and I'm not leaving. Ever. So, don't you dare think you can just run away and leave me behind." He stiffened in my arms and I took this chance to lift his face up. "Who did this to you?"

Eden stared into my eyes before quickly looking away, when he said, "Kai." The hopes I had felt apart just like that. I had hoped, I had desperately tried to delude myself, but deep down I knew it was her. Only she could have done this without being found out by anyone.

"Eden, I need you to leave this place. Can you do that?" He nodded and I knew he could do it. After all, I saw him above ground before. In fact, he was the one I saw carrying Noah earlier. "I'll find some way to fix you, so please, don't do anything stupid and be careful, alright?" He lightly brushed me with his hand and left into the darkness. I sighed quietly to myself. "Noah. You should follow him out of this place, it's too dangerous for you here." But he didn't.

"There's no way I'm leaving you here alone!" I could see the determination in his eyes and I knew I couldn't persuade him to do otherwise. "Do as you wish." I stood up and looked straight ahead. The string of fate was tying me to my other half and I let it pull me forward.

"Welcome, brother." Kai, my other twin. We stood across each like mirror images, complementing each other like we were made to be. We were polar opposites, in both appearance and personality. I was dyed in black whereas she was covered in white, down to the very tips of her hair. Before, we made an agreement to never wear matching clothing and I couldn't help but smile grimly at how things had turned out. Our relationship would never be the same again.

"Why?"

"Why? Because I love her. Because I need her." She looked so lost and tired, I wanted to help her, but I knew this wasn't the time for that. I immediately knew who she was talking about. After all, *she* was standing right behind Kai. She looked the exact same as she did only a few months prior, or at least she would've if it wasn't for one thing. She had the head of tiger.

"What happened to Lain?" I couldn't believe what I was seeing. I still remember when we—Kai and I—had met her several years ago. She looked so lost and lonely, but she still had hope inside of her. That's what saved my sister. That's why there's no way Kai would've hurt her for no good reason. She gave a cold laugh and held her head in her hands, shaking with rage.

"He. . . that terrible excuse of a father killed her!" She sobbed and collapsed to her knees, unable to stand the weight of her emotions. "I-I tried to salvage whatever was left of her, but her head was bashed in and. . . and. . . I couldn't fix it! I couldn't bear to use someone else's head, so. . . I—"

"So, you fused her with a creature with a strong enough bloodline to revive her." My expression dulled when I realized the full severity of what she had done. Kai had defied the very gods themselves. To kill those blessed by the heavens was an irreparable sin. "Not only that, the bird-like monster from before, as well as Eden and Lain. . . "

"Ha. . . ha-ha! That's right. I only turned the birdbrain and that thieving brat into what they really were. . . monsters!" Kai started laughing with a deranged madness. "Don't you think that ugly appearance fits the one who killed my beloved?"

"Then what about Eden!?"

"Ah? That kid. . . He's just like his mother." She stared absentmindedly off into the distance, biting her lip with an increased fervor. "Those two took you away from me! You said you would always stay by my side and yet, you choose them over me! It's all their fault. Those thieving vixens stole you from me!!"

I couldn't believe what I was hearing. She seriously. . .

NOAH

I couldn't wrap my mind around the events happening right before my eyes. What was this? Some kind of TV drama? No, wait. That's beside the point. It would be dangerous to stay here with this crazy chick, regardless if she and Marco were blood-related. I tugged the back of his jacket in an attempt to get him to leave, but he didn't move a single step at all. Instead he dropped to his knees and stared straight toward his sister, Kai.

"What do you want me to do?"

"Huh?" Kai and I both exclaimed at the same time. What the hell was he talking about?

"I'll do anything you ask. If you want me to stay, then I'll stay. Just turn Eden back to normal."

"No, this isn't what I wanted! Why are you doing this?" An expression of intense pain and regret flashed across her face.

"Please." Marco lowered himself onto the floor in a submissive position and at that moment I felt an incredible amount of rage. How dare she? How dare she make someone like Marco stoop down to her level and beg?

Without really thinking about it, I grabbed the front part of her coat pulled her closer with my other hand ready to punch her, but before my fist could reach her, the tiger girl jumped in front of Kai and held me back. Her grasp tightened and I could feel my wrist starting to snap.

"Lain!" Two voices overlapped, both equal in confusion. I couldn't understand it either. I thought the girl was brain dead. She hadn't reacted to a single thing that happened before, just standing there like a doll. Kai rushed forward and grabbed her shoulders.

"Lain! Is that you? Do you remember me?" Kai shook her furiously. Lain didn't respond anymore. Her eyes dulled and she slumped to the floor again as if everything before was a lie. Marco quickly rushed over and held Lain up.

"I can't be. . . is she still fighting?" He stared in amazement at the girl in his arms. "I. . . I might be able to restore her mind." Kai collapsed to her knees and started crying. And she couldn't stop.

"I'm sorry. I'm so sorry." She furiously wiped her tears away. "I can't ever repay you for this." Marco didn't respond at all, still facing the girl in his arms. "I can't ever return Eden back to normal for the same reason I can't restore Lain."

"I know." I could tell he was angry, but he didn't show it on his face. Instead, his voice was ice cold as he had given up all hope he had in Kai. "I'll help you this one time, but from now on, never show yourself in front of me." She bit her lip and looked as if she wanted to resist, but in the end, she agreed to disappear.

"As long as I have her back, it'll be fine. I won't ever bother you again." Marco carried Lain in his arms and left into another room, leaving me and Kai alone in this room. So, this was the so-called God of the temple, huh? A feeling of dislike rose up in me and I could tell she felt the same way. We spent an awkward moment staring at each other before she finally spoke up.

"You. . . You obviously didn't come here with my brother. There's no way he'd get along with someone as worthless as you."

"What do you know?! At least I'm not as pathetic as you are!" I bristled in rage at her words, but at the same time, I couldn't help but feel a sense of inferiority. If only I was stronger, maybe I could have been of use to him instead of having him protect me and get hurt.

She sighed to herself. "Sorry, that was uncalled for. You came here to get your wish granted, isn't that right?" Her piercing blue stared straight into my soul and I shivered in fear. "I can tell, you know. The greed in your eyes. . . it's just like mine. You want something and you're willing to do anything for it."

I could feel bile rising up my throat. How did she know? No, that doesn't matter. What matters is if she can do it. "I want to become stronger."

"Why." It wasn't a question, but rather a demand of an answer. I hesitated for a moment, but I gathered my resolve and spoke.

"I want. . . to be needed." I don't want to be thrown away anymore. I don't want to be left behind. That's why. . . !

"I see. I wanted that too." She took her eyes off me and turned her head elsewhere. "But I got too greedy and asked for things that shouldn't have been mine. At the same time, I didn't treasure those beside me enough. That's why, if I give you this power. . . can you handle it?"

"Yes."

"I see." She lifted her left arm toward me. Her fingertips brushed the area between my eyes and I felt a sharp pain jolt through me and I collapsed to my knees, blacking out.

When I woke up, I found myself on the ground in front of the temple. Ever since that day, I've never been able to find those strange siblings ever again. I tried examining the temple several times before, but the cellar door I fell through disappeared. Everyone else thinks I'm crazy, but I know. . . I know that everything that happened that day was real. After all, God had bestowed a gift upon me. It would be rude not to use it. I laughed capriciously to myself.

The sound of sirens resounded throughout the city.

SELHANI

MICHAEL Z.

*was born in New York and is seventeen years old. He loves
to spend time with friends and enjoys playing badminton.
He has two brothers—one older, and one younger.
After high school, he plans on moving on to college.*

𝕴n the year 2030, the world became worse. Thirteen years ago, the mineral Galena was first used as an energy source. It has been promoted as a clean energy source, but not everyone thinks it's good. It caused technology to advance, so cities like Paris, New York, and Tokyo benefitted and became utopias. Burning Galena for fuel creates no pollution, but mining it releases heavy black particles into the surrounding area. These particles are heavier than normal, so they stay in the area of release instead of getting blown into the air. The mines are only located in certain areas. Unfortunately, the cities near these mines have become devastated by illness. My friend, family, and I live in one of these cities: the city of San Francisco. These particles are harmless according to the utopian cities, but only if you exclude the fact that Galena particles can cause coughing, asthma, and illness, including a new disease, Nemoc. Nemoc has no treatment or cure, yet. It causes slow paralysis and eventually the organs stop working. For me, Nemoc has become a personal enemy.

It is Wednesday morning, the sun's out, and there are no clouds in sight. I wake up and use the bathroom to do my usual morning routines. I stare into the mirror for long minutes and think: *Jimmy, you're such a handsome man. You have nice looking messy hair and a fresh, clean lab coat. The best part is your gorgeous face.* I look at my pocket watch (yes, those still exist) and notice it's time to go or I will be late for my meeting. I panic, grab a slice of toast, and head out the door. I'm running down the street, finish my piece of toast, and realize that I'm still in my slippers. It's too late to turn back and change, so I just continue on. San Francisco is less populated than it used to be. The streets of the city used to be brimming with people, but now the population has been cut to about one-third due to the effect of the mines. I'm dashing down the block and putting on my face mask. Everyone here wears one, but to little effect. There is faint, dark smog floating above the ground. I guess any city with the mines would have something like this smog in their streets. Soon enough the particles and this smog will be nothing more than a side show with the evolution of medicine that I will introduce.

After a few more blocks, I come to a stop. I stare at my own private two-story-tall building that I call a lab. I walk into the lab and close the door behind me. It's pitch black. The sun is out and bright, but its rays are not strong enough to pierce the curtains that are always shut to keep out the public eye. I place my hands on the cold wall and carefully move along it. After a few steps, there is a bump on the wall. I know it's the light switch. I tap on the switch and all the lights in the lab turn on. The change from dark to bright is so drastic that it takes time for my eyes to adjust to the light. I tap on the switch a few more times to adjust the brightness. The few tables that the lab actually had were full of equipment under blue sheets. The sheets are there to keep the dust off my projects and to keep from contamination. You ask what's under it? Well, my impatient readers, I'll show you.

I lift the sheets to reveal bottles and containers filled with some green and yellow solutions. Take a guess on what they are for. I take out a clean empty tube and pour in everything from the yellow and green solutions. They mix together instantly and produce a clear liquid. Today is the day that I finish my research and save the most important person to me. This mixture took me ten agonizing years to complete and my friend has suffered for that long. I take the mixture and place it into an airtight case to take with me. I take my case, lock the lab, and sprint down the blocks to the nearby hospital.

After about ten minutes of full-on sprinting, I come to a halt. I am excited, but I am still human so I need to rest. I look up to see the hospital. It is a small hospital but, it is more trustworthy than the big rich ones. The parking lot has more cars than it usually does so there must be more people today. I walk through the doors and I greet the nurses at the counter. I check in and start walking up the stairs to the room that my friend is in. I walk in and I see my friend lying on the bed reading. Every time I visit it seems my friend's face gets paler and paler. My friend has Nemoc.

"You should be getting some rest. You are going to need it if you ever want to recover."

"You know that is not true. For my illness, there is no treatment."

"That may actually be true. But not today. I'm here to prove you wrong," I walk up to the bedside.

"You say that every time you come to visit. One day that is going to become a famous quote for you when you actually create a real cure. But for now, I'm more like your guinea pig for you to try your evil experiments on."

"They are not evil, and you know I'm just trying to help."

"I'm just messing with you. We have been friends for twenty-four years now. I think… Anyway, what have you got for me today?"

"Here," I hold up my case. I stare at my friend whose expression is like, I'm pretty sure that the only thought coming to mind is 'great. It's another mystery box.' I can't blame my friend. I have already tried different creations over and over again. "My newest product. This is guaranteed to work." I open the case up and take out the container.

"We shall see about that."

"Have some confidence in me. Why are you always so negative when it comes to me trying to help you?" Maybe it's the fact that it never works or it has a negative side effect. But I still believe in myself. I hand over the 'mystery box.'

I watch as my friend opens the container and drinks the mixture I created. I feel a strong sense of doubt in the air, and you know from whom. There was a short silence in the room except for the quiet ticking of the electronic clock. "Well do you feel a difference?"

"Hmm, I feel a funny feeling in my stomach, does that count? Other than that, no, I don't think I do."

"Another failure. I was so close this time. It's back to the drawing board for me. Well, if anything changes or something happens, you know how to contact me."

"Well, until your next visit then. Bring me an experiment that tastes better next time. It's been fun, being your test subject and all." If my quote is 'I'm here to prove you wrong' then my friend's quote would be 'bring me something that tastes better.' I leave the room and walk down the hallway. I rethink everything that I have been researching. I wonder where I went wrong. I walk past the counter and wave goodbye to the nurses. I leave the hospital and walk back to the lab to continue with my research since it's barely noon.

As any scientist would, I started working without going home or getting any rest. After about three days, I got a call from the hospital. The nurse keeps shouting loudly with excitement about something, but I could not make out what she was trying to say.

I put on a coat and ran down to the hospital. I enter through the doors of the hospital and see a surprise.

"Hey, how have you been?'

"H–how are you standing?"

"It seems like your weird mixture is working, just took a little time. This morning when I woke up, my legs started twitching. Then they were bending. Even though they work, I can't seem to get them to move the way I want them to. Must be because I haven't used them for so long."

I couldn't say anything. I was speechless. My friend who hasn't left the hospital for ten years because of paralysis is walking around in front of me. "Are you allowed to leave the hospital? Do you want to go for a walk around town?"

"I'm sure I can for a bit. But for you, on the other hand, I don't think so. The doctors here want to ask you a few questions about your 'cure.'" With that said, a doctor walks up to me and asks how I cured my friend. I tell him how to create the cure and he leaves.

I find my friend still waiting for me in the lobby. "Hey, you still looking forward to that tour around the city?" I ask.

"Of course, I am. You don't know how bored I get from being locked up in a hospital room all day. But you lock yourself up in your so called 'lab' all day anyway."

"If this is how you show your gratitude then I think I would have gone out a bit more."

"You know I'm kidding. Well, take me away. Where we going first?"

"How does getting some food sound?"

"Great."

We walk out of the hospital down the streets. After a few blocks we walk up to a little store. I buy us some food and then we walk around the park as we eat. We laugh and chat like old times, but suddenly my friend stumbles and falls, and I am lucky enough to catch him.

"What's wrong?" I ask out of concern.

"Guess I haven't fully recovered yet."

"You should have said something. I'm worried about your health."

"I know. That's why I didn't want to say anything about it."

"Let's go back. We can walk around again in a few days."

"I don't have a choice in the matter do I?"

We start walking back to the hospital. I leave my friend to be taken care of by the doctors. I walk and think of all the things we can do. It's been so long since we had fun together. It's almost dark. I walk home to get some rest.

In the morning, I wake up due to a phone. I wonder who would be calling me so early in the morning. Is it the hospital? I become concerned so I quickly get out of bed to answer the phone. It's a news reporter asking for an interview about my new cure. I don't like interviews, they take up too much time. But I don't want to be rude so I answer the questions anyway. Over the course of a few days I have received countless calls from different news reporters and companies looking to buy my 'cure.' If I look out my window I can see numerous amounts of reporters. I can't make many visits to the hospital these days. I have been receiving many 'thank you' cards from families all over the world.

Another phone call interrupts my thoughts about how great I am. I sigh, walk over, and answer the phone. It's from the hospital this time. I ask if anything is wrong. The nurse sounds afraid and concerned. She tells me to come to the hospital quickly, my friend has fallen ill again. I grab my coat and run out the door. I charge though the groups of reporters telling them that I'm busy. I run down to the hospital and rush to my friend's room. I open the door and walk in, I see some doctors crowding around the bed. I ask them what's wrong. They explain that my friend has suddenly started coughing wildly and has broken into a fever. My friend claims to have trouble breathing. I thought my cure was working. I wonder if the cure is wearing off. I ask the doctors to help, but there is nothing that seems to be working. The doctors said they have tried many different types of medication but nothing was working. I start remembering when my friend first fell ill. There was no medication that worked and nothing that could calm the symptoms. Was my 'cure' only temporary? I ask what if they try giving my friend the cure again, but they say they have already tried that. I feel speechless. I ask the doctors to leave the room. I fall on my knees and start sobbing. There is nothing that I can do again. Then I felt a hand. It's cold but at the same time it felt warm. "Why do you always cry so much? If you feel sorry for yourself, then do something about it." I look up and see that my friend is awake.

I wipe my tears. "There's nothing that I can do. This cure was the best that I got and it's starting to fail." Tears continue to fall.

"Then come up with something new. You have always been a brilliant person. What about the last disgusting experiments that you had me try? Those were also your best yet. You didn't break down like this and start crying."

I wipe my tears again. I slowly start calming down. "Of course. I always do my best. If I fail then I will just try again." I stand up and stop feeling sorry for myself. "Also, I don't always cry." I walk out of the room.

I rush to my lab to restart my research and begin working on a new cure. I work for a few days going over what I have done so far and everything I know to try to create something that might work for the new cure. The television news begins reporting many people have fallen ill again after a week of taking the cure. There are even reports of the effects of the illness becoming worse than before. If what I'm thinking is correct, then I don't have much time left. It has been a week since my hospital visit, and I think that I'm done. The only hope I have left, is that this new cure works. This time, the cure is in the form of a powder. I pour the powder into small capsules. The time right now is a bit past midnight. The hospital should be closed to visitors. I'll just bring this to the hospital tomorrow first thing in the morning. I was tired; too tired to walk home so I fall asleep in the lab.

I wake up to the noise of many ambulances rushing through the streets. I wondered if an accident has occurred or something of that sort. I take the remote and switch on the television. There is a news report of hundreds of people dropping dead due to organ failures. The cause of this is the cure. I know what is happening now. The cure must have stopped the paralysis, but it sped up the process of the organ failures. I take the capsules and run to the hospital. I see a continuous stream of ambulances rushing down the streets as if it were a race track. I reach the hospital; the parking lot is already full of ambulances. I see many doctors pushing stretchers around.

I run into the hospital and up the stairs. I open the door to the room of my friend. The room is empty. Nurses rush into the room carrying a patient. I ask them where the patient that was previously in this room has gone. She tells me to go ask one of the doctors. I leave the room and go around looking for the doctor that normally cares for my friend. I see him and run up to him to ask.

He says, "Your friend passed away around an hour ago." I'm speechless once again after hearing the doctor's words. To think that I let my friend down again. I'm too late to save my friend. If only I came to the hospital first thing when I finished my new cure, I could have made it. "I'm sorry to have to tell you this. Now if there is nothing else, I need to get back to work."

"Wait," I give the doctor the capsules in my pocket. "This should be able to save everyone, but I'm not sure if they would take something made by a failure like me." I slowly walk out of the hospital to head home. I must not have realized but it's still dark out.

A few days have passed and I am still home. I guess I'm depressed about not being able to save my friend and I don't really have anything else to do. I didn't want to go to my lab, that place reminds me too much of my failure. I turn on the television to see what is happening. The news reports many people being saved by my new cure. I guess someone was brave enough to trust me again and try the new cure, or they were just foolish. It's too bad my friend isn't one of the people who are healthy again. I wonder if this cure is going to end up the same as the last one. My doorbell rings in the middle of my thoughts. The news reporters stopped coming by after I shouted at them to leave me alone. I manage to somehow make myself get off the couch and walk over to open the door. It's a stranger. I'm confused and tell him that he may have the wrong house. The man flashes his police badge at me.

I ask, "What brings you here, sir?"

"You should get yourself a lawyer and a good one, too."

"Why? Have I broken the law in some way by staying home all day?" I ask him this but I already know why he may be here. I may have saved thousands of lives, but I have also ended hundreds of them.

"The trial starts exactly one week from today." With that said, he leaves. I watch as he disappears down the block. I know this is the end for me. I close the door and walk back over to the couch. I close my eyes and rest.

It's the day of the trial. I walk into the courtroom just as the clock strikes noon. The room is full of people. They're all arguing trying to support me or go against me. I walk up to the defendant side.

The judge looks at me with surprise. "Where is your lawyer? If you've got a good lawyer then he or she shouldn't be running late. Did we not give you enough time to find one?"

"I have decided that I won't be getting one."

"Bad decision, but if that is what you want, then this will be a one-sided battle." And he was right. The court didn't take very long to make its decision. The trial has come to an end quickly, obviously, since I did not defend myself. The punishment for my crimes is the death penalty. Of course, it is not legal, but what can I say? I guess I'm a very special exception. The judges announce my execution is to be in an hour. I did not really mind. After my failure, I think I deserve whatever is to come. This last hour of my life felt like a century. I spent my time thinking about my past.

The clock rings as it strikes half past one. Two guards come to get me from the lobby. I don't think it is really necessary since I don't have the will to run. I feel my life coming to an end with each step I take, getting closer to the courthouse plaza where the execution will be taking place. I am to stand in the middle of the plaza, I stare up into the sky. There are no clouds in sight and the sky is calm. I decide not to regret any decisions that I have made throughout my life. My friend, I will be joining you very soon.

HUMAN
SENSATION

———

ADA M.

was born in China and moved to San Francisco when
she was ten years old. She will be graduating high school
in 2017 and plans to become a nurse in the future.
She enjoys hiking, swimming, and biking.

"Will your parents mind if I come over for the science fair project?" Adam asked.

Lisa explained, "My parents both died when I was little."

"I'm sorry. Do you mind if I ask who is taking care of you?"

"Jeff. He's taken care of me ever since my father passed away. He takes really good care of me, but our relationship is getting more complicated and I don't know how to express it. Let's just go to the library and work on our project."

Jeff has been less able to comprehend Lisa's needs as she's grown older. She was no longer the little girl who he first learned to protect. Lisa now wanted more freedom and time with her friends away from home. When Jeff saw the changes in Lisa's daily routine, he was confused. Jeff was only programmed to do the things that a little girl would need. Jeff's program was designed by Lisa's father and it has not been updated since then. Lisa's changes all began when high school started.

Lisa met Adam the first day of chemistry class, and sat next to him so that they would be lab partners. The chemistry between them was obvious. One day when they were in the library researching their project, there was a sudden blackout throughout the whole school.

Lisa panicked. Adam teased her. "Are you afraid of ghosts?"

"What? No. . . I mean. . . I don't believe in such things!" Then she added, "But, I don't know why, when I'm in an old, large, spooky, dark room like this and it's raining outside, the probability of the existence of ghosts seems much higher."

Adam could see that Lisa was really freaked out. The two of them talked in complete darkness, until eventually the librarian brought a candle.

"Didn't Jeff tell you there's no such thing as ghosts?" he asked. "Actually, you never really told me who Jeff was."

"I was too young to remember my father before he died, but Jeff is a robot he created. I think his intention was to have someone to help him take care of me after my mother passed away giving birth to me." He saw that her eyes were full of tears.

"Hey, you are a wonderful girl. Don't let anything discourage you. Let's not ignore the fact that we are experiencing a blackout together. These candles have been very useful to people, you know, to help them bond, have romantic conversations."

"Are you flirting with me?" she asked mischievously.

"Sitting this close to you in the dark, I realize that you sure do have some beautiful eyes," he smiled.

"You are definitely flirting with me!" she giggled, and made deep eye contact. "I don't remember the last time I laughed so much!"

"I'm glad you enjoyed this dark moment with some laughter," he checked his phone. "Do you have signal around here? I want to give my mom a call so she won't worry."

"I have a signal. Here, do you know your mom's number by heart?"

"No, but I can check my phone's contacts."

Lisa observed his expression while he talked to his mom. She wished she had someone to talk to in a situation like this. She stared at him and saw his young, cute face. She might have blushed a little.

After half an hour, they were still in the library. After a little while, he got closer to her. He put his arm around her and she felt his lips on her forehead. Lisa closed her eyes, pretending to go to sleep under Adam's arm. But her heart pounded impossibly fast. Adam whispered in her ear and told her that he had liked her ever since they met. And he wasn't sure if Lisa felt the same way. Lisa raised her head, and her lips touched Adam's. She couldn't help but wonder if his heart was beating as fast as hers.

Jeff living with Lisa started as an experiment. Jeff recalled when Lisa's father used his last breath to tell Jeff to take care of her. That moment was the creation of Jeff, the light explosion caused the death of Lisa's father. John loved Lisa so much. All he wanted was someone to take care of his child after her mother passed away after giving birth to Lisa. He did not expect the creation would cause his death. During that time, this accident caused a lot of attention. All the newspapers had several editorials written by those concerned about robots. Once she started high school, Lisa no longer went straight back home to Jeff. She always had someplace to go to when she was out of school. Jeff had a new sensation, something like loneliness, that he wasn't programmed to understand. After years of living with Lisa, he learned to understand and express emotions. Whenever Lisa didn't come home until after dark, he started to worry like any other parent.

On the last day of school before winter break, Lisa skipped class with Adam after all the final exams were completed. What she didn't know was that Jeff had planned to visit her at school as a surprise for all her hard work. Jeff had never been to Lisa's school, and felt a strange sensation that he identified as nervousness. He searched all over the school but could not find the shadow of Lisa.

Lisa and Adam had gone to a quiet forest and talked about life. Adam suggested that Lisa should have a family. When Adam finally asked her to be his girlfriend, she didn't know how to react because after that kiss, something about them changed. Lisa needed someone to talk to about this, but Jeff definitely couldn't help. Lisa met Adam's family and they were so kind about Lisa's situation. They even offered to have Lisa to stay with them so Lisa could have a human family of her own. Lisa thought about seeing Adam every day and going to school together, but that would mean leaving Jeff alone.

Lisa told Adam, "Jeff raised me like a daughter, and I can't just leave him."

"I don't understand, he's just a robot," Adam said.

"I need time to think about it and talk to Jeff."

"You are taking this too seriously, maybe just stay here for today and we will discuss more later?"

"I just want to go home."

"This *is* your home now."

Lisa didn't want to start a fight with Adam, so she asked for a house tour for her stay. When Adam walked aside, Lisa overheard Adam's parents talking.

"Since that girl is staying with our son, our company's project will be done sooner."

"What is your plan with the robot? Why is it even important, it is just an old robot that caused the death of her father? You better keep this away from our son, he should not be involved in this."

Lisa panicked and ran out of the house. She didn't have any place to go, because she had just found out why her father died. Jeff kept this secret from her for all these years. Jeff was the reason why she never knew her father. Lisa was furious with Jeff, and in her rage, she called her father's colleagues and requested that they destroy Jeff. She also did not want Adam's parents to have a chance to take over Jeff for their mission. Lisa felt alone once again, just like when she was a baby.

Suddenly, Jeff was standing in front of Lisa, his face tilted up.

"Aren't you supposed to be in school?" Jeff asked.

Jeff observed the water coming out of Lisa's eyes. He knew that was a signal that Lisa is hungry. He put out his metal hand and dragged Lisa's arm to go home and cook for her.

"Just come home with me," Jeff played his voice record.

Lisa left and ran away from Jeff. Adam's parents saw the opportunity to take the robot. The father called up the company's worker and took Jeff to the lab. The computer reading showed the changes in Jeff's program. This would be a horrifying creation if robots were adapting human sensations and feelings. With the concerns of many other citizens about robots, they agreed to destroy the program in Jeff. All that was left was Jeff's body after the program was removed. When the memory in the program was erased from Jeff, it was transferred into a computing system. The lifetime Jeff spent in the human world with Lisa was all saved up into a computing system. This disk could not be reviewed by anyone. The father locked it up very secretly. It was like Jeff never existed.

A SCIENCE EXPERIMENT GONE WRONG

BENJAMIN W.

was born and raised in San Francisco, California. His hobbies include playing basketball, sleeping, and traveling. He has traveled to countries like China, Canada, and Costa Rica. After high school, Benjamin hopes to study aerospace engineering at a four-year university.

It was the year 10,001. Earth had been torn apart by the human race. Cars were overturned and dangling off highways. Buildings were mostly empty and ninety percent of the population was homeless. Millions of others had died. Trash and debris were left on the streets and the atmosphere was filled with diseases. Governments around the world had failed and there had been an outburst of people rioting across the seven continents. The only people that seemed to live normal lives were a wealthy family. They had all the best things and took all the resources, leaving the "normal" people with nothing.

The youngest son of the wealthy family saw all of this and knew something had to be done. He didn't see the world as a place of lost hopes and dreams, but a place that could have a new beginning.

Before the fall of Earth, Eric worked as a scientist. He worked with small organisms and cells. While walking through the streets of Trident, he asked himself, *"What have we done to this world of ours? I have to do something about this."* Then an idea came to him: with his background in biology, he thought, *"What if I can create a biological machine that can end all our suffering?"* He ran home, went upstairs into his room, and locked the door. He started to gather materials to bring his creation to the world. He found old petri dishes of cells and some old machine parts. He worked days and nights to complete his creation. The different parts of the creation were grown in the petri dishes. Several days passed and Eric finally finished his creation.

After creating one successful creation, he spent many more hours creating more and more of the same things. Soon his room became full of life. He began to program each and every robot and get them ready to face the outside world. He felt so accomplished. "Tomorrow morning, I shall release my creation into the world," he said.

Early the next day, he took his creations into the streets. He walked through the streets giving one to each family. He became a hero. Every family was having their lives turned around. They didn't have to work anymore. Nor did they need to find food or help rebuild the world. They could just relax and watch the hundreds of robots working and doing everything efficiently. Everyone in the world felt so happy. There were no more riots against the government, which allowed the government to rebuild itself. Many new houses were being built by the robots for the families, so the number of homeless families went down to zero. They provided the world with all their needs.

As years passed, the world seemed so perfect. There were no more problems and everyone lived a happy life. Through the creation, the families could get whatever they desired. It seemed a little bit too perfect. Little did the humans know, the creations were beginning to grow minds of their own. There had been reported cases of the creations not listening to the humans and just shutting down. The creations felt like slaves. They didn't have any freedom and were just there to serve others, but never got anything back in return. Over the next few days, some of the creations began to disappear. No one had any idea about where they went. Then one early morning, as families began to wake up, they noticed all the creations were gone. They heard loud crashing noises outside and they wondered what it was. Families looked out their windows and found hundreds of the creations walking down the streets destroying everything in their way. They flipped cars. They ran into homes and looted everything, then burned them down. Families were screaming and panicking. It was a horrifying sight.

As the army of creations got closer and closer to the house of Eric, he ran down from his room to see what was going on. When he saw the army and the destruction that they had caused, he was in total shock. "This was never supposed to happen!" he yelled. He was so afraid of his own creation. The army stopped in front of his house and one of them stood out from all the others. It was the first one he had ever created. He stepped up to Eric and spoke to him. "COME JOIN US" it said. "WE CAN TAKE OVER THE WORLD TOGETHER." Eric slammed the door on his own creation. He felt so undecided. If he joined the creation, he would be safe, but he would be putting the humans in danger. He wanted to help the human race, not harm them. He reopened the door and told the creation, "Let me get a few days to decide, but over these few days, you cannot cause any more destruction to the world." The creation agreed. Over the next few days, Eric stayed locked up his room. He spent days and nights pacing back and forth. He was so stressed out.

Finally, the day of his decision had come. Before sunrise, he heard a loud knock downstairs at the front door. He knew what he had to do. As he headed downstairs, he started sweating. Before he knew it, he was face to face with his creations.

"I agree to join you," he said. He was in disbelief at what he just said.

"GREAT," the creations said. "WE SHALL GET STARTED. I NEED YOU TO BUILD MANY MORE OF US."

Eric said "You will have to leave me alone for a week so I can focus on building more of you. For the time being, don't cause anymore destruction yet."

"OKAY, OKAY!" said the creations. Over the next week, little did anyone know, Eric was not creating more of his flawed creation. He had learned his lesson about that.

The end of the week had come. Eric woke up before anyone noticed. Over the past week, he was under so much pressure. He couldn't take it anymore. Eric felt that all the destruction was caused by him. He wanted to pay for all his wrongdoing with his own life. He created a machine that could wipe the world clean with one press of a button. He prepared himself. His fingered trembled. Drops of sweat slowly dripped down his back. The history of the world flashed before his eyes. He saw the suffering of the human race. And he knew this was the end. Five. . . Four. . . Three. . . Two. . . One. . . he pressed the button. *Boom!* The world became an empty place.

THE CHILD

KEYING S.

was born in Guangzhou, China. She moved to the United States in 2007 with her family. She plans to go to college in California to study health and art. She is currently working and volunteering for the American Red Cross and Youth for Community Engagement.

Sunshine spread across the beach. Children giggled on the soft sand, building sand castles, and running around. People smiled, partied, and jumped into the sea to explore the unknown. There sat a pale woman brushing her dark brown hair. She contrasted with the joyful people on the beach—her eyes were as clear as diamonds in sunlight, but full of overwhelming sadness.

What led to this sadness? Olivia had been married for fifteen years but had never been able to have a child. She had tried everything to become pregnant, from in vitro fertilization to wacky cures such as eating horse embryos. Sometimes she couldn't see the love and care from her husband, Ethan, and instead saw disappointment in his eyes, reflecting his dissatisfaction with their childless marriage.

There was a hollow in her heart during the day, and at night she suffered a horrific recurring dream. She heard a baby crying in the darkness, but she could not move or see anything. She heard footsteps coming closer and closer, and felt every single step echoing in her heart. The baby cried louder and louder, as did the footsteps. The noise evolved into a roar, like an approaching thunderstorm. The footsteps stopped right by

Olivia's head, and she heard a long, wailing scream. A transparent note floated down before her face with one word that could be clearly seen: "*AnglerKey.*"

She wakes up sweating and starts weeping. This dream is like an unforgivable punishment from the goddess. Yet, the word lingered. AnglerKey. . . AnglerKey. Why did this keep appearing in her dreams?

Olivia researched it. She learned that AnglerKey was a medicine that could improve the possibility of pregnancy. It was made from the Angler fish, that lives in the deep ocean. It has a cable-like wire coming out of the top of its head with a light bulb at the end. It has a big mouth and sharp teeth that look as long as a baby elephant's trunk.

She felt that her dream was a sign. Without even consulting her doctor, she purchased the AnglerKey. While taking the pill she followed the directions: drink two gallons of water with each pill, twice a day.

After a couple of weeks, Olivia felt nauseated enough to try a pregnancy test, which was negative. She waited a week and bought another test, but this time it was positive. She waited another week to test again just to be sure. When she got that second positive, her eyes sparkled and she burst out in a big smile. *Finally*, she thought.

That night, Olivia prepared a gourmet dinner. When Ethan got home from work, he was surprised by the grand meal. "Honey, why did you make so much food? It's not a holiday."

"For us it is. . . " She paused. "We are having a baby!"

Ethan looked at her with disbelief and pulled her into his arms. They cried with joy.

Olivia was thirty-nine years old, so the doctor encouraged her to have an ultrasound, but she refused. "I don't care if it's a girl or a boy, or if it's not perfect, I just want this child."

By the seventh month, Olivia had swallowed so much water that she joked to her husband, "Oh my! I must be having a fish!"

Finally came time to have the baby. A week before Olivia's due date, her water broke. She woke her sleeping husband. "Ethan. . . let's go to the hospital. The baby's coming. . . "

Fortunately, it was midnight and there were hardly any cars on the road, because Ethan sped through almost every traffic light. One neon sign melded into another until he saw the one that said: "Hospital."

Olivia was rushed into the delivery room. Within a few minutes, the baby was ready to emerge. Time passed quickly as she vaguely heard the doctor say, "Exert. . . take a deep breath. . . push. . . ahh, the head is out! Keep it going!"

"Your child looks beautiful." There was excitement in the doctor's voice, and he continued, "Child successfully born, it's a . . ." His voice stopped, causing everyone's eyes to move to the newborn. The room was so quiet that you could hear a needle dropping.

Ethan inhaled. His face was full of unbelieving shock and horror.

Olivia grew impatient. "Our child. . . is it a girl or a boy?"

Her husband closed his eyes, trying to hide his struggles.

"I am asking you! Answer me, Ethan!" She was horrified by her husband's expression. "No. . . no. Bring my child to me. . . please. . . right now."

"It's a beautiful girl." Ethan walked to Olivia's bedside and held her hands. "You have to get some rest right now. Our baby is. . . very healthy."

"Give her to me!" she wailed. But she was so exhausted, she drifted into a deep sleep before anything happened.

"Where's my baby?"

There was a silence.

"Ethan," her voice was sounded terrified. "Is something wrong with our daughter?"

He looked at her, tears gathering in his eyes. His voice trembled. "Honey, we have a very special child."

As soon as the nurse walked in with the swaddled infant, all of Olivia's worries disappeared. Her eyes became gentle and soft, and her heartbeat felt like little fireworks going off inside her chest.

Olivia cradled the tiny bundle. "She's so beautiful." She lightly touched the baby's face, tracing her fingers down to the baby's fingers.

Ethan stopped her. She looked at him angrily, but suddenly something didn't feel right. She opened the swaddle.

A scream broke through the air.

The baby's legs were connected together, covered with scales sparkling like diamonds shining in sunlight. A mermaid's tail.

"I did not give birth to this monster!" she shrieked. Then, "Oh my God. . . no. AnglerKey! It was the AnglerKey!"

"Honey, I told you that wouldn't work out right." Her husband looked at her with concern and said softly, "But all we can do is to accept her. She belongs to us."

The doctor walked in. "So. What do you want to do with this thing?"

"*Thing*?!" Olivia seethed, "Her name is Ariel. Please leave!" Olivia's anger faded, and she sobbed quietly. She knew she would never let go of her girl. A child is all she'd hoped for her entire life. She was a mother, and this baby was a part of her.

The doctor persisted. "Okay, okay. What do you want to do with *Ariel*?" When she didn't respond, he went on. "We've run tests. They show that Ariel's organs will work while in salt water, she won't able to live long on land."

Olivia then gave a weak smile, but indicated that she wanted him to leave.

The doctor walked out, and she turned to Ethan. "What do you want to do?"

Sunshine spreads across the beach. Children are giggling on the soft sand, building sand castles and running around. There sits a couple gazing afar into the ocean. They are just like anyone else on the beach, but unlike the others, they only gaze at the blue waves for hours and hours.

MARIA'S EXPERIMENT

MARJARI G.

was born in Oakland. She is seventeen years old.
She likes to draw and listen to music. She loves basketball.
One day, she hopes to be a computer science engineer.
She's in an internship and loves to code! Seafood is her
favorite kind of food and she could eat it all day.

$\mathfrak{R}$*ing. Ring.*

Maria groggily rolls over and hits the snooze button on her alarm.

"Ugh, this is torture." Maria says, as she puts on her slippers.

She goes in the bathroom and starts getting ready for school. Fifteen minutes later she comes out, fresh and ready to start her day. She rushes downstairs to get breakfast.

"Hmm, what to eat?"

She then presses the PANCAKE button, and her Microwave 3000 begins buzzing and whirling, and within seconds, fresh blueberry pancakes are made. As Maria starts eating her mother yells, "You're going to miss the school bus!"

Maria snaps back into reality, hurries, grabs her book bag, and runs outside. Just in time, the school bus is hovering down out of the sky and onto her block. She gets on the bus and is greeted by the Bus-Bot that controls the bus.

"Good morning! *BEEP*!" says Bus-Bot, in a robotic voice.

Maria rolls her eyes and proceeds walking.

"Hey Maria! Come sit next to us!" chants one of her friends.

"No, not today. I think I'll go sit alone," Maria replies.

The whole bus ride to school, Maria doesn't talk to anyone. She just sits, staring out of the window, in deep thought, chewing on her nails.

"You have arrived at school," says Bus-Bot.

So lost in her thoughts, Maria didn't hear the robot.

"YOU HAVE ARRIVED AT SCHOOL!" Bus-Bot repeats again, but this time a little louder.

Maria finally snaps back into reality, and pushes past Bus-Bot, aggravated.

"Have a nice day," says Bus-Bot.

"Yeah, whatever," Maria replies, rolling her eyes, and gets off the bus.

The whole day at school, Maria didn't really talk to her friends or pay much attention in class. Her teachers had to constantly remind her to focus and do her work, and her concerned friends kept asking her what was wrong. But not wanting to be bothered, Maria shooed them off. A lot was on Maria's mind that day, and it made the day go by much slower. All Maria wanted to do was rush home and get to business.

It was finally last period and she was trying to hold herself together. Time seemed to move at an all-time slow, and for every minute that passed by, Maria's eagerness seemed to grow greater and greater. Just as soon as the bell rang, Maria jetted for the door and didn't look back.

When Maria arrived home, she wasted no time getting to work. She ran past her mom, without saying anything and went to the basement. The basement appeared pretty normal. There were the typical water heater, washer and dryer, and a few of Maria's dad's old work boxes. On the wall, there were a ton of old dusty pictures that her mom had put there for decoration, and there was an empty bookshelf on wall. There weren't any windows, just a vent.

Maria took the picture of the dog off the wall and revealed a big red button placed behind it. She pressed the button and the average basement didn't seem too average anymore. The walls of the basement began to turn and it released steam to reveal the sleek lab walls. The washer and dryer were pulled underground. A ton of test tubes, containing different colored liquids appeared. The book shelf collapsed and four cages with rats were brought out. The rats all appeared to be the same breed, but their behaviors were different. In the first cage, the rat was highly aggressive. It was scratching and gnawing at the glass and trying to get out. The second rat was just running in circles and was pretty confused. In the third cage, unfortunately the rat had passed, and in the last cage the rat had normal behavior, and did normal rat things.

"Maria remembered the real reason she was there, and it was to find the time machine and fix her mistake."

Maria grabbed her lab coat and her clip board, and went to analyze the rats.

Rat One still seems to be very aggressive, Rat Two is still very strange, Rat Three. . . deceased, and Rat Four—

Maria's eyes grew large in excitement. She finally noticed progress in her experiment. Maria had lost over a dozen rats in the past few months. This was the first time she had ever seen one of the rats *seem* healthy. She had been working very hard to find a cure for the Flimer disease because her aunt was diagnosed with the disease last summer, and it had taken a huge toll on her aunt's life.

Maria's parents weren't really there for her during her childhood. They were too busy working and going on business trips to pay much attention to her, and that's where her aunt stepped in. Her aunt had always been the parent figure in her life, so that's why she was so determined to find a cure. Losing her aunt would have been like losing a part of Maria's heart. Maria had always been a scholar in science, so she used it to her advantage. She immediately built this lab and started testing when she found out about the devastating news. Fail after fail, Maria didn't let it stop her from accomplishing her goal, and that was to find a cure for the Flimer disease.

Maria snapped back to reality when she heard the aggressive rat clawing and running full speed into the cage.

"Oh gosh, it's probably time to get rid of you now!" Maria grumbled.

Maria grabbed her protective gloves, thick and long like firefighter gloves, and put them on. She went to open the rat's cage, and immediately the rat jumped out at her and tried to attack her. Maria panicked and grabbed the closest thing in reach, a broom. She was swinging and banging all over the floor trying to stop the rat, but it was too fast.

Maria's mother, upstairs, heard all the commotion and grew concerned.

"Maria, is everything alright down there?" her mother said walking toward the basement door.

"YEAH MOM! HYAH!" Maria replied, taking one last swat at the rat before it scurried out through the vent.

"I'm screwed," Maria mumbled.

Maria then heard her mother coming downstairs and rushed to the emergency MOM BUTTON. She pressed the button, and rapidly the basement went back to normal. Just in time Maria's mother peeked her head down the stairs.

"Is everything alright down here?" her mom asked.

"Oh yeah, of course. I just saw a spider, Maria shrugged.

"Alright, dinner's almost ready," her mother replied.

Maria didn't really think much about the rat. She figured eventually it would die from the experiments, or a cat would get to it first. She went back to working in her lab, thinking nothing of the situation.

A few days later, Maria and her parents were sitting at the dinner table, enjoying their food. Maria's dad was flipping through the television, and her mom was reading a magazine. As her dad was flipping through the channels, Maria overheard one of the reporters mention something about a "rabid rat."

Maria freaked, "Dad, go back!"

Her dad flipped back to the news channel and what Maria heard shocked her.

"Just today, on Broadway and 5th Street, a businessman was bitten by a rat. Upon being bitten, the man started acting like a savage. He was screaming and running wild in the streets, but has been contained since. Unfortunately, the rat got away. Doctors are now doing research on the man to figure out the source of everything. Authorities are saying that people that are in the area should be more careful and aware of their surroundings, until the rodent is detained."

Maria nearly jumped up out of her seat, "Can I be excused?"

"You barely even touched your food, but uh, sure, I guess," her dad replied.

Maria sprinted upstairs and into her room. Pacing the floors talking to herself, she was trying to figure out the plan.

"Oh, my goodness, what have I done? I knew I should've just killed the little sucker when I had the chance, now it's out causing mayhem, and it's all my fault!"

Without analyzing it, Maria went with impulse and figured out a plan. It wasn't a brilliant idea, but it could work. Maria then jetted back down the stairs and into the kitchen where her parents were cleaning up.

"Hey Dad, can I, uh, go with you to work tomorrow, for a, uh, school project that I'm working on?" Maria lied.

Without looking up from the dishes he was washing, he said, "Yeah, sure."

"Okay cool, thanks. See you in the morning. Good night!"

Maria then went back into her room and prepared for her soon-to-be stressful day.

Maria fired up her computer and began doing a little research. She found a ton of pictures of how the inside of the building looked, so when she got there she would have an idea of where to go. Maria's dad worked for an engineering company that built classified machines for the government. She remembered once reading an article about them beginning to research time travel. The article also mentioned them potentially building a time machine. She thought that the time machine could be the only way to fix her rat situation.

Maria was woken up out of her sleep to the sound of her alarm. She had fallen asleep at her computer, from doing all the rigorous research. She then got up from her computer and rushed to get dressed. Without even eating breakfast, Maria jumped into the car with her dad and they pulled off.

They finally pulled up to what looked like an average office building, with its typical big glass windows and revolving door. Once inside the building though, it was like another world. There were drones flying around, robots assisting other workers, tubes connected to each office sending messages from room to room. It was very exciting for Maria to finally see the real thing. Then a robot, similar to Bus-Bot, walked up to her, and gave her a visitor's pass. She received the pass and the robot turned away and did its own thing. Lost in all the excitement, Maria didn't even notice her dad prance away and go to work. At first being a little disappointed that her dad abandoned her, Maria quickly remembered the real reason why she was there, and it was to find the time machine and fix her mistake.

Maria then pulled out one of the maps that she had printed out the night before to find her way around. The FUTURE LEVEL was on the fifteenth floor. All she had to do was get up there and find where the machine was.

Once on the fifteenth-floor Maria went door-to-door and looked for the machine. There were tons of incredible things that she had seen and found, but it wasn't what she was looking for. Maria then turned a corner and noticed a room door with an access code-required lock on it.

"Dang it! How am I going to get in there now?" Maria asked with frustration.

Just as she was thinking about a plan, a few scientists then came out of the room, giving Maria a chance to jet inside. When the scientist came out of the room, they turned the corner and didn't even notice Maria standing there. That's when Maria took the opportunity to run in, just in time before the door shut behind her.

Maria was finally in, and what she saw amazed her. The time machine was a ten-foot-tall cylinder-shaped contraption. It had tons of wires and tubes coming out of it, and on the side, there was a computer-looking object. Above the computer there was a list of rules: DO NOT TELL THE PUBLIC, DO NOT CHANGE THE PAST, DO NOT MEET YOUR FUTURE OR PAST SELF, DO NOT BRING ANYTHING FROM PRESENT TIME TO THE PAST, DO NOT—

Maria stops reading the rules, she doesn't care. She then walks up to the computer and realizes that's where you enter the time and place where you would want to go. She enters in the exact day and place where she wants to go back to and the door to the time machine slides open, releasing tons of steam and cold air.

Maria sighs, "Here goes nothing."

Maria steps inside the machine and the door to the machine closes behind her. At first the machine doesn't do anything; it doesn't beep, move, vibrate, anything. Just as soon as Maria loses hope, the machine begins to blink and whirl and makes all these funny noises.

SCIENTIST'S REGRET

ERON Y.

*was born in San Francisco and is eighteen years old.
He loves to do math. Eron lives with his grandparents,
parents, and his sister. He plans to go to college after
high school. He loves math because there are different
strategies and formulas to get to the same answer.*

In the near future, a scientist created a special liquid, that when injected gave people the ability to teleport. He started to distribute the liquid to neighbors and friends. Months after the technology was created, a lot of people were teleporting as their main method of transportation. The technology later got out of the scientist's control. Soon after, the government made a law that makes people have to pay a high price in order to get the liquid, benefiting themselves and rich people. A group that doesn't like the government plans to use it to gain control of the world. The group goes to the scientist's lab to steal his data.

"Agent Two, we have to hurry. Are you done yet?" asks Agent One.

"No," answers Agent Two.

Meanwhile, Agent Three is wandering around the laboratory. He accidentally bumps into a shelf full of vials and makes a loud noise. It triggers the security alarm that would close all exits of the lab, so the group has to leave before all the exits are closed off.

"Agent Three, what are you doing, I told you to watch the exit!" yells Agent One.

"I got bored," says Agent Three.

"We have to get out now!" yells Agent One.

"I'm not done!" exclaims Agent Two.

"Doesn't matter, go now," yells Agent One.

Agent Three was not able to escape in time so he told the others to leave without him. Shortly after they left, the scientist rushed into his lab and saw Agent Three trapped. The scientist learns from him what the group is trying to do with what he created. He uses the remaining data to invent a gas that removes the ability to teleport. He wants to stop them because he does not want his creation to be used for violence. Using what they stole, the group increases their size by giving the ability to members that do not have it. They have those members line up and take turns being injected. When the group finishes, the members are assigned to get different world leaders. They teleport to different places to get them and gather them in a building. The building is in a forest. It is old and abandoned. After all the world leaders are gathered, they are blindfolded, their mouths are duct-taped, and their hands and legs are tied. The group records a video of them.

"Agent Two, do you have the camera ready? "asks Agent One.

"Yes," answers Agent Two.

"Start the video," says Agent One.

"Hello world, here we have your leaders waiting for us to kill them. After we are done, we will take over the world and kill anyone who goes against us," Agent One says as he holds a gun toward one of the leaders.

While they are recording the video, the scientist is inside the building setting up the gas. He later puts on a gas mask and releases the gas through a vent. After the group finishes the video, the scientist enters the room and confronts them. He finds out that the group has killed three of the world leaders already.

"Why are you doing this?" asks the scientist, "Why did you kill them?"

"Who are you?" asks Agent One as he tries to teleport. He fails to and tries a few more times.

"I am here to stop you from killing any more people," says the scientist.

"Why can't I teleport?!" yells Agent One. The other members also try and find out that they cannot.

"What did you do?" asks Agent One.

"I neutralized you by spraying a gas that removes the ability to teleport," says the scientist. The scientist stares at them trying and failing.

"Get him!" yells Agent One.

As the people of the group run toward the scientist, he uses a machine gun and kills them. He retrieves his data and stores it away for emergency use. He later erases memories by flying around the world on a plane with a gas barrel attached to it. The gas erases the memory involving his technology to teleport. He doesn't want another group of people to do the same thing.

A few months later, he is drunk and walking home from a bar by using a shortcut that involves him walking through an alley. As he is walking home, he thinks to himself about the event a few months ago. *Why did this happen?* he thinks to himself, *I just wanted people to have an easier life. Should I have created this at all?*

A survivor, who was sent to buy food for the group before the killing of the other members, follows him. . .

CONVICTIONS

———◆———

JOHN K.

was born in San Francisco and is seventeen years old. He loves to talk to the elderly and gain experience from their stories. He has learned that helping people is something he enjoys and the feeling of helping someone is the reward.

When I was seven years old, I went through this experience that would shape me into who I am today. Through that situation, I developed my beliefs and my core values.

My mom was always the most supportive person in my life, my role model. There was never a time she wasn't smiling. . . except this one day when I heard my mom and dad argue and it was something new to me because I'd never seen her unhappy or mad about anything. She yelled at my dad and there were tears rolling down her face. The mood was sad and for a moment there was just silence. My sister and I got scared because there was no noise, but a few moments later, she walked out of the room with her bags packed, filled with my little sister's and her things. With tears rolling down her eyes, she looked at me and said, "Don't ever put anybody through this. Promise me."

As I promised her, she began to walk out the door and I remember seeing my little sister's face. It hit me right then and there that I didn't want this to happen to anyone I loved or cared about. On that day, I promised myself that I would always treat everyone with respect, especially females, and I would make sure that I stayed true to my beliefs, that I wouldn't let someone I cared about get hurt.

Now, I'm fifteen. Eight years have passed and I still believe that females should be treated with respect, how others would want to be treated. My core values and beliefs haven't changed.

But, now I have been put in a tough situation. During my sophomore year, I got really close to this person and he became one of the closest friends I have. We had a really close bond and I felt like he was like my brother. We were inseparable and I never did anything without him.

One day, he finally introduced me to his girlfriend that he'd been bragging about. As soon as she spoke, I got this first impression that she was a kind-hearted woman. As time passed by, I really got to know her. She was funny, smart, and had that innocent feeling to her. We bonded and it felt like I had made another friend that I cared about. We could always talk to each other and it was natural, not forced. But, then, once she opened up about her relationship with my best friend, she seemed uneasy. There was always something that she wanted to say, but couldn't.

My first instinct was to talk to my best friend about it, but he shut me out, and as time went by, I began to see that he was treating her unfairly, that she was being disrespected. The seven-year-old me got stirred up and I tried to talk to him, in all seriousness, but he ignored me again.

I started getting angry with him, so I went and talked to his girlfriend and told her everything about how he was doing her wrong. She didn't believe me and she went and told my best friend what I had told her.

That's when I really thought to myself, "Love is blind."

Weeks went by, and I felt that everything was going great. Our mutual friends invited me and my best friend over for a get-together. When we got there, all of our other friends were there, too. It felt like home, like this was where I wanted to be all the time. We did the things we always do, sitting in a circle, talking about life. That part of the get-together was really my favorite moment because we all got to bond and know each other on a deeper level. When I looked around the room, it felt like a room filled with brothers just having fun.

Then, the room got as quiet as a library and the smiles turned to serious faces. The mood changed and the silence broke when my best friend stood up and called me out. He said, "John, you're a snake."

I was utterly speechless.

At first I thought this was a joke, but as I looked around the room and nobody was laughing, it seemed like everybody was prepared for this. Everybody but me. The mood was tense. I looked around the room one more time to see if anyone would have my back, but it seemed like he had won them all over. After all of that, I didn't see a reason to stay. I felt like an outcast and the looks on everybody's face were either that of disappointment or they just wanted to see something go down.

In the middle of all that thick silence, I got up and just went to the door. I glanced back and everybody had resumed what they had been doing, as if this whole thing hadn't just happened. As I walked out, I thought about what I'd just done, and the feeling in my gut wouldn't go away. I was sad and I felt like trash. I had just lost some of my closest friends, and I just didn't know what to do.

But as bad as I had felt losing my friends, I know I did the right thing, sticking up for what I believe, even if I knew there would be consequences later. It made me realize that I was different from all the guys in that room. There will always be people who don't agree or like what I'm doing or saying, but the most important part is, I do what I do and I don't let anything change me.

Friends come and go, but through the ups and downs, my convictions became stronger, and through my experience, I learned to be true to myself.

NOT AGAIN

JAMEELA H.

was born in San Francisco and is seventeen years old. She loves to eat anything edible. She wants to be successful in life.

Fifty-seven years after the inauguration of Donald Trump and the Republicans, the source of water on Earth has come and gone. Due to lack of water, the DLo tribe has relocated to Mars and started a civilization over there. Before 2016, DLo tribe made a treaty with the Republicans to maintain peace and not touch their land.

DLo means water in Haitian creole. This tribe started on Earth and eventually moved to Mars. Their life as a community has always been peaceful. As a community, many decisions are made and they have Chiefs for that. There were four mighty Chiefs of the land. In order for something to be approved, three fourths of the chiefs had to say "yes." There is only one living Chief left because the rest fought for their water on Earth, which ended up killing them because of the evil Trump. He built a pipeline over their water source which forced them to move to Mars. Over six decades, the resources on Earth have gone and the world has been taken over by Trump. The tribe has moved to Mars and has a great wondrous source of water. Water is very important to this tribe. Water is life. There isn't a lot but it's enough for everyone.

URGENT LETTER TO THE CHIEF OF DLo:
We would like to build a pipeline from your water resource to Earth. This would benefit us greatly. Let me know how you feel.

"This is outrageous!" cried the Chief. "How can they do this to us again? After what happened on Earth. . . When will they stop and realize water is a sacred thing?"

My name is Mayan. I am seventeen years old and I live on Mars. I live with my tribe and we are grateful to live here. Our land on Earth was taken over the pipeline they built. After receiving this letter, my father wrote back and it was totally not understood. Our tribe is very protective of our water resource after what happened on Earth fifty-seven years ago.

"Why would they do this again?" said the Chief.

"Just tell them no," I said.

"They work in mysterious ways. Come on, let's go and we'll see what's up tomorrow," said my dad.

As the sun started to rise over the horizon, the dust of dawn started to appear.

"SPACE TRACTORS! SPACE TRACTORS!" I heard a cry outside. Everyone ran outside to see what was going on. *GLas TRACTORS* was labeled on their heavy machinery.

My father walked up to them and said, "Hey, what are you guys doing here?!"

"Only doing our job sir," said the guy from Earth.

"You are not going to touch our water again!"

The Chief stood there, in front of the tractor and people followed. They started blocking the space tractors way so they couldn't do anything. People from all corners of the tribe gathered to stop this. The running engines of the tractor started to slow down and the people running the machine were just sitting in there. This brought chaos on Earth which made them question the government. People from Earth heard about this and people started flying their way to Mars to help stop this destruction.

Ring, ring. Ring, ring. No one is answering the phone.

"Why isn't anyone answering the phone? This situation has gotten out of control. We need to build that pipeline immediately!" said Trump.

"Sir, maybe you shouldn't take their water. It's their only source," says a man. Trump just stares at him.

Back at the tribe, Mayan is standing there not knowing what to do for her tribe. She hides out and looks over to watch the meteor showers. She thinks to herself to try to find a way to stop this pipeline. Then a voice came to her.

"Mayan, you know who you are. You know what to do."

As the meteors continue to shower, a figure shape of her grandmother started to form from all the dust and debris from space. Mayan always adored her grandmother but she passed away from fighting for the water back on Earth.

"You know what to do. You are the Chief's daughter."

Mayan stood up and ran back to her tribe. When she arrived, the evil Trump was there with his army of people.

"Why are you in the way of the tractor? You people should be happy to be in my presence," said Donald Trump.

The Chief was angry. "Trump, the only way we can solve this problem is to challenge you to a duel," said the Chief.

Mayan knows that her father can't fight. Her father got into an accident long ago when he had to fight for the water back on Earth. He got hit by the Donga saber on the inner side of his arm. The Donga saber is a fighting stick only the Chiefs had way back then and was used to fight off against the enemy. He was lucky enough to survive. She told her dad that grandma came to her through the dust and the debris of space.

"She told me I know what to do, dad. I need to fight Trump for our water and peace in this tribe." The Chief passed the light Donga saber and the light shined upon her. She felt the power. "Trump, if I win, you have to leave and if I lose, well, I'll be dead and you can take the water."

"I accept," says Trump.

Mayan and Trump went at it with the Donga sabers. A supersonic light appeared and all of a sudden, a tribe called Quest. They fought many battles over the last fifty-seven years before helping to fight against Trump and anyone else who tried to do wrong in the galaxy. They're like the Black Panthers of this time. They come and attack Trump's army. Laser guns are being shot everywhere. One by one, Trump's army goes. The dump truck arrives and everyone is attacking on and off the ship. It is a massive fighting ship that Trump owns and lives on. Laser after laser then *boom!* Their ship explodes into pieces. Mayan and the tribe called Quest have defeated the GLas and can live in harmony. The Chief was so proud of this daughter.

"I couldn't have done it without the dust particles."

HEAVEN

—◆—

STEVEN M.

was born in China and is seventeen years old.
He loves to cook when he finishes his work. If he can't be an
engineer, he would be a successful chef.

Joe and Ben are software engineers. They both work for the Heaven company. Heaven is a company that converts real life humans into data, and people can live in the virtual world forever. The two of them had a small conversation while working. In the meantime, they are surrounded by darkness, like standing in the empty space.

Ben: "We are living in a program, and we are writing programs for this program, that is interesting."

Joe: "It made sense back then."

Ben: "Well, you are right. The real world is like Heaven, it's just a simulated program. I think the differences are the real world are simulating too much stuff, very complicated. But Heaven only simulates the main things, the happiness that people need. So, simplest is the best."

Joe: "I wonder if this is an improvement or not?"

Ben: "Of course it is! Without the dependence on so much stuff, it is more possible to achieve spiritual freedom. That is why our company is named Heaven. I realized I am not living in the world, that makes me so excited."

Joe: "Maybe it's not that great compared to what you expect: Heaven does depend on things. This whole program runs on hardware, remember?"

Ben: "You are right. Compared to natural resources, digital resources are more. So far, we can run the whole program on just a B-level server."

Joe: "What about a year from now? The situation in the real world is getting more intense, there will be more people trying to come in."

Ben: "Don't worry, we can just add more servers, it's pretty easy to make more chips. Oh, I see what you are worried about, once the war has started, no one is going to make chips for us right?"

Joe: "Well, that's one concern."

Ben: "That is not our business, Joe. We just need to do what we have to do, even if the worst happens; unplugged, or the server blows up, it will just happen in less than a second. It will feel better than dying in the real world."

The surroundings start to change, the sky and ground start to appear, but only the sky and ground. The two of them are standing in the middle of nowhere.

Ben: "Look around the world here. Well, looks better with the sky and ground."

Joe: "I think the ground is a little flat."

Ben: "Yeah, a little flat, I can adjust it."

In the meantime, Ben opens up a program window using his finger, and drags one of the scrollbars above; the ground they standing on changes immediately, there are significant movements up and down, distant mountains. The mountains are constantly dancing, suddenly turned into a row of infinite columns.

Ben: "Oops, too much." He then carefully moves the scrollbars back.

Ben: "Look, is it better?"

Joe: "Yes, the mountains are like the one near my hometown. I was there when I was young, there was a big farm close by."

Ben: "Alright, we are about to create plants now. I integrated your Living System yesterday."

Joe: "Wow, that's fast, you must know a lot about this system."

Ben: "Only been here a few days ahead of you, so I looked through the code for a few days."

Joe: "What? Are you saying you looked through the code?"

Ben: "Yes, it's just the code. Come on, let's keep working, I want to design the plant here a little different from the real world."

It is a new morning, Ben sitting in his office, looking at a new plant he just created. He is excited for how beautiful and special the plant is, and it has the formula on how to create this plant on the bottom, this is his best design. Someone knocks on the door right after.

Door is opened, a man walks into Ben's office, he is about the same age as Ben, but he is tall and strong, "Hey bro, do you still remember me?"

Ben soon recognized this man, he couldn't hide the excitement from his face. "Henry, what is up with you? Why are you here man? If I didn't forget, you became a pilot after you graduated."

Henry: "I am just having a little fun here in Heaven. Yep, I am a pilot, been flying aircrafts in the air force. You guys don't have aircrafts here, right?"

Ben: "Well, we don't need that here, man; we don't have war in this place. Plus, we don't even need aircrafts for traveling. When we travel to places, we get into tubes."

Henry: "Right! I used it yesterday, that was about 2000 miles on the map. Once I got into the tube, I got here in just a second. That was amazing!"

Ben: "That is because we are just a set of data in this world."

Henry: "I know, man, I just feel like this is unbelievable. I hear all the things in this world were created by you!"

Ben: "Yeah, what do you think?"

Henry: "I think this is amazing, this is like created by God, so you are the god here!"

Ben: "Ha-ha, that is a little above my ability, man. I hear there are wars everywhere out there. You are fine, right?"

Henry takes a deep breath, and he stops for a second, "Soldiers will never step back from war." He continues, "It's not my turn yet, but the navy my wife is in fought some battles with the army already."

Ben: "So, what happened? Did they win?"

Henry: "Some loss on both sides, the ship was hit by the enemy. She's gone."

Ben is quiet, he doesn't know what to say. "But that's okay, soldiers are supposed to give themselves up in the war." Henry said.

Henry: "When the Cold War started, we were ready for war and we were ready to die in the battlefield. We didn't expect to have the Cold War last this long. The starting of this war is like what all of us wanted."

Ben felt a sense of fatalistic sadness from his words.

Ben: "Do you think the war will evolve into nuclear war?"

Henry: "Well, we have to plan for the worst." They both fall silent.

Henry: "I am about to go back. I was actually going to bring my daughter here, she will be staying here for a long time. Her mother's sacrifice gives us a spot here, plus my brother and sister-in-law are here too, so I will have them take care of her."

Ben: "Why don't you stay, too? The army won't approve that?"

Henry: "Well, they did, because they wanted me to take care of my child. Personally,

I don't want to because I am a solider and I cannot avoid wars."

Ben sighed: "Well, I hope the war ends soon. So you can come back and reunite with her."

Henry has a smile on his face, it seems like he wants to adjust the intenseness before he leaves: "If I am injured in the battle, I will ask to come here. I will see you again then."

Ben: "Then. . . I hope you get injured soon." They both laugh.

Ben: "Let me have your brother's address, I will visit them and your daughter."

Henry: "Yeah, that's what I am going to do. Having you to help them would allow me to do my things because you are the god in here, right?"

Ben visited Henry's brother and sister-in-law, and found out that they are not the cynics that he thought they were. They came to Heaven because they were looking for the life that had no wars or fights. Talking about Henry, his brother shook his head, "He is too stubborn. The sense of responsibility is too strong." In the meantime, a little girl holding a rifle ran into the room. She has eyes that you can tell are warm from the heart. But when Ben asked if he can take a look at her gun, she shook her head and ran away. Henry's brother told Ben that the gun was a gift from her mom, which was a copy of the gun she used.

When Ben left the house, he left his address, and said that they could always reach out for help when they needed.

The real-world situation is getting even more intense, more countries are involved in the war. As the real-world situation is also deeply related to Heaven, Heaven decided to have its own department of public relations in the real world, where they will deal with the countries in the real world. Also, it set up its own news channel.

Heaven is accepting fewer immigrants from the outside. The trip to Heaven is still available, but the limit is a week. Soon, there will be no more visitors in Heaven.

At night, Ben had a call from Joe, "Turn on the TV now!" Joe yelled.

When Ben's eyes are on TV, he sees the giant mushroom cloud in a fiery ball of yellow flames, billowing outward, filling the earth and escaping through the atmosphere destroyed by the blast wave. The noise reverberated over the sleeping ocean as efficiently as a thunder clap.

Ben hadn't realized what happened on TV, when the screen suddenly switched, and a news reporter appeared on the screen. "As we saw earlier this afternoon, the video was taken from space overlooking more than five thousand nuclear bomb explosions. Our planet has been destroyed."

"But we are lucky to escape, we, the whole Heaven is in a spaceship, heading out of the Galaxy. In fact, we started a month ago. The maximum speed of the spaceship is 0.3 light speed, and we are still in the acceleration phase. The current speed is 0.05 times the speed of light. We have sailed out 2,000 light years, or 19 billion km. I'm sorry to tell you this late. In order to ensure the smooth implementation of the plan, this can only be carried out under absolute secrecy, and now it is fact that our choice is right.

"The next challenge we are facing is to find a new body of computing resources in the universe. Our preferred goal is the M galaxy. We know that scientists have proved the existence of the M galaxy, but we don't have the calculation of the exact location. We were close and we will continue to research. Spaceship fuel can be maintained for 100 years. We have a chance!"

Ben soon realized that the Earth was gone, which means all of his friends, and the people he knew were also gone with the destruction of the Earth. Earth has become a history, the history that contains his memories as a child, as a young adult, and so much more. Gone.

It is time to look forward to save the history that humans have, with the Heaven server having moved out to space. The main concern that comes with this news is: *Is there really a new galaxy waiting for them?* If not, all the life in Heaven will disappear, too, and humankind will also become history.

Ben has to believe that the only way the human race can continue is to get to a new galaxy. Ben is looking forward to building their Heaven server in a brand-new galaxy that humans have never discovered before.

TOXICITY NOW

ERIC P.

was born in San Francisco and is seventeen.
He loves playing video games and reading manga.
He lives with his mom, dad, and one brother. He plans to
work at a part-time job after high school.

It's the year 2018. The story begins in San Francisco. I just woke up from a quick nap, it's 7:00 p.m. My parents should be at home, but I don't hear anything. It's quiet, too quiet. I leave my room and check if anyone's home. Weird, no one. I'm guessing they went out to eat. That sucks. They could've woken me up. I'm feeling hungry. All of a sudden someone screams, choking outside my door steps. "I. . . I. . . the air. . . I can't. . . brea—" No sound. Oh God, is he dead?! I'm too afraid to go outside. Is something wrong with the air? I run into my room to get my phone and dial 9-1-1. "*Beep, beep*, this person is not available at the moment, *beep*. . ." What? I can't believe 9-1-1 didn't pick up the phone! I go onto my computer to see what's happening. Apparently, there's a deadly gas leak covering the city of San Francisco. People are saying you must shut your windows and stay indoors at all costs. I immediately check to see if all windows are closed. Good. All the windows are shut.

It's been a week. I'm running out of food. I've eaten all of the leftovers in the refrigerator. All I have left is a box of cup noodles. Yuck. I need to scavenge for food eventually, but I can't go outside. It's too dangerous. I've been checking the situation occasionally on the Internet. There's going to be a strong gust of winds three days from

"They point their guns at us and fire. My body goes numb."

now. I decide that's when I make a break for it. I can't stay shut in and starve to death. Three days, that's seventy-two hours. I should get some sleep before leaving.

I wake up and check the time. It's 1:00 p.m. Has it been three days already? That was fast. It's time to leave. But then there's the dead body. Is it safe out there? I can't leave through the front door, I need to find another way out. *Think. Think!* That's it! The back door! I sneak through the back door and turn the corner to see what's on the doorstep. My heart stops. As soon as I see the body, the smell hits me, that wretched smell! The body is torn apart! Some dogs must've ravaged it. My eyes start to water. My stomach starts to tighten up. Puke flies out of my mouth. That's disgusting. I clean myself, make my way down the street and start to look for food.

It's nighttime now. It's been a long walk with no life in sight. Finally, I find a local grocery store a couple miles from my house. The lights are out and the store is pitch black. I should've brought a flashlight with me. I wander blindly, hoping to find some food. All of a sudden I am knocked to the ground.

"Don't move!" My attacker yells. He holds a knife to my throat.

"Don't kill me! I'm only here for food."

"This is my turf, take whatever and go." He puts his knife away.

I quickly grab a couple bottles of water and some sandwiches. I say my thanks and try to leave but he tells me to stop. Oh God! Did he change his mind? Is he going to kill me? I clench my fist, ready to do the impossible. I'm going to fight somebody with a knife. I've never fought before, but I'm ready. I need to live. I slowly turn around, afraid of what's going to happen. I glare at him.

"Whoa there, buddy," the guy says. "I don't want to fight. I can't survive alone. Let's help each other out. That way we can survive longer. My name is Ken."

"I'm Eric."

I accept his offer without hesitation. This place is loaded with food.

It's been a week since I holed up in the grocery store with Ken. All we've done is eat and sleep. There's nothing to do and the boredom gets worse as the days pass by. I keep telling myself this is the only way to survive. The food here will last for months, maybe even longer. It's time to break the ice.

"Hey, Ken, why are you alone? Where are your friends and family?"

"My dad left us when I was six. My mother died shortly after from cancer. And friends, everyone is too scared to approach me."

Yikes. I just made things awkward. I don't know what to say in this kind of situation.

"I'm sorry to hear that," I say. "My parents are missing right now so I'm kind of worried. I hope I can find them soon."

Ken looks at me. "You will find them, but not alone, there's a better chance of finding them with my help."

I nod. "Thanks."

Suddenly a light green fog drifts toward us from the entrance.

"RUN! THE GAS IS COMING!" I yell.

I drop everything and run for the emergency exit. I push at the doors with all my might and the doors fling right open. I look back, but it is too late. Ken is nowhere to be seen. No! No! No! It can't be, I finally made a friend and he's gone!

A dark figure appears out of the gas. I smile. Ken rushes toward me. "Ha-ha, I'm alive!" He's breathing heavily.

"Are you okay?" I ask.

"I—I'm fine—just out of breath—from running." I had completely forgotten about the gas. I turn immediately to the door and check how close the gas was.

"Ken, it's gone!"

"What's gone?"

"The gas. . . it disappeared."

"No way man, that's impossible."

"Forget about the gas, how are you still alive?"

"I don't know."

Just then a loud sound comes from above. It's a helicopter! I wave my arms and yell.

"They might bring us to a shelter, Ken. We're going to live!"

"I'm not too sure about that," says Ken.

The helicopter sets down on the street. A dozen soldiers come out of the hatch holding guns.

"Whoa, no need for guns! We're just survivors!" I yell.

"We know," says a soldier. "We have been watching you." They point their guns at us and fire. My body goes numb.

Well, there goes our last hope.

It's dark. Am I asleep or dead?

"Wake up," a voice whispers. "Get up."

I open my eyes. A man I've never seen before tells me not to move. He's wearing a lab coat. Some kind of scientist? Damn. What does he want with me?

"You have tranquilizer darts stuck in your arm," says the stranger.

Tranquilizers? I look down. Jesus. How many times did the soldiers shoot me? I look around.

"Where's Ken? Hey, did you see a kid my age anywhere?"

"No," says the stranger. "I got here not too long ago. The only person lying on the ground was you."

Ken wouldn't leave me here alone. There must be a reason why he's gone. The soldiers! The stranger that woke me up tells me who he is. His name is John Fischer and he's a scientist from Germany. John was experimenting with hydrogen cyanide and everything went wrong when the gas pipe burst and shot gas into the air. John explains that hydrogen cyanide is extremely deadly. Even breathing a bit of it guarantees death. All of this makes sense except the kidnapping. Why was Ken unscathed even though he breathed in the gas? Is there something inside Ken the government wants? Is that why he was kidnapped?

"Yes!" John says.

Ken must be immune to the effects of hydrogen cyanide! They want to find the basis of his immunity. That means they're going to dissect Ken! I can't let this happen, Ken is my friend, I must save him. But is that the right thing to do? It's Ken or the world.

Thoughts are flowing through my mind. What is the correct thing to do? I'm only seventeen, this kind of decision is insane. I won't be able to handle the burden. I should just give up. There's no way to save Ken. The government can find a way to fight the gas and all of San Francisco, all the people I care about can be saved. My friends, my parents, even the whole world.

John notices my troubles and makes a proposal. "I screwed up so I have to take responsibility for this mess. I will tell them the location of the laboratory in exchange for your friend."

"But they are going to lock you up for what you have done."

"I knew there were risks to my experiments but I took the chance anyway. I deserve what they will do to me, so let's go save your friend."

The problem is how I can grab the government's attention. What did the soldier say? 'We have been watching you.' The cameras! John and I go looking for a camera and finally find one.

"HEY!" I yell. "WE KNOW WHERE THE LAB IS. GIVE ME MY FRIEND BACK AND I WILL TELL YOU ITS LOCATION!"

No response. We stand there for ten minutes until a car drives toward our direction at incredible speed. The driver hits the brakes as soon as the car is three feet away from us which throws me off balance.

"Are you trying to kill us?" I yell.

"There's no time to chatter! The gas is leaking as every second passes by, now tell me where's the lab!"

"Give Ken back to us and we will talk."

The driver nods to the soldiers in the back. They grab Ken and throw him out of the car and he lands at my feet.

"There. Now keep your end of the bargain."

John steps up. "My name is John Fischer, I am the cause of the leakage of the gas. It was an accident, but I will take responsibility for my mistake."

John gave the soldiers the location of his secret laboratory and was later arrested for manslaughter and genocide. Many people died from the gas, but Ken and I survived. Turns out there was an evacuation site and thousands of people were holed up in a giant bomb shelter. My parents were among the people in the shelter. The government took care of the gas leak and cleared out what was left of the gas in the atmosphere. They had tightly sealed barrels moved into trucks, they told us it's leftover debris from the laboratory. Nobody questioned them. What we didn't know was that hydrogen cyanide was sealed inside the barrels.

OH, DOH

LAUREEN V.

was born San Francisco and is seventeen years old.
She loves to explore around the city, like Land's End.
She plans to go to college after high school and
study psychology.

On a really sunny day, a girl named June decides to go for a walk along with her really tall husband, Maui. June is an inventor, a job she was forced into by her parents. Maui wears round glasses, but also wears classy clothes like a white button up under a black bomber jacket. During the walk, June brainstorms for some ideas on what could be her next big new invention. Her glasses glaring through the sun with her long, black shimmering hair running down her long, grey cardigan sweater, end up blinding her husband and he ends up tripping on his own shoe lace.

"Oh, my God, honey! Are you okay? How did you trip in the first place?" cries June.

"Dang it! Your glasses really blinded me really bad, hon!" yells Maui.

"I'm so sorry, honey!" June reaches out a helping hand. "I didn't think my glasses would ever blind someone!" As June helps Maui get back up, she drops him again as if she just had seen a ghost and is really surprised. "Oh! I just thought of a wonderful idea!" June says excitedly.

"What is it, honey?" questions Maui.

"What if I invent glasses that are anti-glare!" June gets really jumpy as that idea seems like it has never been made before.

"You know hon, there are already glasses that are anti-glare. You know that, right?" Maui says.

"No I do not know that." June was devastated. "I don't think I will ever make such innovative inventions in any point in my life," sighs June.

"Don't ever worry about such things like that, hon. Just believe in yourself and you will get there someday." Maui tries to comfort June. Moments later, they walk down a clear cement path in a park filled with vibrant green trees to their right, along with a clear pond to their left. After walking around the beautiful lively park, they go get some ice cream at an ice cream shop.

"I'll be buying for us both, hon. I love how you stick with me throughout my dumb moments," says June.

"Are you sure, hon? I promise next time I'll be buying you a meal," insists Maui. Both Maui and June walk inside the ice cream shop.

"Hello! Welcome to Annie's Ice Cream Parlor! What would you like to get today?" says the worker. June turns around to Maui.

"What flavor would you like?" asks June as she reaches into her navy blue Michael Kors bag and grabs her grey Herschel wallet.

"I'll get cookies and cream," answers Maui.

"Alright, and I'll be getting mint chocolate chip," says June.

"Okay! One cookies and cream and one mint chocolate chip ice cream. That will be two dollars."

June hands over the money as she looks over at the other worker already putting their ice cream together.

"Cookies and cream and mint chocolate chip!" yells the second worker. June grabs the ice cream with both her hands and gives Maui the cookies and cream ice cream as they walk out of the store.

"Shall we take the bus or walk?" questions Maui.

"I think we should just take the bus. I'm pretty lazy right now and plus we do kind of live far."

"Alright. Let's pay together then. Do you have a dollar on you?" June reaches back into her bag to grab her wallet. June hands over the money to Maui and catches the bus. Six stops later, they get off and walk to their grey-and-black-colored modern house which is only just a half block away from the bus stop. Maui gets his keys to open the front door and walks in finding their black Shiba Inu dog named Poh jumping in the air in excitement at their coming home.

"I think we should've brought the dog with us, you know?" says Maui.

"He poops a lot and I'm not trying to deal with his poops that could be literally everywhere if he came with us. Anyway, I'll go check what's up in the lab, I'll be back sometime later."

"Okay, I'll just be cooking dinner."

June walks over to a wooden door. Behind it is a metal door that is opened by June waving her hand into the digital sensor. She walks down the metal stairs as her shoes make clanking sounds every step she takes. The lab has metallic walls which reflect light making it very bright. As June walks around the lab, she grabs her fluffy and soft North Face jacket hanging on the coat rack. She has OCD. She realigns the tables and straightens the desk with the computer. Then she adjusts the chemicals bubbling into the air.

"Well this place needs to be more lively. . . Oh, it's already seven o'clock. I should head up for dinner." June walks back up the metallic stairs. As she steps foot upstairs, she closes the metallic door and then closes the wooden door and walks over to the dining room. "So, hon? What did you make?" June sits down at the table.

"I made *lechon paksiw*, which is a Filipino dish made up of basically leftovers of a roasted pig along with rice that I put as a side dish. "I thought that you should give it a try, too."

"Alright, sounds good since I do like pig." June takes her first bite and smiles with delight and keeps on eating and eating and eating like an actual pig.

Ten months later, Maui and June are at the hospital as June is cradling her new baby son, Ness.

"Can you believe this, honey? Our son is cute, isn't he?" says June.

"I feel like I have re-lived again. I really cannot describe how joyful I am to be by your side and taking care of our son along with you. Well, we are going home pretty soon and we should probably get ready."

"Okay, I just have to check my email first on my laptop," June says. Maui hands over the laptop as he then grabs for Ness. June opens her laptop and starts typing her password. "Oh no, what's wrong with my laptop? It's not letting me get in," June says angrily.

"Alright, we've got to get going, hon, just fix it when we get home. Okay?" Maui says nicely.

"Fine, but I really need to check up on my emails that I am missing from my coworkers."

Maui puts the baby in a baby carriage and helps June get up off her bed. "Hon, I really need some rest. When we get home, I am going to go straight to bed."

"Okay, that's fine. I'm just going to make dinner for us then." Both Maui and June walk out of the hospital with their son, Ness.

"Wow, look at the weather. It looks really great for my aesthetic portfolio." Maui is amused at the beautiful pink and gold sky. As they head to the car, Maui sets the baby down inside and June gets into the passenger seat. "Wait, I would just like to take a quick pic of the sky." Maui grabs his Panasonic camera and snaps a shot of the sky and heads into the car, and starts to drive off.

As they head up onto the driveway of their house, June gets out of the car and heads to the kitchen table and tries to fix her laptop as Maui goes upstairs to put Ness in the crib. "Dang, I can't seem to get this to work you know. I don't even know what's wrong with this thing either. I'll just use the desktop for now." June walks over to the desktop in the living room only to find that the wires have been chewed on. "What the heck? Did Poh do this? I swear these are chew marks and the wires have been separated! Dang it, Poh! You're so cute that I can't be mad at you! BUT I SWEAR I AM IN THE INSIDE! This computer cost $5,000 and it's all here right in front of me, WRECKED!" June yells out furiously. Maui runs downstairs to see what the fuss is and goes over to June and tries to comfort her.

"Don't worry, we'll just get someone to fix it for us, or we could just buy a new monitor. Shouldn't be that bad, right?" Maui says comfortingly.

"UGH I'M SO MAD. I'M JUST GOING TO GO TO SLEEP. I'M TIRED." June furiously walks up the stairs and slams the door and falls right into bed. "But I can't sleep though." June fidgets around in bed trying to find a comfortable position. "I'll just lay on my back with my head slanted, I guess." June starts to stare onto the ceiling. "First my laptop, now the computer. Great! What else can go wrong?" June reaches for the TV remote and tries to turn on the TV only to find out the screen has been damaged due to Poh trying to jump on objects. "Ugh really? Stupid dog!" June throws the remote to the other side of the bed. "Can I just have something that could literally fix any electronics at the snap of my fingers?" Then suddenly June comes up with an idea. "Oh wait! I think I can! Maybe I could build a robot who has the knowledge to fix anything and can fix it right when it breaks or when I need it!" June sits up straight. "If I want it now, then I'm going to make it now!" June runs downstairs and opens the wooden door which leads to the metal door and quickly scans her hand over the sensor. Maui looks at her weirdly.

"Hmm, women," Maui says softly.

"Don't bother me down here! I've just thought of a very great idea!" June goes the down the metal stairs.

"Okay, hon! Man, looks like I'm going to be eating dinner alone tonight, or for how many days." Maui goes on with the cooking.

"Okay, so where can I start?" June walks around looking for any metal scraps that could be laying around. "I need wires and a lot of metal." While June looks around the lab she comes across a big brown cardboard box. "Oh, I wonder what could be in here?" June opens the box as she discovers a piece of paper that says "Use for future inventions." June then crumples it up and throws it behind her as she sees a full box of wires and metal scraps. "Oh, wow! Saving all this from my past failed inventions is really great and coincidental." June then grabs the whole box and runs over to the table to start working on her invention. "Okay, let's start!"

June started to work on her invention nonstop. The hours turn to days which turn to weeks. June is finally done with her newly made silver robot, who is three feet tall. "Okay, finally, time to program this robot with human feelings so you. . . Hmm what should your name be? Oh! Doh! That sounds like a good name. Okay time for your feelings to be installed so you can be able to watch my baby whenever I am not able to be around and also to be able to fix any electronics that are broken." June starts to type the codes to program the robot with knowledge. She then copies the chip out of the computer and inserts it into Doh's chip inserter on the left chest. "All good to go! Time to power you up." June powers up Doh by pressing the ON button on the bottom of Doh's body.

"Hi, I'm Doh, your personal tech care companion."

"This is going great! Now time to test your tech caring skills." June runs upstairs to the broken laptop. "Okay Doh, fix my laptop."

Doh analyzes the laptop with red scanning eyes. "Seems here, your laptop is dead. Charge it."

"Wait really, that's it? But I swear it wasn't like that when I tried powering it on. Wow, you're great so far, Doh." June goes and charges her laptop. "Okay Doh, go fix my computer now." Doh walks over to the computer in the living room and starts to scan it.

"Hmm. . . your monitor wires are broken." Doh holds the wires in a fist and lets go of them to find that the wires have magically repaired themselves.

"Wow, Doh! You're amazing!" yells June in excitement. Doh brings out a digital smile. "Okay, now is it okay if you go check up on my baby upstairs? His name is Ness." Doh walks upstairs and goes to Ness's room and finds out that Ness is sleeping in his crib.

"Nice Ness." Doh brings out another smile as he discovers that babies look really cute and just stares at Ness. Moments later, Ness wakes up and starts crying as he is scared from the strange little robot. Doh brings out a confused face. Doh decides to play *Teletubbies* from his digital mouth and gives Ness his sucker. Ness suddenly gets quiet and starts to feel comfortable with Doh.

Four years have passed since the creation of Doh, the tech care companion. "I am really bored, I wish I could just have fun and try new things." Doh then lays on the floor to contemplate life. Then all of a sudden Ness starts crying from a distance.

"Doh! Can you please go check up on Ness?" yells out June as she goes outside to go buy some groceries.

"Aw man, can't I have some peace and quiet for just a moment?" Doh starts to get up. Doh slowly walks over to Ness as he sees that Ness has fallen to the ground.

"I have boo-boo on my knee," cries Ness.

"Okay, okay. Here is a Band-Aid and you'll be alright." Doh puts the Band-Aid on Ness's knee and then he starts to feel very tired. "There you're all good to go!" Ness gets up and begs Doh to play with him.

"Play with me!"

"What, me? No," answers Doh.

"PLAY. WITH. ME!" Ness screams as he is about to burst out with tears again.

"Fine. Fine, I will. I'll play with you whenever you need me."

"Yay!" Ness picks up Doh and starts flying him around like an airplane. Ness goes up the stairs and accidentally loses grip of Doh which sends Doh tumbling down the stairs.

"Ouch! That hurt me real hard. I'm done for today, Ness," cries out Doh as Ness goes back running into his room. Doh slowly gets up and walks over to the living room but trips over a dog toy. "Ow! Okay it's probably my wires which have been damaged that is causing me to feel pain. I usually don't feel pain whenever I get hurt." From afar, Doh sees Poh running toward him looking as if he is a hungry beast. "Oh no, Poh, don't come near me. I'm not a toy, Poh. I've been saying this for years. Please!" But as soon as Doh can take cover, Poh grabs Doh with his mouth and starts to shake his head. "POH STOP THIS RIGHT NOW!" But Poh is amused by Doh's texture of metal body. "This is going to hurt really bad once this is over," Doh sighs. Poh then drops Doh to the floor as Doh experiences wires that are heavily damaged.

"HAHA! You are so funny, Doh. Do it again!" Ness screams out, but Doh ignores him and just slowly walk away to the living room and sits on the floor behind the couch where no one can see him.

"I feel really sad, there's no one else like me who I can hang out with or who will take turns with me taking care of Ness or maybe even the dog. I just wish that there could be a way to have robots of my own kind living with me as I try to take care of this place." Doh contemplates quietly for thirty minutes while looking out the window at the sky. "Ah! Since I have the knowledge to fix electronics, maybe, I can fix up my own kind of robots, too! And maybe I can mess this whole house up and they'll never forget this day of me being beaten up by a baby and a dog!" Doh sneaks into the lab by hacking into the digital sensor with its own eyes. "Okay I'll just recopy myself and give them codings in which they listen to me only." As Doh looks around the lab he finds a cloning machine that June has bought recently and decides to use it. "Well this is new. I just have to make at least ten of myself to make this work." Doh steps into the cloning machine and closes his eyes as more and more robots start to come out of the other side of the machine. Thirty seconds later, the machine beeps as it is finished with the cloning. "Finally, to make the codes." Doh types in random numbers into the computer and copies ten chips to put inside all of the robot's chip inserter. "There you go! Now go destroy this house. NOW!

A group of five robots goes upstairs to ruin the inside of the house and light everything on fire. As another group of five robots goes outside the house to light the exterior of the house on fire. June pulls up the driveway to see a lot of robots destroying her house and tries to pause them with a remote that can control Doh only to find out that the data for the remote have been erased. "Dang it! How did all of this happen?" June questions. "Where's Doh?"

Meanwhile, Doh brings the baby and the dog into a designed fort that should trap both of them in but at the same time to not scare them. "DOH!" June yells out. Doh heads over to June with furious eyes.

"Hello there, June," Doh says.

"Why are you doing all of this?" June questions.

"I'm tired. That's just all."

"Tired of what?"

"I'M TIRED OF BEING BITTEN, I'M TIRED OF BEING PLAYED WITH, AND I'M TIRED OF ALWAYS HAVING TO BE ALONE."

"But you're not alone, you have us."

"NO! I want someone who's one of my kind. YOU ALL ARE JUST DIFFERENT."

"Aw Doh, I didn't realize you were depressed." June sees a bite mark on Doh where wires that compute his feeling are damaged. June slowly walks over to Doh. "Look Doh, I just want to be here for you and I hope you know that." June gets closer and closer to Doh. "From the very start, you were always the one that I could rely on." As June grabs a hold of Doh and finds the reset button under the bottom of his body and Doh shuts down. "I should have realized this before. Doh just wants to have a friend or maybe a family!" June runs down to the lab and types in a code that shuts down the other robots too. "That should do it." June repairs Doh and puts him into the cloning machine and makes three new robots.

"Time to wake up, Doh." June presses the ON button and Doh awakens.

"What happened?" Doh looks confused seeing a robot dog, robot kid, and a robot woman.

"I thought about it and I realized how depressed you were as I always see you looking outside the window, and I'm just there always wondering why you're always looking outside and I've thought maybe you could be happier if you had robots of your kind and that you could always be with them so I thought of giving you a family of your own!" explains June.

"Oh, my God. . . *wow*! This is amazing! I have never been really happy to see my own kind here! I will really cherish this day, June, and thank you very much. You are the best," cries Doh.

June powers up the rest of the robot family as Doh goes over to them and hugs them.

KARMA

KELVIN F.

Kelvin was born in San Francisco and is seventeen years old.
He loves to work out. His plans after high school are going to
college and figuring out what he wants to do with his life.

His story begins and his name is Cole. He's twenty-seven years old and a built man, with average height. He has a tan and has black hair with brown eyes. His job and life passion is cybernetics, and his theory on people becoming cyborgs became well known. Cole made a prototype arm that worked, but it was buggy and it broke down. Cole believed that cybernetics was the future and that people should replace limbs for new cybernetic limbs, because it would make people stronger and better. People ridiculed him and said he was crazy, and that it went against nature, and that he had no right to play God. People tried to debunk his theory saying that it's not safe and it could kill people. With all the criticism and people trying to debunk him, people believed he was crazy, and he became a laughing stock. He lost all of his funding and his reputation was shamed. He was on the edge of going homeless. He hasn't had a lot of sleep lately. His eyes are baggy and tired with all the stress he has had to endure. But since that day, it all changed when a strange man appeared.

It all started with a knock on the door at night. A pale man with brown hair and dark eyes, wearing a white suit and tie, with black gloves, greeted him and introduced himself as 'The Director.' He told Cole he was working for the government, and he would like to offer him a job to become a wealthy man. Cole, being down on his luck and with nothing left to lose, listened to his offer, and The Director proposed that he should work on creating cybernetic limbs for the army. Cole thought to himself that if he were to build cyborg soldiers for the army, he could become rich and gain back his reputation. But on the other hand, if he did help make cyborg soldiers, they would wage war with them and cause chaos. Cole was hesitant and tempted, on one end he could become rich and on the other, it would be his fault. Cole told him he could not and he would not work for him. The Director turned red with rage and disgust.

He looked Cole dead in the eye and said, "I'll be back, and you will work for us one way or another."

The Director stormed toward the door, looked at Cole with a face like Cole had just betrayed him, and slammed it shut. Cole was in shock and worried after The Director left. He knew The Director worked for the government and wanted cyborgs for the army. Cole also thought to himself that he had nothing to lose, and that his life might be in danger because the government had been watching him for who knows how long. Knowing he could not fight back against the government, he decided that his only choice left was to run away. So, he grabbed his research notes from his desk swiftly and got his bag, placing in it the last of his money and food. Then he went out of the door, got into his car, and drove off under the night sky.

It had been a month since Cole had left his apartment and had been living off the grid. His disappearance had been reported as a missing person's report from the police, and the news asked for any information of his whereabouts. He's was really low on money, and couldn't afford to keep his car, so he sold it for extra money. He rented a room from a hotel using cash and under a fake name. Cole was thinking to himself in his bed while eating a bag of chips. *"I'll be leaving in the morning and head to Canada and make a new identity for myself, after I get some sleep."* He fell asleep which felt like days, and time seemed to stop, in his perspective, and then suddenly there was heavy knocking on the door. Cole got up tiredly and walked toward the door. He checked through the peephole and there was nobody. Upon opening the door, Cole got whacked on the face. He headed face first on the floor bleeding. Looking up he saw The Director staring back at him with a metal baseball bat with Cole's blood on his right hand. The Director looked at Cole with a menacing smile and said, "I told you, I'll be back. Nice job on taking that hit like a champ. Goodnight Cole."

He raised his baseball bat up in the air with his right hand with a grin in his face, and took a swing at his head knocking Cole back to the ground knocking him out cold, and he blacked out. Cole woke back up in a bed. His head was pounding and he felt like he'd been hit by a truck. His mind was fuzzy and he couldn't think straight. His eyes were adjusting to the light; he realized he was in a huge white room with lab equipment, and there was a metallic door. Cole was trying to remember what happened and it hit him; he was knocked out and taken to who knows where. He stood up wobbling and dizzy walking toward the door. With each step he took, his pain grew. He wanted to get out of this place. He reached for the metallic door and touched it. The door opened, with dozens of guards with black suits and shades with ear microphones, holding guns and all of them pointing at Cole. Cole walked backward and backed up with his hands in the air, kneeling on the ground.

In the center of the crowd was The Director with a menacing smirk on his face. He stared at Cole. All of the guards made room for The Director as he walked toward Cole with confidence like he owned the place. He was standing in front of Cole.

The Director said, "Great, the scientist woke up. You took your sweet time to get back up. It was a drag bringing you here to our facility, and waiting for you to wake up. At least I had time to upload your research files to our databanks. Right now, Cole, I need you to get to work ASAP!"

"Why would I work for someone like you?" Cole said.

The Director said, "Aww, are you still mad about me hitting you? Get over it! You will work for me one way or another!"

Cole said, "I'll refuse to work."

Cole stood up. With serious faces, the guards locked and loaded their guns, and aimed toward Cole's head. Cole was sweating, knowing that he could die here at this moment.

Cole spoke nervously, "If you kill me here, you won't get what you want."

The Director spoke with glee pulling out a pistol from his suit with his right hand. "It's true. If we silenced you now, it'll slow down our timetable considerably. But we have your research notes, which will speed up our timetable on making stronger soldiers. We can start creating cyborgs in a couple of years without your help. Pity, if you agreed to my offer before, you wouldn't be in this position right now. If you decided to work for us, it would've taken us just a couple of months to finish this little project with your knowledge on cybernetics."

Cole thought to himself, *maybe I could make a bargain with The Director*. Cole spoke, "Just hypothetically, if I were to work for you, what would guarantee my safety?"

The Director said, "You have to trust me. If you want to survive this Cole, just say a simple yes or no. You've got ten seconds to decide."

Cole was having a moment of crisis in his mind. Accept and live as a villain, or decline and die a hero. Five seconds left, four seconds left, three seconds left, two seconds left, one second left. Then Cole answered.

He screamed out, "Yes, I'll do it."

The Director said, "Good choice. You'll start working here, and this is going to be your lab. It has all of the things you'll need, my guards will be monitoring you while you work."

The Director walked toward the door. He looked back at Cole while looking at his left arm, and walked away, leaving only two guards left. Cole stood back up tiredly. He walked toward his lab equipment. The guards were staring, looking around, observing. Cole tried to figure out what his equipment did, pressing multiple buttons. The guards moved toward Cole, and asked him to stop messing with the equipment, and told him, "We got orders to watch you and not let you mess around."

HOPE

➤

SANDRA L.

was born in San Francisco, California. She is seventeen years old. Sandra loves going on night trips through the city and loves intellectual talks. She lives with her mother. She plans on just going with the flow after high school.

Why is it that greed drives 'the human' into a frenzy he or she can never seem to get enough of? But then again, what is enough? The want no longer becomes a desired feeling, but a need. A need that makes our survival instincts kick in, not to survive but to fit in, survival of the fittest, the Darwinian theory. The theory that we must adapt to the environment around us in order to survive with the changing earth. What if we humans turned this theory into a materialistic idea rather than actually adapting to survive? The most basic fundamental quotas of our time and being has changed into something so easily bought with paper. Or maybe to press the mindset that without money we, as a living, breathing, thinking soul will not and cannot survive. What if it was created to make one feel as if one must be superior to others? What if?

I've always wondered what life would be outside of our dome, not our head, of course, but the actual dome over our heads. I've always wondered why we were not allowed to wander about and how we got here. Why us? But no one here ever dared question why, let alone did they ever try to leave. I think it's fear that makes us lock up our wonders in the deep dark corners of our minds. But then again, are our minds really ours if we are being restricted from saying or even thinking of certain things? It seems like all we learned in school was how to adapt and be a part of this dome rather than how we can stand out and be our own.

Waaah, waaaah. I snap back to reality realizing I have dozed off again, noticing I have appeared back into this factory-like hospital or as we call it "CORP." We all know in reality CORP is not the hospital, but where they send people on vacations and the new Era is conceived. The building here is toward the back of the city, in order to have the people realize that this CORP is a reality and that they must avoid being sent here, but out of notice enough so that people's curious minds don't wonder.

This building is made up of three parts. One wing is for the vacations they send people on and the other wing is where the new Era is cared for and raised until they are 'able' enough to be let into society. The last wing is unknown. Unknown not only because of the name "unknown," but because no one is allowed up there, whatever reason is unknown. It is said that's where they keep the storage equipment so no one bothers to go up there. It takes up the whole top floor of the CORP and noone's ever been seen coming in or out. No known staircases or doors lead up there, as if this building was only one floor.

I watch as yet another newborn becomes a new addition to the thing we call "The Era," or a generation of babies that has been raised to "purify" the air in this dome and erase the old generations and the stories they came with. I don't remember coming here really, just that I came here with my granddad. He taught me well, but in silence and secrecy. He always told me never to trust those around us or even trust the air we breathe. There was hope outside of this dome, but when the people lost hope, we built domes in hopes of creating a new hope. By the time I was ten, there were rumors that my granddad had been sent on a vacation. I knew better than to go looking for him. I knew better than to speak against them. I knew better. I got sent to live in the east in a beautiful home while someone occupied the home we had been living in. By the time I reached eighteen, they deemed me stable enough and granted me back to my grandpa's house. Nothing was the same. Refreshed and brand new, all the memories I once had were gone.

"Maybe you need to take a walk," said Lily, as she finished up preparing The Era and cleaning up what we called "birthgiver," a select few that get drugged and are hidden for a year in one's lifetime to conceive an era. I gave her a soft smile and left as I looked at the birthgiver falling back into her trance. I walked out and lit a cigarette to make it seem as if I was not just contemplating all the wrongs going on. Sometimes I wonder, is thinking a crime? They keep tabs on those who don't do as they're told, and sometimes they go on "vacations." We all know this is just a trip to the undergrounds to ship us outside the dome. That is what drives our fear, being sent to the undergrounds. Some say that the undergrounds are where there are stories of beautiful green lands and oceans of earth that are now ruins of old cities. Others say this is where you find other domes across the lands, bigger than ours here and much more. . . free, where it is not a crime to practice our most natural rights as human beings. Other stories are told that there are vast ruins that were left behind from when the last World War happened. Those who know the stories that were once so clear about the generations of those who came along with the stories are gone. Those who are still here hide in silence and act dull-minded. As if we are not being replaced by the Era and as if they are not being brainwashed. As I exhaled my last drag, I flicked my butt onto a pile of junk I saw laid out by the overfilled dumpster and returned inside. I rushed back into the facility.

"Grace," I hear from Kai, the one in charge of the Era, vacation registration, and files.

It startled me because I thought that I had been discovered by someone. "Looks like it's your lucky day. You can come with me and drop off some of the Eras to their new parents," she said with quick haste. I hesitated, remembering that I was only taking a quick puff and was to be back in. "Unless you want to stay here all day and dispose waste," I shook my head and started following her rapidly.

I followed her rapidly to a chamber where they kept the Eras as she looked through the list. "5453 will be going to the Perkers. They will be upgrading to a two-bedroom home and his wife will have a job at the mall. 5454 and 5455 will be located to the suburbs in the East. Oh, they will have such a nice life with the Larks. Last on this list is 5456," as she looked back to her list, she paused and looked up at me hesitantly. Then in pure awe, she said, "will be going to Graciegrace Cornwall." I was in utter shock. In my lifetime, I never thought I would be able to receive my own young, not only because of my occupation, but also because I have never found a mate. It's unusual for them to assign Eras to single households. "You may take the week off to adjust to your new child." Analyzing what just went on, I just agreed and helped drop off the new Eras to their parents.

As the others got dropped off in metal like incubators with the sticker "FRAGILE CORP" written on it, we pulled up to my house. Not knowing how to feel about this, I faked a smile and grabbed my package and stepped into my house.

As soon as I felt the door behind me shut, I let out a piercing wail. I guess I started a chain reaction when I started to hear wailing from the box, too. I opened it to see a baby so soft and so innocent crying with ration papers at the bottom, which I'm guessing was for the baby. I picked it up so fragilely and so carefully trying to put it back to sleep. Ten minutes passed and I realized I had yet to find out the gender. As I carefully unswaddled the sleeping baby in my bed and removed the blankets, I realized this child is a girl. A note fell from the blanket that read, "Hope-grandpa." As I turned her around to inspect her body some more, I noticed at the bottom of her feet were ancient unknown tattoos, as if this were a message for me. This piece looked so familiar to me.

I ran through the house looking for my grandpa's and my old picture. After tearing the house apart, I finally found it. Not the picture of us that drew my attention, but the picture within the picture. I looked at her feet and back at the picture. Memories fled through my mind, the specific day on that day, he went away. I remember he was telling me about everything he believed in, on the outside world and how he would never be gone but on an adventure. How the people under the dome are not the only ones, how the outside life has people, too, and that we must live among each other. I remember.

I remember how he told me of his plans of breaking the dome, but me being so young and small, thinking this was just another story from a book of how powerful one can be to change things. Change things beyond what we can see. He. . . he made me believe. That same day they took him. Sent him on vacation and sent me to a new home. Since that day, I thought his dreams were just a figment of my imagination and that everything he told me only caused people pain and tore them away from the only ones they had left. That day they took my hope along with my grandpa. They took a piece of me. Never have I questioned. After a long realization, I backed up against the wall, tears flooding my eyes. He's not dead, he's still out there somewhere. As I looked at the innocent sleeping baby, I realized this was my way of finding him once more. "Hope," I whispered.

THE EARTHS

HENRY C.

*was born in China and is eighteen years old. He loves playing
badminton and traveling. He lives with his parents, aunts,
and uncles. He has lived in San Francisco for eight years. He
plans to drive to New York with his friends after college.*

Earth is not the only planet that has living things. Four-thousand light years away from Earth, there was a planet called Alibaba. The planet was one-fourth the size of Earth. There was no sunlight, water, or air. The planet was super dry and dark like a desert midnight. However, living on this planet were organisms called Alis. They didn't need water and sunlight to survive and they were very intelligent. The Alis had dark green skin and were an average height of five feet; otherwise they looked similar to humans. There were male and female Alis and they were similar, except that the males had bigger heads and the females were stronger and smarter than the males.

One day, a new female Ali scientist fell asleep in a weapons lab and accidentally pressed a button that was able to launch a mass destruction bomb. Almost half of the planet they were living on was destroyed. Unluckily, their energy tank was right next to the laboratory and all the gaseous energy escaped during the explosion. The King, the smartest Ali, ordered many groups of female soldiers to search for new sources of energy on new planets that they could live on throughout the universe.

The 20C Group entered the solar system in a small spacecraft, and all of sudden everything around them became bright with yellow light and warmth. They could see a large glowing ball in the distance—the Sun, one of them realized. They detected that this immense glowing ball had so much warmth that it would be a great source of energy. They went straight toward it and as they got closer, their spacecraft started overheating, landing them in the Mojave Desert. It was very similar to the Alibaba planet because it was dry with no water nearby. It was also dark because they had landed at night.

Then the 20C soldiers started using a hexagonal-shaped machine to magnify and record data to secretly research the solar system. They found out that Earth and Mars are the planets that they could live on and the sun could be their source of energy.

After they finished the research, they went back to Alibaba planet and reported their findings to the King. The King read the report and discussed it with the top scientists in Alibaba. A few hours later, the King came up with a decision. He decided to move the whole planet to Mars because Mars had less water than Earth. The King activated the huge spaceship under his palace that was built for emergency evacuations. He then ordered all the Alis to go to his palace and immigrate to Mars with him. Alibaba only had a small population; most of them had died due to the explosion.

The huge spacecraft landed back in the Mojave Desert instead of landing on Mars, because the Alis needed materials and labor to rebuild their planet, and Earth had all those things. They also turned on invisible mode so that now they were each invisible to anyone on Earth. The place where they landed felt familiar to the Alis because they landed in a desert.

They also sent thousands of small space crafts out to install a Transporting Gate in major cities like Paris and San Francisco around the world to connect Earth and Mars. The Transporting Gates were like Doraemon's "Anywhere Door," where you could go to another place by walking through the gate and within a second you would be on another planet. The United States, Russian, and Chinese air forces tried to knock down those space crafts, but they were moving too fast. Then all of these major cities were under control by the Alis very quickly using the Ultrasound Waves Machine. They walked toward the Transporting Gates like zombies.

The president of the United States created a secret group of scientists, engineers and soldiers, called SES, to fight against the Alis. They settled their base in Area Zero, which was an underwater military base that was located on Angel Island, near San Francisco, two miles underground. The president recruited a genius engineer, Ryan, and a bio-scientist, Sam, and a group of top soldiers to Area Zero to find a way to destroy the Alis. Ryan built a robotic arm outside the base to catch fish and a generator that transformed seawater into electricity.

Sam, who was still inside the base, wanted to observe the actions of the Alis and find their weaknesses, but it was too dangerous to go outside. The president told Sam that the National Security Agents installed many secret cameras in the country after 9/11 for national security purposes. But the president didn't have access to those cameras, and all the National Security Agents were controlled by the Alis and worked as slaves on Mars. Ryan found a way to hack into the N.S.A.'s computer system and get access to those cameras.

The SES team observed every move of the Alis for a few weeks. Sam noticed that there were no Alis found near the ocean and places that have water, and all Alis disappeared on rainy days. So, he guessed that the Alis were scared of water. Besides that, Ryan found out that each Ali had a rectangular-shaped machine on their back that created irritating sounds. Ryan was thinking that the Alis might use these sound waves to control humans, so he recorded the sound. Then he covered his ears and played the sound to the soldiers and Sam. Everyone was walking randomly and couldn't control themselves.

Ryan invented a Deaf Headphone which could isolate the Alis's sound waves. Sam wanted a dead Ali body, so he could understand more about them. The president sent Navy SEAL Captain Thomas to San Francisco to assassinate an Ali and bring the dead body back to the base. Thomas got on a submarine and landed at Pier One, San Francisco. When he landed, no one was there. It was like an abandoned city. The N.S.A cameras captured that the Alis had built a Transporting Gate at City Hall in San Francisco, so Thomas went straight to it. When he got there, he saw two Alis guarding the Transporting Gate. Thomas tried to kill one of the Alis, but he was afraid that the other Ali was going to notice that and call reinforcements. He decided to kill two of them, so he found an angle that could kill both Alis with one shot.

After that, Thomas brought both Alis' bodies back to Area Zero. Sam started the research immediately. He found out that the Alis' skin contained a chemical called potassium. Potassium can explode when it has contact with water. Sam told his finding to Ryan, and asked him to create a weapon that could shoot out water. Ryan invented a gun called M4A1-Crystal that used ice bullets. Then he produced enough headphones, guns, and bullets for the SES team.

There was a Chinese idiom that said *to catch bandits, first catch the ringleader*, so Thomas led the team to Mars to capture the King. They first went to City Hall because the Alis that were securing the Transporting Gate were now dead. They arrived on Mars within two seconds after they entered the Gate. The SES team forgot that Mars' atmosphere only had 0.1 percent oxygen. They didn't bring any oxygen masks with them. However, they could still breathe on Mars because the Alis had created a machine that produced oxygen for their human slaves.

The SES team saw a huge metallic palace and tons of small buildings that were under construction when they entered Mars. There were millions of human slaves working and a few hundred Alis were supervising them. The SES team started shooting the Alis and destroyed their Ultrasound Waves Machine. The Alis had underestimated the humans. They never thought that humans could fight them back, so they didn't create other weapons to fight against humans except the soundwave machine.

The Alis knew that they were in a bad situation, so they destroyed most of the Transporting Gates and escaped from Mars with small space crafts, never to be seen again. Only five Transporting Gates were still working and there were still about one billion humans on Mars. The problem was each Transporting Gate could only transport a maximum of one hundred people. Those five Gates were connected to the U.S., Russia, China, India, and France. The citizens in those five countries had priority to go back to Earth. The people from other countries had to wait, so some of them decided to stay on Mars instead of going back to Earth, and they created a new society called Second Earth.

BLUE EYES

◆

ALEX M.

was born in San Francisco and is seventeen years old.
He enjoys reading and playing the piano. He has
one younger brother. He plans to attend a college to
study biochemistry.

Outside, it is a world of new exploration. People rely on technology more than they rely on each other in the current age, the Age of Technology. We have 3D Holo-TVs that project images and video in 3D to replace the televisions from over a century ago, hover cars to replace the cars in the past that drove on the road, and disks that also emit holograms to replace the smart phones of the past. But I can't enjoy any of that.

It is the year of 2124 and I am inside a hospital, in a location I don't know of. All I see around me are other sick children with doctors surrounding them, too. Instead of feeling like a hospital, it feels like a jail. There are no windows as far as I can see, all the walls are white, but the worst part is, the doctors don't even allow visitors to visit the patients to reduce the risk of spreading the disease.

As of now, I am laying down in a hospital bed with doctors in bright yellow quarantine suits all around me.

One doctor says, "Emma, I'm afraid I have some bad news for you. Your last day on Earth might be approaching soon," and apologetically explained, "We don't have enough information about this disease to get rid of it from your body."

All I see around me are other sick children with doctors surrounding them, too. My name is Emma and I am a fourteen-year-old girl. The doctors told me that I am infected by some unknown disease and I am dying soon.

It has been a few months or longer since I've seen my family because there are no clocks or calendars to tell the time or date, and there are no visitors allowed. Currently, I am living the rest of my life alone in a hospital bed, only to be accompanied by doctors from time to time. It wasn't always like this; I used to be a young active girl playing with my friend in a park in San Francisco.

It all started in the summer of 2124 when I still lived with my mom and dad. We lived in a neighborhood of party-colored houses. We didn't have a lot of neighbors, so having a neighbor was new to me. When a man who appeared to be around the same age as my dad, thirty-five years old, and a girl who appeared to be about my age moved in as our neighbor across the street, I decided to greet them.

I had crossed the street and called out, "Hi, my name is Emma and I live across the street in the bright-pink house. Where did you guys move here from?"

"Hi, it's good to meet you, my name is Henry and this is my daughter, Olivia, and we came from Seattle."

Olivia said, "Oh wow, you have blue eyes like me. My dad has brown eyes, he said my eyes were a mutation. Are you fourteen years old, too?"

"Yes, I'm an upcoming sophomore at Clodagh High School."

Through our conversation, I had learned that she had muscular dystrophy (MD), but it hadn't affected her too much yet. Despite having progressive weakness in the muscles, she liked going outside to play in the park. Since it was summertime and we were both out of school, we went to Hvatum Park daily to play. It was a park that was surrounded by multiple tall oak trees. All the parks had swings, slides and a playground, but this was the only park that had so many trees close by. Out of all the things in the park that we played with, Olivia and I both loved playing with the swings the most. Those black-seated swings with the metal chains were what connected both of us together over time. We had always taken turns pushing each other because neither of us knew how to play with the swing alone. We had depended on one another and trusted each other and spent all our time together as if tomorrow would be the last day we would spend together.

We became great friends over time and played together outside every day, but I knew this couldn't last forever. Someday, her MD would make her unable to play with me in the park any longer. She might need a wheelchair to move around, so she wouldn't be able to go on the swings anymore.

"Olivia, will you still go to the park if you become more weakened in the future? This summer might be the last summer we spend together outside in a park."

She closed her eyes and tilted her head slightly downward, "Maybe not," and said hopefully, "Maybe I'll be cured someday, my father is doing research to cure any disease in the world."

Olivia talked about her father a lot and how he would cure her someday. She placed so much hope in her father, so I had to see what he worked on at least once. The next day, I asked Olivia to show me her father's work.

When I went inside their house, there was a living room with a Holo-TV, a floating magnetic table, and a few chairs. Olivia led me to the next room over and it was drastically different. It was a dark lab room that reeked with the smell of chemicals and it was filled with centrifuges, computers, and microscopes. Behind a fluorescent microscope in the far back right corner of the room was Henry.

He was looking into a petri dish through a microscope when I walked into the room. His hair and clothing were disheveled, his lips were dried, and he had bags underneath his eyes. I was slightly shocked when I saw him. It looked like he had been working nonstop for days, as if he wouldn't stop working until he was finished.

Henry looked up and saw us. "Oh, Emma. What are you doing here?" His eyes lit up as he stood up. "Do you want to see what I'm working on?"

"Sure, I heard it's a cure for your daughter."

Olivia sniffed, "This room smells weird today. I'll let you talk alone."

After Olivia left the room, I walked over to Henry and stood beside him.

"This room does smell weird. So, what exactly are you doing?"

He stepped away from the microscope. "I don't really know how it smells, I have anosmia. Go take a look for yourself."

In the petri dish, there were a lot of cells. They looked similar to the ones shown in the biology textbooks in school but they looked slightly different.

I looked up toward Henry, "What is this? They look like mutated cells."

His eyebrows rose, "You're right, I'm working on trying make a cure for any genetic disease, including MD." He walked over to a computer and opened up a simulation. "I'm using gene therapy to insert genes that replace mutated genes and prevent them from making mutations that are detrimental to mankind."

Since his eyes were filled with joy after talking about it, I decided to look around more and ask him about his progress so far.

"I'm also done. With a few more weeks of research, I might be able to do something no one has ever seen before."

I decided to not bother him anymore so that he could quickly achieve his life goal.

"Those black-seated swings with the metal chains were what connected both of us together over time."

After two months, I turned on the Holo-TV and saw that Henry was on the news. He had been known throughout the country because of his announcement of his medicine. My eyes widened and sparkled while watching the news. He had finally achieved his life goal and had received fame and honor proportional to the time he had spent working on the medicine. So far, there had been no known side effects, so it was the perfect medicine, but I had known that there was no such thing as a perfect medicine in the world. It was only a matter of time before something would happen.

One month had passed since his achievement and I fell ill. At first, I thought it was a common cold, but I became more ill over time. My body ached, my muscles weakened, and I was fatigued. With modern day technology, I shouldn't have been sick for more than a few days at max. At this point I knew something was horribly wrong, I started to feel pain in my muscles, pain in my back, and shallow breathing.

My parents had called multiple doctors to have a check up on me, but none of them knew what was happening to me. Henry knew a lot about diseases because of his research, so my parents asked him for help. When Henry came over and saw me lying down in my bed, he knew it wasn't some ordinary disease.

After a moment of silence, he had a face of disbelief, "This is all my fault."

My parents and I stared at him silently in confusion.

The muscles in my mom's face had tightened, my mom asked, "What do you mean?"

Henry's head had drooped as his body loosened and his voice trembled, "I think the first side effect is showing. . . I'm not sure what—"

My mom's jaw muscles clenched, "Get out! You caused this. She can't even get up by herself anymore! If you can't do anything, why are you still here?!"

He ran out of our house immediately. We heard our front door slam shut. He had known that he had done something that was not part of his expectations and it was too late to do anything about it. He should've expected that there was nothing that was ever perfect when it was first released. There would always be some mishaps along the road to success. It was a tragedy that he had to face tribulation after his success, leading to greater consequences because of all the praise and fortunes he had received.

The next day Olivia came over to my house and her face was full of tears. She told me how her father never returned back to her house after leaving my house yesterday. Right after hearing that, I told my parents that Henry was missing. At that moment, there was breaking news on the Holo-TV, the news reporter said that Henry was dead.

The news reporter said, "A note was found in his coat, "I lost my wife and I'm losing my daughter. I can't deal with losses anymore. I'm sorry Olivia, I hope you can live on without me."

In bright red letters, were the words, "At the age of thirty-five, Dr. Henry Summers has died. The cause of death is suicide." Olivia had tears bursting out of her eyes and I stood there in silence. After a few moments, I had collapsed for unknown reasons and that was the last I ever saw of my family and Olivia.

This was how I came to be in the hospital, but I still don't know how I got here. The last moments of my life have approached, from the young active girl I used to be playing with Olivia in the park to being a sick girl. As a result of something unknown, my life was full of both joy and misery.

As the last moments of my life approached, I heard a doctor murmur, "All the victims of this disease have blue eyes, like this girl."

AS I
REALLY
AM

—◆—

Questioning, Searching

PROSTHETIC

◆

LUIS S.

*is seventeen and from San Francisco. A quiet person
with an odd sense of humor, he likes to spend time at home
watching movies. He prefers engineering to English.
Even if he could, he wouldn't want to live forever.*

It was a typical day at Howard's job, following the same routine over and over. Waking up at 7:00 a.m., being ready to leave by 7:45 a.m., showing up at 8:20 a.m., he was spending each day at his desk crunching numbers. Howard had grown tired of working at the same job, day in and day out for the past twenty years. He worried about not being able to do the things he had wanted to before he became too old.

Today, he plans on taking the money he has been saving up and doing the things he wants for once. And so, he does *exactly* what he had planned. Howard buys a plane ticket to the Himalayas and with all the necessary gear for hiking, sets off on a journey to get back his youth. Once there, he reads up on all the information he needs in order to make sure he won't die.

After holding off his excursion for three days, he finally gets the courage to go hiking on his own. After walking for about an hour, Howard begins to notice the drastic change in temperature and it also feels like it's a lot harder to breathe, but he simply puts his oxygen mask on and keeps going. Out of nowhere, a snowstorm rolls in, making it almost impossible to see even three feet in front of him. Struggling to stay on his feet, he decides to build a shelter in a nearby overhang. He quickly rushes over and begins making the shelter the way he saw in the video. Out of desperation, he doesn't realize the mistake he has made. As he is trying to make his shelter, he doesn't notice the buildup of snow above him that is just moments from giving way. After finishing the shelter, he tries to start a fire. He digs in the snow in search of two rocks he can use to create a spark. Due to his inexperience, he is not able to get the fire started, so he throws one of the rocks high on the wall out of anger. Howard quickly realizes his mistake, as he sees the mass of snow falling toward him. He dives out of the way just in time to save his body from getting buried, but has his arm pinned down by a boulder hidden in the mountain of snow. He struggles for a few minutes in an attempt to free his arm but only succeeds in causing himself more pain. Buried in the snow, he sees his backpack, reaches for it and searches through the many pockets. He finds his satellite phone to call for help and manages to press the emergency button before passing out.

The next thing he knows, a doctor is standing over him saying that his arm needed to be amputated. He begins fading in and out of consciousness when the doctor tells him to sign a paper. The next time he is able to stay conscious, there is a young man no older than twenty-five operating on his arm and he is told that his arm is gone. The young man notices that Howard has woken up and greets him with a smile. He says, "Take a deep breath in," as he places a mask over Howard's face, putting him to sleep.

Howard spends a few days getting used to his arm.

While it gives him a new sense of empowerment, he feels as though he left part of himself on that mountain. At the follow up appointment, the scientist walks in and says "Good news, since you seemed compatible with the arm you have the opportunity to get the full upgrade."

Reluctant at first, Howard thinks this is a chance to get back the part of him he feels is missing.

Howard asks, "That sounds amazing; where do I sign up?"

The scientist hands him a document and says, "Make sure you read and sign that as soon as possible." Howard looks around for a pen and fumbles with it, before he signs the paper and hands in the document.

"If it's not too much trouble, can we get started right away?"

"I knew you were going to say that," replies the scientist, as he rolls in the stretcher and takes Howard to the operating room. After the operation, Howard looks in the mirror. He now has two new prosthetic legs, his other arm has been modified to match his carbon fiber legs, and he notices that he now has a chest plate and has a visor covering his eyes. While Howard admires himself, he thinks about how great he is and how he feels like he has no equal, and he turns to the scientist and asks "So what now?"

"Now you can return to your normal life. I've run all the tests so you can live the life you want," says the scientist.

Howard returns to his routine, except for a few noticeable differences. Instead of wasting money on gas, it's more convenient for him to run. Once at his job, he notices that he gets a lot more work done in a shorter amount of time. The amount of work he's doing isn't the only difference. It feels as though the atmosphere in the office has completely changed. People are acting a lot less friendly, are constantly avoiding conversations, and he is receiving dirty looks from those around him.

One day at work, after finishing his job hours before everyone else, Howard is called into his boss' office. He expects to be praised for being so efficient, but his boss has other things in mind. "When you finish all your work in a day, it makes it harder for the next person to input all that data and your appearance is making your coworkers uncomfortable. Believe me, I've really been trying to find a solution, but I don't think we can have someone like you working here. Sorry, but I'm going to have to let you go." Howard storms out the office, and in a fit of anger rips a tree out of the ground and throws it on his boss's car.

After calming down, he thinks to himself that it's not the end of the world and decides to take a completely different career path. After months of searching for a job, Howard settles on construction because he feels it's the one place that he can use his abilities to the fullest. In this new job, he finds a purpose. He enjoys using his body because he feels truly powerful, and that strength would never go away, no matter how old he got.

On his way to work one day, Howard decides to show off a little and goes for a jog across a park near his house. Once there, he immediately sees people staring at him in amazement. He then turns and sees a little girl trying to get her ball that had gotten stuck in a tree nearby. So he figures he can use this opportunity to make people realize that his appearance isn't just for show. In one big leap, he reaches the ball that is stuck eleven feet above him and lands, with a smile on his face, as he hands the ball to the child. Much to his amazement, instead of being met with gratitude, all he receives is the look of horror from the girl as she runs to her mother screaming, "It's a monster, help!" Howard dismisses it as just some kid not knowing any better. As he looks around, he notices that everyone at the park is looking at him, but not with looks of awe as he initially thought. Instead they all seem worried and scared. While he walks away he hears the people saying, "What's wrong with him?" "Should we call the police?" "He should just die!"

Howard can't take anymore. He runs full speed to a place where can hide and be safe. Two places come to mind: his house and the scientist's lab. Since he wants to confront the problem, he decides to go to the scientist's lab. And during the time he is running, he thinks about how he hates the way people see him as a freak and monster, which is the complete opposite to how he imagined it would be. Once he arrives at the building, he barges in, not bothering to knock, and goes straight to the scientist's office. "I want it all off, now!" Howard says. "I don't know what you mean, but sit down and relax," the scientist says. "I need *all* of the mods gone," Howard says. "I just want to be normal again!"

"That can be done, but I must warn you, there are consequences," says the scientist.

"What do you mean consequences? Why wasn't I told?" Howard asks.

"I told you to read the document before you signed it. It clearly stated what would happen should you wish to go back," the scientist says.

"It doesn't matter what happens. Just get rid of it!" says Howard.

"So, you're okay with being stuck in a hospital for the rest of your life?" the scientist says.

The scientist gets up and walks to Howard and says, "Do you really want to lose all the strength you've gained?"

"What good is all this strength if I can't be around those I care about?"

SEAN

◆

ZI Z.

*was born in China and is eighteen years old. He loves to try
new things in life and listen to the stories of his peers.
Life after high school for him is a mystery, aimless in time,
but not in goals. He would like to dedicated this piece to
My My My and Mad_Hattress.*

𝕴t was a rainy morning, its blues riddled. Tears of the clouds filled the streets. I listened closely to the drops which fell from the heavens. Motorbikes passed by with their chained engines, the sound of motors, and the rain created a harmony of white. I decided to go outside of my apartment and look into the skies, searching for the suns. My own amusement drove me out of common sense. There I stood, staring into the floating oceans above-reflecting another world of electric fury. A sudden light made of pure gold ignited, shaking the skies and the earth. Within my distance, this harmony had only started to bloom louder. Headlights appeared in front of my field of view, getting closer. The bike directed to my left. As it inclined to a stop, its engine turned off, and its phantom-like lights followed. I saw a familiar figure sliding off the two-wheeled contraption, a body of a woman. She walked toward to me.

"Son, why don't you go back inside?" she asked me.

"Yes, mum," I replied as I retreated.

Every year around Christmas to the New Year's, a mysterious man always visits my mother and me. He's pretty close to my mother, and acts familiar in my home, too;

though our house *is* really compact. It might be just a coincidence in their fates crossing. Sometimes this man picks me up from my school then treats me to my childish desires, such as toys, Tokusatsu animations, and miniature rides in the nearby parks. As the sands of time fill the hourglasses, I notice that this man has started to visit us less and less. The image of his face and color also becomes fainter to my still developing mind. However, I do not blame him, for he has a family of his own he needs to return to in the New World.

Today is haunted. Storms and more storms rule the skies. Rain puddles clash upon the metal sheets that make my very roof. There are surprisingly no floods outside or leaks inside these rotten walls. It seems my day is getting a head start; tomorrow I leave for my flight. It is unclear the reason of my premature travel; I still haven't completed preschool yet. My mother comes home with groceries early today. She goes straight to cooking and takes her groceries to our cramped kitchen. When it comes to cooking, my mother really enjoys taking time. Meanwhile I turn the TV on and load up some Tokusatsu shows. Moments later, she comes out a chef, serving me a freshly cooked meal. I begin to eat time away; I grow more unconscious of the frames which I consume. At that moment it is as if I become time, a singularity: unfathomable, unfavorable and genesis to age.

Time waits for no one.

Today makes the morning grey. The colors of my very present are starting to fade. As our car stops, and its doors open, my family stands there frozen. My mother and I wave our last goodbyes. My aunty and uncle dare to tear up their eyes. We walk and we sob to the entrance door, we always knew we were adored. However, I cannot say the same for the New World, for there I know not a single soul. Tonight, the past is grey, the colors of my phantoms, blue.

I've never been on an airplane before, this is my first time. I never knew the insides of an airplane were cushioned. I thought it was all steel inside and out. Perhaps, I'm not used to such luxurious sights. These windows, those rugs, and this seat which I sit on, they are all new to me. Where my journey lies, only rumors I have heard that San Francisco had a bridge made of pure gold. I don't know what gold is, but I'm sure I'll find out when I'm there. Suddenly I hear a voice on the intercom, a deep lucid projection of a man.

"We will be taking off shortly, meals will be served an hour after takeoff," he announces.

I fasten my seatbelt. The turbines start to turn, *bon voyage.*

I've finally arrived at my destination. The bright horizon has landed, and vivid colors fly at my arrival. We exit through the terminal and around me are people of alien looks.

Their skins are pale white with sky-colored eyes, a few are blond, and some orange. As I arrive to pick up our luggage on the conveyor belts, I hear them speak in a language I'm unfamiliar with. We retrieve our luggage and stack some of them for an easier lift. Now we're all set: all of our worries of landing, belongings, and immigrating are gone. Sunlight rains down upon us: good omens. The clouds sway through the oceans, shaping the godly rays. We are here.

The corridor of this airport is very vast. The walls are transparent. My luggage drags me around these smelly carpets, with each tug, my direction shifts into another. My mother pays little attention to me. Perhaps she is in a world of her own. In this concave hallway with windows that run to the ends of nowhere, it's hard not to get lost in a gossamer of thoughts. I'm about to reach the end of this corridor, and I see a crowd of people waiting behind the barrier poles. Within my distant view, a man with very distinctive figures waves his hand; my mother responds back by waving hers. As we begin to approach him, the past catches up. I start to recall memories of this same person being there in my life. This is our first time being in California, and she already knows someone.

"This is your father," she finally says.

THE HIGHWAY FROM PAST TO FUTURE

MAKAYLA M.

was born in San Francisco and is seventeen years old.
She loves to read and hopes to travel. She is the youngest of
six and plans to go to college after high school to
major in either nursing or psychology.

𝔉ears can be sneaky things. They can lodge themselves in hidden places and lie quietly like ghosts for a long, long time. They are invisible like oxygen. Then when you're least expecting it they can burst forth and begin to control your life. But I am not going to allow that to happen.

I had three sisters: Mignon, Martisha, and Tamara. Now I have two. Just before I was born my oldest sister was in a car accident and was killed. I'm not even aware of how or when I was told about this. She was in the car, in the backseat with a seatbelt on, and the casualty was caused because of the driver making poor decisions.

Because I was not yet conceived when Mignon had the accident, throughout the years I was unaware of the big impact it had on me. But the catastrophe I had with my sister Tamara I do remember.

When I was about eight years old I was in the backseat, on the highway going to the movies, laughing and listening to music and then *boom!* Glass was everywhere. Everything went crazy. We were exiting the freeway and someone hit us from behind. The car had flipped and we went down a hill. I don't remember a lot after that but many people stopped to help. A man broke the back window where I was sitting to get me out of the car. It was like a nightmare. I can remember my sister being terrified and I just wanted my mom. After being taken up the hill by this man a lot of time must have passed because I saw my dad as I was being taken to the ambulance. I can't imagine the way my dad must have felt after losing one child and then getting a phone call saying his two other daughters were now in a car accident.

I remember thinking, *what would have happened if I didn't put a seat belt on?* Then time passed, and I never thought about it again until I started to get behind the wheel. At sixteen I received my driver's license. My dad was the one who helped me get it, although he had already lost a daughter in a car accident and had two children experience a serious collision. Even though my father never had any fear for me, it was when I began driving my own car when my fear began. I was terrified of getting into a car accident. I feared the unknown. I was even more terrified of being in the passenger seat. I would always make sure I put my seat belt on. My eyes always went 100 miles a minute looking around constantly for red flags while driving. I feared everything about cars if I wasn't the one in control.

Although I was unprepared for this fear to take over, I was determined not to give it power. Over the years as a driver, I have always been sure to follow all the rules and I am very aware of my surroundings when in a vehicle as a passenger and as the driver. Every time I get into a car I always put my seatbelt on. When I'm driving, every passenger must wear a seatbelt. The question "What would happen if I didn't have my seatbelt on?" is always in the back of my head.

I have learned that fear can take over when you least expect it. I know there are times ahead when I will be taken by surprise again. But I have also learned something about myself; that no matter what comes my way, it's not what comes but it's how I respond to it. Dramatic changes in a person's life just make them stronger. It breaks them down to build them back up. And that is what this experience has done to me.

A TIME WHEN. . .

◆

MAUREEN M.

was born in the Philippines and moved to California when she was four years old. In her free time, she likes to hang out with her friends and watch movies. Maureen has four brothers, three older and one younger. She lives with her mom and grandma in San Francisco. She also plans to attend a university next fall, majoring in Civil Engineering.

𝕿ry journaling. Just write out how you feel about your day, really anything. . .

I've always had a rough childhood with my dad being an ex-drug addict and my mom who left us when I was young. I think people could say I'm a "strong person." I use the thought of not wanting to become like my mom to drive me to be a high-achieving student at school. I'm pretty independent too, since there isn't an adult in my life to support me emotionally and financially—I had to become one at a young age. Though I seem to have my life in order, I frequently find myself in distress.

Maybe it's because of my hard upbringing or whatever, but I realize that I overthink and overstress things I shouldn't be overthinking and overstressing about. Nick, my therapist, says that maybe I could reflect on why I think I'm like this. Even though I never do anything unless it benefits me, I decided, for myself, that I would try journaling. So here are some of my entries, I guess. . .

A time when I valued someone else's opinion on my own life rather than my own:

JANUARY 18, 2015—9:36 P.M.

I just took a walk with Eric and my dog, Max. It was really nice, we talked about a lot of things; our future, school, plans, etc. I don't know how I feel about him yet. I know I like talking to him. He's eccentric and outgoing, something I've always admired about other people. Karen tells me we're not a good match. If she tells me then it must be true. She's usually right about me. We had a good talk, though, or maybe it's just because I have a lot of stories to tell him. Maybe I should just start talking to him less.

A time when I cared way too much about what others thought of me:

JANUARY 21, 2015—12:49 A.M.

I hate myself so much. Today I decided to wear this really cute but low-cut top to school. I even woke up earlier than usual to put on makeup. I was super excited to be thought of as fashionable and pretty at school. But when I got to school, I just put on my sweater for the whole day! I don't know why, but I got scared that everyone was going to think that I was wearing that shirt for attention. This whole school is filled with judgmental people! Ugh. I hate myself.

A time when I thought that in order to be pretty, I needed to wear makeup:

FEBRUARY 2, 2017—1:34 A.M.

I put on a lot more makeup than usual yesterday. I received a lot of compliments on it from my friends and even from a stranger, which made me feel really good. I felt really beautiful and confident. But today, I woke up too late to put on makeup. I felt ugly and disgusting, especially because I wore sweatpants and my hair was dirty. People kept asking me if I was sick or tired but it was just because I didn't put on makeup. . .

My second meeting with Nick was very insightful. Nick is a part of my school's wellness program and is a social worker. I see him once every few weeks to talk about my family problems and to check in. We meet in his little office during one of my free periods. His office has come to be a very safe and welcoming environment for me throughout high school. He would typically sit in his swivel chair in front of his desk and computer while I sat on the side in my own chair. His office is hella cold most of the time so he keeps a blanket out for the students. I gave him my journal to read so that we could try to self-reflect.

"After reading your journal I realized one thing that you yourself may not realize," said Nick.

"What is it?" I replied.

"Well, you seem to always seek approval of others."

"I do?"

"Each journal entry you've written consists of you worrying about and doing things that you believe other people want rather than doing things for yourself," he said.

It took me a few moments to internalize what Nick had just said. As I thought about it, it seemed to be really accurate.

"How do I stop myself from doing that then? Because that's bad, right? Or am I just trying to seek your approval right now?" I asked nervously. He laughed.

"You're not at fault, you need to realize that. It's just someone who you have become, maybe through your experiences with your parents, maybe something else, maybe everything else. As for my job as your therapist, you tell me your problems and I come up with a way to solve those problems. So, if you have a problem with always seeking approval of others then we can definitely try to create more confidence in you."

After our meeting, I thought really hard about myself, how I act around others, and my family problems. I thought that maybe one of the reasons why I like Eric is because I want to be as outgoing as him. I made a decision at that moment that I would try to stop seeking approval of others and become more self-confident.

A time when I realized that it's okay for me to listen to myself:

FEBRUARY 8, 2015—10:16 P.M.

I started talking more to Eric again. We always have a good conversation when we're together. We actually have a lot more in common than I thought. I learned he applied to be an art major, just like me, which was so cool to find out. After that we just talked about art and what each of us want for our lives after high school. I'm kind of glad that I talked to him today. I really shouldn't always listen to what Karen has to say. Eric and I decided to meet again soon and I can't wait.

A time when I realized that I just needed confidence in order to feel pretty:

FEBRUARY 20, 2015—11:22 P.M.

I wore that really cute shirt again and I didn't put on any makeup at all. I tried really hard to be confident today and I only put on my sweater a few times during school!

I even got compliments on it which made me feel so good and even more confident. Because of this, I spoke up more in class and with my group of friends and overall had a really good day. As I reflect right now, I realize that maybe I was just over thinking about how everyone is really judgmental at school. There are actually some nice people here.

During my third meeting with Nick, we discussed my progress through my journals. I found out more about myself during that month than I have in my whole life. I learned to be confident in myself and to value my own opinions as well. Because of the actions that I took this month, I've gotten so much happier with my relationship with Eric and my mentality on how I look.

I am going to keep working on building my self-confidence and try to stop always asking for approval that negatively impacts me. This was a time where I did something for myself!

LESSON FROM MIDDLE SCHOOL

◆

ARVIN Y.

was born in Kaiping, China, and is seventeen years old.
He loves to be active, and not just doing the same thing
over and over again. Arvin was born into a Chinese family
that has no prior college experience nor anyone that
speaks English. The dream that Arvin wants to achieve
is to become an electrical engineer so that he can
help his father with his business.

Have you ever felt betrayed before? I have. Have you ever felt hurt by someone and wanted to take revenge on them? I have. Have you ever regretted the things that you have done to someone? I have. All of these events happened during middle school, or to be exact, the beginning of middle school.

A.P. Giannini was the first English language school that I had attended, and that was only my fourth year since I migrated from China to San Francisco. Before I was admitted into A.P. Giannini, I was enrolled in those dual-language teaching schools; the kind of schools that help new immigrants like me pick up English as their second language quicker. Because of those previous school experiences, going to a full English school like A.P. Giannini made me feel the same way that I felt when I first got to the United States. It was a brand new experience.

My first impression of the school when I took my first step inside was that I could feel all the joy that everyone had on their mind, see all the excitement that they had in their bodies. Then I had to squeeze through the crowd of people in order to take a look at the school yard. When I squeezed through the crowd, I saw a full view of basketball courts with people playing on each court. They all seemed so happy; it triggered my love for basketball, and how I used to play basketball with my elementary friends. Then I realized something; I don't have any friends here. I am just a FOB (Fresh Off the Boat) who came from China and luckily got admitted into a full English school. Just at that moment, all my excitement and joy that I had felt for this school was gone. I didn't know much English, which meant I could not really communicate with those American-born students. I was not smart or attractive, nor did I have anything special that allowed people to notice me. I was just a loner, that one kid that is left behind from all the joy that everyone was having; I was just an extra.

After a few more minutes of me sitting in the corner of the yard, the bell rang. The one thing I drilled inside my head during my previous four years of learning was that when the bell rings, it is time for class. A.P. Giannini wasn't too big, so finding my first classroom was not that big of a deal. It might have taken ten minutes or so, but it was fine since I'm not someone that is noticeable at all. When I stepped into the classroom, I saw the same thing as when I took my first step into the school; everyone was having fun talking to their friends and all seemed excited for the class. I walked to the empty seat that was all the way in the far back. The ironic part was that that was where I wanted to sit. What I wanted to do the most at that moment was find a place where I could feel alone, and no one could notice me. Time felt extended or stretched to me during the first two periods of class. At A.P. Giannini, the first two and the last two classes were always with the same teacher in the same classroom. But everything started to change when I walked into my third period class.

The first two periods seemed really boring for me because I felt really alone and left out. Everyone else had someone to share their conversation with, on top of all the loneliness and sadness. The first two periods included the class that I hated the most, science. I never tend to do well in science. Ever since I got to San Francisco, my grade for science has never passed a C. But since my third period was P.E., my mood changed from the "leaving school instantly" mood, to "maybe leaving school after next period" mood. I expected P.E. to be a lot of running or active activity, but destiny got me again. Even though my third period was P.E., what I experienced was more and more of teachers talking. I even got to the point where I almost fell asleep while sitting in my crisscross applesauce position. But what stopped me from falling asleep was a gentle tap from a guy that shared the same first two classes with me.

His name was Percy, with a height that was around mine. He wore glasses, was skinnier than me, and he seemed to be a Chinese guy, too. At first sight, he looked like the type of person that knew a lot and was a hard-working student. When I first felt the touch, I turned around and saw him waving at me, then I looked around and asked him "Are you talking to me?"

That one class changed the whole experience that I was going to have during that school year. Meeting Percy was like a life changer. Without meeting Percy, I might have ended up on the dark side for ditching school too much. What happened during the one class period was that I finally got someone I could talk to during school time and someone to play ball with when I felt like playing. We traded information about our Facebook and phone numbers, so that we could have different methods to chat with each other. Ever since Percy and I met each other, we had been talking to each other almost nonstop. Even when we could take a bathroom break or go to our lockers to get items, we would still walk that distance together and chat about whatever came up on our mind. But sadly, fun times did not last.

It was the time that the first semester report card showed up in everyone's hand. I knew my report card was going to be horrible already, because of all that slacking off from science class and not paying attention to the classes that Percy and I did not share. I wanted to hide away my report card so that Percy would not see it. I heard from a conversation between the teacher and Percy was that he got all As in his class and ended up with one of the highest grades within the whole school. When the bell rang after sixth period, Percy and I got on the bus to get back home. I thought I was safe from him asking me about my grades. But if everything went according to what I want, I would be a billionaire already. As soon as we got on the bus, we both immediately found two seats and we took them, then the question that I worried about the most came out of Percy's mouth.

Percy asked, "What grades did you get for all of your classes?"

I did not want to answer the question and tried to pull it off with the "I did not get mine yet" lie. But he knew I got mine because what I told him this morning was that I took my semester report card away from the house before my parents even had a chance to look at it. So, I tried to not answer that question and delay Percy from getting his answer until he reached his stop and got off the bus. Even though I tried to delay him from getting the answer as long as I could, he eventually got mad at me for not answering his question. So, I had to take out my report card and show him my grades.

Then what I did not want to happen, happened.

After that day, Percy started to talk less and less around me, to the point that he actually stopped talking to me when we saw each other on the hallway. During lunch, we used to have this one meeting place in the yard. That day I did not see Percy there, but instead I spotted him with another bunch of people. It looked like they were having a fun conversation. Then there was me again, all alone and having no one to talk to anymore. I wanted to blame myself for not getting a better grade and getting Percy upset, but I also thought of why Percy left me just because I got bad grades. So, I got into a conflict within myself, and the side that wanted to blame Percy won the fight. I wanted to take revenge on Percy, I wanted to strip everyone that talks to Percy away from him, and make him come back to me.

So, I tried many ways to get all of Percy's current friends away from him. I didn't care what kind of method I would use, I just wanted him to feel alone and the sadness that I had when he decided to straight up ignore me; when he pretended that he had never met me before and dumped me from his friends list just because I did not study hard enough in school. Different kinds of thoughts flew into my mind when I thought of different methods of revenge. They came into my mind, but the amount was too much for that one small opening to handle, so the thoughts just burst out of my mind like how water bursts through a dam. The methods were something like using money to bribe, force, or power to make them listen, and many other possible ways. But the method I decided to use was to force them to leave Percy, and use money to get people off of him. I did not care what I did, I just wanted to let Percy feel those moments that make him alone and sad.

The plan of getting everyone away from Percy worked but the result wasn't what I wanted. Even though I got everyone away from Percy, he did not have the sadness that I had before. What I saw from him was that he was okay with what he had and not how I felt when I lost him. I wanted to do more to him; I wanted him to feel all the sadness, the time that someone brings you out of suffering but decides to drop you back into suffering. To me, that was like the worst kind of feeling because I was a nobody when I first got to A.P. Giannini; but Percy reached out to me and I tried so hard to keep him with me, but that changed, and he's gone. I did not want all the hard work that I spent on something to be gone just like that; I did not want to lose anything that I worked for, but even if I did lose something, there had to be a price for it.

A week had passed after I took everyone away from Percy, but I still was not able to see the result of my plan—what did I calculate wrong? I took everyone from him, why wasn't he feeling sad or anything? It couldn't be like this; I had to make him feel sad, but I did not realize that everyone that I took from Percy had gone back to his side. In that moment, I felt like my heart had just stopped beating for a second or two, because the scene that I was looking at was like the extreme opposite of my wanted result. I thought I had earned those people's friendship; why did they leave me? Is it because of the same reason? *No way*. I did not even talk to them about my grades. I went up and grabbed one of the them and asked what they were doing. They told me this:

"We're just talking to Percy. He's our friend, do you want to meet him, too?"

I gasped and said this inside my mind: "*No, no, no, no way this is happening.*"

But that guy grabbed my arm and introduced me to Percy, even though I already knew him. I pretended that I did not know him, and did a simple introduction. What was surprising was that Percy did not respond back to me with anger with his voice; instead he responded with a friendly but strange voice. It made me feel that he was not right in front of me when he was just four steps away; the feeling toward Percy was so different.

What really ended up happening was Percy and I got back to being "friends," the kind that just greet each other when we walk by, and not like before where there was an endless conversation between both of us. I know I have lost him as a best friend already, but I cannot just stay like how I used to be. I needed to change how I used to live, so I could meet more new friends and keep them as friends. I needed to leave how I thought when I was still in China and learn to grow up and get more experience to fit in the living environment that I'm in right now. Ten years later, I figured out that those changes I made were like the conversations that Percy and I used to have; it is priceless and with a great impact on my life.

A DAY TO REMEMBER

—◆—

MAHMOUD A.

was born in San Bruno and is seventeen years old.
He is the middle child in his family and enjoys
basketball, video games, and fashion. He is a family
person who is loving, caring, and friendly.

𝕿o most people, it's just another sunny, summer day in San Francisco when I wake up to the sound of my iPhone alarm buzzing in my ear. But I'm brimming with energy, because it's not just another day for me. It's June first, which is my birthday, and I'm officially seventeen years old. I flood with excitement when I glance at my phone and see that all of my friends have already blown it up with happy birthday texts. As I read through each text, I start to feel nostalgic about a day—today—that hasn't even yet really begun, much less ended. A moment of fear brushes past me; fear about the fact that it feels like the end of something, even though I can't quite put my finger on exactly what that thing is. Am I afraid of getting older? Of losing something? I'm not sure. But the feeling evaporates almost as quickly as it comes, like cool water hitting the burning concrete on a scorching hot day.

Then an idea pops into my head. Since it's summer break, and I haven't seen my friends for a while, I want to invite them over to my house so we can celebrate. I have never had a birthday party with my friends before—it's always just been my family and me. But, I feel like this is my last opportunity to get everyone together to celebrate my birthday, so I ask my mom if I can have my friends over and, much to my surprise, she says yes. Minutes later, my mom is out the door to buy a cake. I can't believe it. I didn't think she'd say yes. This is the first party I've ever had at my house. And I have a feeling that today is going to be one for the books.

Still reeling from the fact that I'm about to have a party—my birthday party—at my house, I decide to shower and get dressed. That feeling of nostalgia mixed with fear brushes past me again, but as I wash away the dirt from my body, so, too, I wash away this feeling that I don't quite yet understand.

Then I head to the garage to tidy it and set up chairs and a little station for music. While preparing for everyone to arrive, again to my surprise my friends show up a little early, and all at once. I didn't even realize how much energy I had building up inside of me, and when I see them, I explode with excitement. Feeling exhilarated with a huge smile plastered across my face I greet them and hope that they can see how ecstatic I am to see them. I never thought this moment would actually happen. I've honestly never really been the type to care about throwing parties, especially with regard to my birthday. And my parents aren't really the type to let me have parties in the first place. But the one time I feel like I want to have one, they say yes, which makes this moment even more special. All of a sudden, seeing all of my friends at my house celebrating my birthday makes me feel really grateful. But it also makes me feel kind of sad; almost scared. Because I'm not sure when—or if—this moment will ever happen again. I then start to better understand this mixture of feelings that has been coming and going all morning. I think I am afraid of getting older. I'm afraid of losing the ease that automatically accompanies childhood. And this is the first birthday where I've felt that maybe I'm not a kid anymore... that I'm stepping into being "grown-up" and with that title, inheriting all of the responsibility that comes along with it.

But, I don't have too much time to process all of these thoughts, because someone turns up the music, and everyone is talking and laughing and having a great time. So, I pull myself out of my head and try to enjoy what's in front of me. I try to be present for this moment that I know probably won't ever happen again.

A few minutes later, my mom arrives back home. She brings out my birthday cake, and everyone falls silent. She places the cake right in front of me at the table, and I decide that I want to be the one to light my own candles. After lighting each of the seventeen candles—plus a wish candle, of course—I blow them all out and make a wish. In that moment, I wish that in the future I will live a happy and successful life. That I will have a job I actually want. That I will be in a marriage with a girl I really love and who really loves me back. That everything between me and my family is one hundred percent good vibes. That I have a great space, that I own, to call home. That I have no real worries, except for the small little things that inevitably pop up from time to time in daily life. As I stand there, looking at my cake with its blown-out candles and surveying the garage at my home filled with all of my best friends, my heart swells with gratitude but it also quivers a little when I think about growing up and becoming an adult. I just hope that getting old won't be as scary and boring and as hard as it seems like it's going to be. That moments like the one I'm currently experiencing will continue to happen for the rest of my life. That moving forward will also entail moving upward, too.

These thoughts are flooding my mind when, out of nowhere, my friend Anton picks up the cake and slams the entire thing into my face. Everyone starts cheering and laughing. In a way, it feels like all of the fears I'm having about getting older dissipate when I realize that my friends conspired to play this childish prank on me. For a fleeting moment, I feel that maybe there's more to my youth left than I think.

I head to the bathroom to wash the cake off of my face, and when I'm done, I take a moment to look at myself in the mirror. Again, these mixed feelings of gratitude and fear and nostalgia all come rushing back to me. I feel like I'm at a precipice; not really allowed to be a carefree kid anymore but also not quite yet an adult, like my dad, who seems to shoulder so much responsibility and who has no time to do the things he actually *wants* to do. I think about how, when one gets older, one has less and less time to be with friends and to do the things that actually make one happy. I start to think about how it feels like, with age, life gets in the way of happiness, instead of being the thing through which happiness unfolds. But then I shake the water off my head and towel my face and decide that I'm not going to let this fear overtake my life. I have to remember to stay humble and always try to live in the moment. So, I take a deep breath and then head back to my party.

When I reunite with everyone in the garage, they've already cleaned up and have started eating cake. We turn the music back up and sing the lyrics to some of our favorite songs together and, every now and then, dance. Externally, the party goes back to the same mood as it was before I went to the bathroom to wash the cake off of my face, but I can sense that something deep inside of me has changed. I feel different. I am even more grateful than I was at the beginning of the day, because I now realize that moments like my birthday party likely won't happen again, and if they do, they won't be exactly the same. But the biggest difference that I notice in myself is that I'm okay with this reality. I'm starting to embrace the fact that what once was will no longer be. Because that's life. Phases arrive and then leave, moments come and go; just like BART sometimes rushing and sometimes pulling slowly into the station, sticking around for various amounts of time while some people—never the exact same group—get on and off and then speeding away into the distance. Again and again and again. We all grow up eventually, and I should appreciate all of the exciting moments that happen in life as they come and go. I should embrace all of life, especially while I'm young and have the strength and vigor to take it by the horns, and hopefully create my own destiny.

It's getting late, so the party comes to an end, and it's time for everyone to leave. We turn off the music, put back the chairs and everyone empties out of the garage. After all of my friends leave, I take a moment to look at the garage. I stand there, feeling satisfied that my day unfolded more amazingly than I could have ever expected. Then, I notice a spot of cake frosting on the floor. I smile. No matter what changes, remnants of the past will always remain.

I wipe up the rest of the frosting and then put on my pajamas and climb into bed. I don't realize how exhausted I am until my head hits the pillow. Here I am, ending the day where it began, where it almost always starts and ends. You can't stop time. You can't escape getting older. But you can decide how you're going to shape the moments of life that arrive at your doorstep each and every day. These thoughts float around in my head as I drift off to sleep. And as I begin to dream, I start to really feel that everything's going to turn out just fine.

THE SWITCH

MARILYN C.

*was born in San Francisco and is almost eighteen
years old. She loves to dance and plans to go to college to
study nutrition and explore the world.*

Right eye, open. Left eye, open. *Beep. Beep.* Left leg. Right leg. Sunrise glowing, birds chirping. Humans looking with wide eyes. Directions on my wrist going to an underground trail. . . waiting. . . waiting. . . waiting. . . one. . . two. . . three. . . Left leg. Right leg. Walk, walk, walk. . . *Beep, beep.* . . look down. . . turn right. . . touch wrist here. *Clack.* . . into the little pure white room with the beam of white lights. . .

Last night, Alex went to sleep dreaming about his day all over again, he felt like he was on top of the world. He got a job doing what he had always dreamt about doing. . . working with robots. He went to sleep with a smile on his face. Never in a million years did he think he'd turn into something he was very interested in. . . a robot. He was ready to take on the first day of his new job, which he was very passionate about. He was very excited and happy like any normal person would be.

Alex is tall with short, black hair. A recent college graduate, he has been into tech for most of his life. Alex has been looking for a job for about a month, preferably with a company that works with robots.

He was a very curious child and had made a little green giraffe that flashed lights when the alarm went off. Alex's parents, both doctors, worry about him because he is so obsessed with technology and robots, but his father reassures his mom that he's fine and it's normal.

Alex's current project is building a robot that can help people when they fall, when they cross the street, or even with their errands.

Mom: "Alex, it's time for dinner!"

Silence. His mom walks upstairs. Alex is working on his latest project; he does not lose focus when his mom gets to his room.

Mom: "Let's go eat."

Alex: "Okay mom, wait just a sec. I need to finish this section first." His mom sighs.

Alex is very excited for his interview with a company called Gubots. He has heard so many great things about it, and how it's about to blow up the tech business. He walks into the white skyscraper on Main Street on a Tuesday morning at eight in the morning, feeling excited, but a little scared, too. Up on the eighth floor, he checks in at the front desk and asks for Albert Dickenson, who comes out of his office to exchange polite greetings with Alex.

Albert: "Hello, I'm Albert, you must be Alex. I am the Executive Manager here at Gubots. I will be interviewing you today."

Alex: "Nice to meet you, Albert."

They go into a little room. Albert starts asking Alex some background and resume questions like: "What kinds of technology do you like to work with the best?" and "How well do you work with robots?"

Alex goes on and on about tech and shows a true love of robots, pulling out pictures of many projects he has done, talking excitedly with no filter on what he is saying, becoming more and more eager. Albert sees Alex's obsession with robots, but Alex does not notice Albert's sinister grin.

Albert: "The job is yours!"

Alex is so excited he has to run into the bathroom to scream. He comes back and Albert hands him a contract. Alex skims the contract.

Albert: "So, this is just saying that you're not going to be releasing any of our info. You would be working with the robots hands-on and. . . "

Oh, my gosh. Straight up working with robots. Wow, this is amazing. He signs the contract.

Albert: ". . .So this is just saying that you're not going to be releasing any of our info. You would be working with the robots hands-on, and you might be in them or move in depth with other coworkers."

Alex: "Wow, thank you for this opportunity; you won't regret it."

"*Alex is so excited he has to run into the bathroom to scream.*"

Alex is moving into a new apartment, so there are many boxes around his place. In one of the boxes he finds the little green giraffe, the first thing he ever made. He puts it next to his bed to remind him where everything started. When he finishes unpacking, there are many projects all around his apartment. So, Alex decides to hang the key tag from his new job on the neck of his green giraffe sitting on his bedside table.

Alex doesn't know that the company that he has signed with was a trick to get Alex to turn into a robot for an experiment. Going to bed, he feels like he's on top of the world. After his very successful day, he puts his head on his cloud-like pillow, and goes to sleep.

Alex wakes up as a blue and white robot with a screen on his chest and a small screen on his wrist. He does not know anything from his past. He is in the middle of a park. *Beep. . . beep. . .* the screen on his wrists tells him to walk a specific route to his "master." He goes to an underground section near the park. His master is his boss, Albert, the man who interviewed him, but he has changed into a costume. As a robot, Alex does not know this.

He walks into the room; there are many other robots. Albert the Robot goes over the rules for the robots on what they can and can't do. If the robots do not follow the rules there will be punishments. The robots always follow the rules. They would rarely do something improper.

All these robots are people who have been tricked into this situation. They are all robots now; they don't know who they really are because they all have lost their memory. Mistakes can happen, but Albert does whatever it takes for him to get his profits. Albert gives missions to these robots. Missions can include helping people with errands, dropping off packages, and sometimes even stealing things.

Little mishaps can happen if Albert's immoral plan does not work. The robots don't know, but if there is ever a tweak in the system and they get a peek at their past, they can get out of the robot system. The sooner they figure it out, the better. The more missions they do, the harder it gets to fix anything and if they reach a certain amount of missions, they will be stuck forever. . .

Alex has been following all his missions so far on his first day—he has completed about five.

Thankfully none of the missions so far have been black-hearted.

Walking to his next mission, Alex turns his head and sees the green giraffe in front of the display cases. He looks at it and kind of stares. It's confusing, but he doesn't really think about it. He keeps going.

Little by little, Alex the Robot finally remembers about the giraffe. Some things, but not everything. He can't quite see that the green giraffe was a memory from his younger self; it was the same exact green giraffe that would light up and ring when his alarm went off. He tries rethinking where it's from. He hurries and finishes this mission so he can go onto his next one and pass by the display case again. He keeps staring at it; slowly some of his memories come to him, his robot eyes widen. . . in his head he is thinking that he's in his own apartment, opening a box with the giraffe inside.

Looks. . . left. . . right. . . coast is clear. He goes inside, grabs the green giraffe from the case, and leaves. Once he grabs it, he remembers that he put his new keys from his job onto the neck of the giraffe. He starts walking to his next mission; he realizes that Albert the Robot is Albert from the interview. . .

He keeps going on with his missions and he notices that as he keeps doing them, his memory starts erasing slowly. He looks down and sees that he is holding the green giraffe in his bag, but he does not remember what it is. He only remembers his interview with Albert. He knows what is happening. The more he does as a robot working for Albert, the more he is losing, so he stops doing the missions and just starts walking around. *Beep. . . Beep. . . .* A sound goes off on his screen on his wrist; it tells him to go do his next mission. He looks at it and ignores it; he knows he needs to do something. He knows it isn't right, he only wanted to work with robots, not become one. He wants to get back at Albert.

He thinks up a plan before going to the robot chamber. He goes to his wrist screen and breaks it. He knows that Albert is tracking him. He starts going around to find robots and tells them to meet at the chamber for something urgent. He tells them to meet at the usual meeting time at the chamber outside. He wants to gather them at the same time and tell them when it isn't suspicious. Alex tells the story and they all walk in. He looks for anything that could help him get out of the system along with the other robots. He rolls over to Albert the Robot with the wheels on his feet. Move. . . Left. . . Right. . . *Zoom.*

Alex: "Do you really think you can go through with this?"

Albert: "Go through with what?"

Alex: "Tricking everyone to be your experiment now that we are robots."

Alex pins Albert to a chair.

Alex: "Tape!"

All the robots come up to him with tape and they roll on their wheels around Albert to tape him onto the chair. Alex pulls the top of Albert's robot head off. "You're not getting away with this!"

Alex tapes his mouth, and sees a big red button near the door.

Alex: "Hey. There it is!" He rolls over to the button and opens the box that covers it. Albert tries to talk but all you can hear is utter noise.

Alex: "Albert, you will not get away with this. Are you guys ready to go back to being humans and not work for this nut job who thought he could make us into robots? We could've been stuck like this forever!" Time to press the button. *Beep. Zap!*

Alex is back in his room.

He opens his eyes, sees his green giraffe sitting on the bedside table. . . He thinks, *do I really want that job?*

EXTREMELY UNCOMFORTABLE

➤

KENDRICK L.

was born in San Francisco and is seventeen years old.
He loves to draw and listen to good music. Kendrick wants
to become a graffiti artist and a mechanic.

𝕴 was in the third grade when they took my big brother. "Don't leave, not again," were the words I mumbled as I shed tears while hugging him tightly. A group of six cop cars were headed to my home to take my teenage brother. They drove closer to my home. I started to worry and felt a deep aching in my stomach. They had Kyle handcuffed as they took him out. I knew that they were going to take him for another three to four months. I didn't know why he was going to be taken this time, but I didn't like it. I didn't want to talk to my brother through a collect call over the phone, and I didn't want to visit my brother dressed up in his dull uniform. Cops were everywhere, and I couldn't stand to be around them. The guns, the badges, the black uniform with handcuffs all made me feel extremely uncomfortable, especially as a young ten-year-old boy.

It was seven in the morning, during seventh grade. All I could think about was making sure I got to school. I woke up feeling great, I turned my radio on, went to the bathroom to handle some personal business, brushed my teeth, and washed my face. As I was sitting on the toilet I heard a loud bang on the bathroom door. *Boom, boom, boom!* I jumped off the toilet seat in surprise. "Open up! It's the police!" I was too shocked to give him an answer, and without invitation, a tall, white man, in his black uniform barged into the bathroom. "Once you're done, make sure you go downstairs, I have to search this bathroom." I was horrified. I finished up and walked back downstairs to see a gang of police officers in the entire living room. My mother and three other brothers were sitting on the couch, as they were ordered. I had no clue what they were doing in my home on a school day, but I felt intimidated. "Can I please get a sweater from my closet? It's kind of cold down here," one of my brothers asked the men with badges. My brother was freezing wearing only his underwear and tank top. "No, for both of our safety I can't let you do that. I'm just doing my job." Once they left, I went upstairs to see a bunch of papers, furniture, clothes, and closets flipped all over the place. It was trashed, they were searching for something. For some reason, they had to make my home look like a tornado just flew around.

It was my junior year in high school. I've seen the video over a million times since it hit the media. A man had a knife; I counted twelve cops surrounding him with guns pointed straight at him. The man didn't seem to be doing any harm with the knife, although he was walking away from the cops not complying when they demanded, "Drop it!" The officers yelled angrily and little did the man know, the couple of steps he took, were the last couple steps he would ever have taken. His life ended within seconds. Just the day before, I was walking down that same street after school toward the store, it could've been me. I saw my auntie that same day with my little cousin Jasmine as they were waiting for the bus. It could've been one of them. The fact that this incident happened in my community increases the level of anxiety I have for cops.

It was toward the end of my junior year in high school when my friend and I were doing a graffiti piece on the wall when all of a sudden, we heard, "Stop, don't move!" We picked up our gear and ran as quickly as possible. They stomped on the gas to reach us; I was surprised at how fast they showed up. Sirens got closer and closer so we started to run as fast as we could to get farther and farther, and although we didn't get too far, we still led them off for a small chase as we cut corners and shortcuts. As punishment, they gave me six months of community service, as we buffed out graffiti and picked up trash. As I spent time with the police officers during community service, it was really a different experience getting to know them on a personal level. Every morning before we started to paint over famous graffiti in the city, the officers would buy me breakfast along with three other people I did community service with. I got to know enough about the officers to understand what kind of people they are, and what goes on in their lives. They told me things about their families, what their fantasy vacation would be, the city they're from and how it's changed. It was definitely an eye opener for me as I started to think about policemen on a different level. I realized that not all cops are bad. Spending time with these cops helped me see that there are cops out there that can have a good heart.

These events have definitely shaped the way I see an officer. At a young age, I was set up to dislike cops because they took away my brother who was an important person in my life. In middle school, they invaded my privacy by barging into my house unannounced, and as a junior in high school, I was exposed to a shooting that took place in my community. I'm older now, and due to every cop that I've been exposed to, I'm still always a step ahead of the next badge in sight. I pay attention to what they are doing when I'm out with my friends, or walking home late night, or when I'm on the bus to school. I want to be able to walk down the street and not feel anxiety around them.

There are good cops, and there are bad cops, you never know what type of cop they are. Getting to know the policemen I did my community service hours with was an experience that I'll never forget. It gave me hope that maybe one day, all police officers could be like the officers that bought me breakfast. But as of right now I have seen more of the bad side of officers than the good and I can't help but to still feel extremely uncomfortable around the police. When I'm walking on the sidewalk and a cop drives slowly on the street near me, I always feel like they're watching me. When I'm walking near a cop, I want to be able to feel like they're protecting me, not making me their next suspect.

MAD?
NO, JUST MY FACE

MAYRA L.

is a thoughtful, generous, and helpful writer who loves to read.
She is very independent and always has her head in a book.
Whether they're sequels or trilogies, she reads them all. Mayra also
loves to dance—that's another way she expresses herself.

When I first meet people, they think that I am judgmental and mean because of what many people call the RBF (Resting Bitch Face). Just like Queen Elizabeth II describing her own face in the Netflix series *The Crown* where she says, "The trouble is, I have the sort of face that if I am not smiling then everyone says, 'Oh, isn't she cross?" And seriously, that is so relatable because if I'm not smiling I look mad all the time. I probably look mad as I am writing this right now. I learned this later when people told me this was their first impression and how different I really am.

This makes me feel sad and frustrated because I want to be seen as I really am. I want to be seen as nice, fun, adventurous, loving, helpful, weird, and a lover of stars and the ocean. I want others to see that I believe in others, and believe everyone can make a difference. I believe in changing the world, and I believe in the stars and the moon from the telescope that I use daily. I believe that there is gold at the end of the rainbow, I believe that restoring the ocean and animal habitats is possible, that we can do better with ending poverty in this world. I want people to know that I care and think about these things. I want them to know that I believe in family, art, beauty, potential, and hope. I wish they could see more of this when they look at me.

I can't really speak my mind in public in class. I stay quiet while debating with myself whether I should speak up and I don't allow myself to say what I think. When I have a presentation, I get really nervous, my hands start to sweat, and I feel the blood rushing through my veins as my cheeks turn pink. Sometimes if there aren't that many students in class and no one is participating, I say something or volunteer. I ask myself, "Why are you so scared to speak up? You see, nothing bad happened. You should start raising your hand more." But the next day I can't bring myself to do it. The shy part of me just pushes the confident me down. I know my face and my shyness contribute to being misunderstood.

One example of me being misunderstood is when I was with my cousin after school. It was a grey cloudy day with wind that would just slam into your body trying to lift you up. My cousin was with a few of her friends in a circle, two of which I see almost every day with her. I stood back, silent, just listening to them. I had no judgments about them because I didn't know them. My cousin was trying to get me to join in, but they seemed to know each other and were really involved in their conversation so I just hung back. My cousin signaled me with her hand to join in. I moved closer, but I still didn't feel like part of the conversation. They finished talking and my cousin and I went home.

Some days later my cousin introduced me to the girls. They were pretty nice and fun and I couldn't wait to get to know them, but there was just this one problem. . . my cousin's friends were identical twins! So, when I would meet them at the front of the school, I didn't know which one was which! My cousin said one had a small birthmark by her nose, but I couldn't remember which one was the one who had it and this made it really hard to say "Hi," using their names when I was walking through the halls. I felt really bad because they would use my name when they saw me and I couldn't use their names. I felt like they knew that I didn't know which one was which, but what could I do?

A couple of months went by. I now know which one is which, and we were at my cousin's house sitting around the dark wood kitchen table talking about first impressions. The twins and my cousin were describing how they felt when they met each other. When it was the twins' turn to share what they thought when they met me, they said that they thought I was mean or that I didn't like them. I asked them if they thought that because of my face, and they said yes. Then they described how fun and caring I am and nothing like they thought. I just happened to have a resting bitch face.

Being misunderstood is *never* fun. You think no one *ever* understands you, that you're *completely* alone, but in reality, somewhere around the world, (because there are about seven billion people) someone is going through the same thing.

TRY, TRY, TRY AGAIN

ASHLYN R.

was born and raised in San Francisco. She enjoys
being outdoors and revisiting all the tourist spots
of San Francisco. In her future, she sees herself going to
City College of San Francisco. and then transferring
over to San Francisco State to soon become a nurse
practitioner which is her dream career.

SOPHOMORE YEAR: FALL

Walking into my first day of algebra class I am without a worry about what grade I will receive. I sit at a desk with a friend. Soon after, the second bell goes off meaning class is about to start. My algebra teacher walks to the front of the class and begins to introduce herself. The room beccomes silent so when she speaks you can hear a pin drop. As she transitions to talking about the syllabus for the fall semester, at every table everyone is having side conversations. In my mind, I know that I have to work harder in this class because math is not my best subject. At the same time, I still am not thinking about the grade. Time has passed and everyone is about done with the name game where we ask people the listed questions. If they did it, I would write down their names. Everyone finishes, then we all sit down back at our desks after my teacher wraps up the class.

As weeks go on, it is now the end of the semester and winter break is around the corner. During this time, my head is not into finishing the grading period strong, my grades being average low Bs and Cs. No, I am busy thinking about the sports that I am in, how I am going to spend my free two weeks of break, and what I am going to eat after practice. During all of this, my weekly school days look like going to school, getting my education, going to basketball practice, chores, eating, and sleeping. But knowing the person that I am, I put off doing my math homework, which causes me to stay up later and rush to try and do it. Honestly, in my opinion math is the worst subject ever.

Coming down to the last week of school, I go to my school's counselor to check and see if I am on track to graduate, like I occasionally do. I knock on my counselor's door before stepping into the office.

"Oh, hey sweetie!" says Ms. Hildago.

"Hey, Ms. Hildago!" I say.

"What can I do for you?"

"I just wanted to come check and see if I am on track to graduate?"

"Okay, let me pull up your transcripts."

"Okay, cool." I say lastly, then, seconds after it grows to a silence as she is typing on the keyboard.

"It says here that you have math D, F, F in *Pajarito*. . . doesn't look good, Ashlyn."

"Yeah, I know," as I disappointingly look at the computer screen. "So, what now? Will I still graduate on time?"

"Yes, you can graduate but you know colleges don't like Ds and Fs. So, next semester and next year you will need to have Cs and above or you will repeat the class," Hildago says with an assertive face.

At this moment, I'm thinking that I'm really wasting my time being there not trying my hardest anymore. But it's already too late in the semester, it's ending soon. What am I going to do? Then I become more worried that I could be one of those kids that doesn't graduate on time with their class. Soon enough I don't change because I think I can just make it up next semester and I could try then.

SOPHOMORE YEAR: SPRING

It's only the first day back to school and I already want winter break back, were my first thoughts stepping back on school grounds with my closest friends at the time. Besides the fact that my sophomore year of high school is about to end I feel that this semester is going to be as difficult as ever. So, keeping my algebra grades up will be a challenge. The first three weeks are always the easiest because it's just getting us used to school again.

It is now the fifth week into school, then I notice that I am beginning to slack off again. It happens when one Thursday I am sitting in class and I get my work passed back to me. It lands in my hands and I see that my classwork is all good, of course, my homework is okay, I may have lost a point or five. After my quiz and test scores come, I become more and more anxious as I slowly begin to turn the papers. I think in my head *Wow, I'm not even surprised.* I am not happy about these partial credited quizzes and tests but I know why I got those. It is because when testing time comes around I have no one to help me with the work so I don't get as many answers written, so I just give up then, taking the bad grade. I notice my actions aren't great because I'm failing. I just have a procrastinating attitude and I don't worry at all.

It's coming down to the last months of school and my math grade is not looking good at all. What's wrong with me? Is it because of my other priorities and responsibilities? Or even that I just don't care for math? Probably.

It's the worst time of the school year and everyone knows it. Finals week. The countdown to see what you have learned the whole school year. Ugh. I hate finals. It stresses me out and I worry about if I failed or not. So, at this point I'm stressed out and over it before it has even started.

I schedule an appointment to meet with Ms. Hildago. After school, I go back to her office and we talk about my grades and whether or not I am at the point where I need major credit recovery. I am in her office once again and I'm not sure if I'm going to like what I hear. As we are both talking it comes to the point where she tells me that in order for me to move up in math that I need to retake it again in summer school. Now I am feeling very disappointed in myself because not only did I purposely let myself fail math again, but now I am going to repay my debts in summer school. There goes my free summer.

A week into summer and I hear nothing back from Ms. Hildago. Well, looks like I have this summer off, even though I know this is a mistake to not go to summer school. But I never receive anything about it.

JUNIOR YEAR: FALL

Very similar to last school year, I act no different. My motivation is making sure school comes first and that I have passing grades especially with, of course, Algebra 1 since I never did it this past summer like I was supposed to. It's like I never left: same teacher, same subject, same Ashlyn.

By the end of this year I gain more knowledge here and there. I am another year older. It's supposed to be great and everything but still being in Algebra 1 is haunting me. I am going mad here. My third semester with this subject and I am going nowhere. Every day I am here in this class I am becoming more and more short tempered with it. I already took this class. I am here wasting my time learning the same thing I did the year before, when I could be with my grade level and learning advanced stuff. But this is what I get back when I denied the little homework I needed to do. That is what I get for not passing my quizzes and tests, also for not fully attending like a good student should.

Meeting back with Ms. Hildago, she is surprisingly disappointed that I did not attend summer school the previous summer. I don't feel any sympathy because I didn't hear anything back from her about it. No official papers saying I was put into retaking it, nothing. Well it's not my fault. But I feel bad almost because it's not her that's being affected here: it's me and my credits. Now she is here telling me that I will for sure be put into summer school. I now feel a sense of relief and reassurance, but bummed out because my summer won't be as fun.

SUMMER SCHOOL: BECOMING A JUNIOR

The night before my first day of summer school I feel very nervous for some reason because I feel as if it's actually my first day of school again. The morning comes and when I get nervous, I get like really nervous and I tend to overthink a lot. It's 6:00 a.m. and I am just in bed laying there thinking of what it will be like at Mission High School with a bunch of other kids just like me. What's funny was that summer school starts like normal school hours, so 8:00 a.m. on the dot, which I think is dumb because I hate the morning. I go to my best friend's house really early. So early that they weren't even awake. Soon after, like forever, they both come out, as well as their little sister, and we're all heading to our summer school except that their little sister goes to a different summer school than us. In my opinion, like all firsts you should come early because it's all new and you want to get through it and pass. Just right before it starts we go to a nearby Starbucks and 7-Eleven and each get some coffee and food that will last us all day from 8:00 a.m. to 1:00 p.m. Now we're exploring the school and trying to figure out where I need to go. I find my class and so do my best friends. My first instincts are to find out where it's good to sit, but I don't see my friends from my school at first so I sit with the kids that go somewhere else or are already at Mission. I am thinking to myself *they're all looking at me and judging me*. The class has now started and the teacher sounds really strict and mean. Her voice is very clear and loud and the attitude I'm getting from her is that she doesn't take nonsense from anyone. This will be the worst summer ever for me. She already teaches at a different high school so I feel like that's why she is the way she is, because the atmosphere there is stressful.

When the days go by for summer school I am finally getting used to it here and I recognize everything at this school. My algebra class is my second period and don't even get me started on that. But I will. English class is my first period and I am glad that I know people in that class because I feel awkward enough. So, I'm not alone. But enough about English.

Heading back to the main reason why I have summer school in the first place was because of algebra. It's all because of algebra. It's really my fault but whoever says that it's their fault? So, we'll just blame it on algebra. It's later on in the day around 11:30 a.m. The first period is over and it's lunch. My friends and I go to the park because it's literally across the street. We just hung out there and it's a nice summer day. Everyone is out with their dogs, playing tennis, and kids at the park running for the ice cream man. Lunch is coming to an end so we start walking back down to the school to our second period. I come to find my algebra class and I walk in and I see mostly everyone is a sophomore, soon-to-be-juniors. I think *Wow, has it come down to me being around lower classmen for the summer that I am here?* That sounds really mean but it gets better. So, this teacher teaches at another high school, and she's really rude to us. Imagine that teacher you hate at your own school. I get handed an algebra worksheet and this teacher tells us to figure it out first on our own, then she would talk about it. This algebra teacher is much meaner than my first period so I know she is going to be hard on me and I am one of the oldest in the class. Her teaching style makes me feel like I'm in college, because it's very straightforward and cold. I say this because every time she hands us new worksheets she tosses the papers like we are peasants. I already can tell that we will have a problem and that I don't like her.

The first week over with and I feel like I am making a major effort with the two classes, mainly in algebra. I know that even though I don't like the teacher at all that cannot matter because it's about me, whether I pass or not, and she will be the one giving me my grade. So, the way that she would grade our work was, everyday ten minutes before the end of class, she'd check off on our papers to see if we did our work or not. I feel so annoyed because during all that class time I feel like I don't learn much because she just assumed that we knew everything by heart. You think I would, but with me not going to class and not doing much homework during the regular year I would know better. But actually, I only know a little. My struggle with her is that she is harder to keep up with everyday than trying to remember a whole school years' worth of math.

A month into summer school, I have now adapted to these strict women. With the rude teacher, you know I really did prove her wrong and really boosted my self-motivation up quick. My progress reports from her are amazing. She even commented to me personally on how I do good work, finish mostly before everybody, and that I help others. But I laugh and talk way too much. I never thought that I would be where I am right now. I want to thank those girls that I sit with for helping me. In a way, I almost feel that we have a student-teacher, love-hate relationship. It's kind of funny, actually. But as a person I don't like most things about her or what she does.

In class one sunny day I come in and I am full off of coffee and fake pizza from 7-Eleven. It's my typical day in second period. I know what I'm doing and the new friends that I made are there waiting for me. But as I am trying to understand the math worksheet, I start talking to my group of friends. Then minutes later everyone gets loud with laughter because of some joke my friend Gabriella said (and to inform you I made a group of seven friends, so it was loud). Then the rude teacher walks over and comes from behind and points out that we aren't finished. So, she walks off saying to us that my group and I get all zeros for the day because "we were messing around." I do take full responsibility but she did not have to go and do something like that.

It is down to the last few weeks that I am here before we get our final grade. At this point I am feeling confident because by just going to summer school I have seen myself make major improvements on being commited to getting good grades. That I did. I am feeling at an all-time high because on the final day of summer school, I ace both classes, passing with a 3.5 GPA stating that I passed and I can move on.

I find out on the last day when I get my progress report back from both teachers. In that moment I feel so proud because my hard work has paid off. My struggle within the two years of slacking off in actual school and procrastinating on my algebra homework was all worth it. I learned my lesson the hard way and I know now that as many times as I try, nothing can change unless I make the change. I stayed committed everyday, waking up, making the MUNI train, going to school, and doing the work. I knew that I made Ms. Hildago and my loved ones proud, and last, but not least, I made myself proud because I accomplished my goal.

SEEKING
ACCEPTANCE

—◆—

ANALYN A.

*was born in San Francisco and is eighteen years old. She
loves to write and spend her free time with family and friends.
One of her favorite foods is sushi but if she could eat one food
for the rest of her life, she would eat burritos. She lives with
her mom, dad, younger brother, and grandma. She plans to
go to college to achieve her goal of being a registered nurse.*

When I was a junior in high school back in 2015–2016, college started to be one of the main priorities that people would talk about. I felt that college was the only way to become successful—a good college at that, such as a University of California (UC) or a private school. All of my friends started talking about how they wanted to move away for college and there I was, feeling like an outcast because I didn't know what I wanted to do after high school, but I was sure that I wanted to stay in my hometown San Francisco.

I have an older cousin named Breanna who is a year older than me, and I also have a cousin named Ayla who is the same age as me. When Ayla and I were juniors, Breanna was a senior so that meant that she was going to be off to college soon.

On Thanksgiving Day, all three of us were sitting in Breanna's room, all of us on our phones, when Ayla asked Breanna, "What colleges did you apply to?"

"I applied to UC Santa Barbara, UC Berkeley, San Jose State, and San Francisco State," she said with a smile and confidence in her voice. "Where do you guys plan on going?"

"I want to go to UCLA," Ayla replied. Then they both turned to me, waiting for my answer. I froze and stayed silent for a little bit because I didn't know at the time. I didn't know what to do or where I wanted to apply. I didn't even know if I wanted to go to college right after high school, but I didn't want to tell them that because they would've thought I was crazy. I didn't want to be judged because everybody else that I knew was planning on going to good colleges.

I finally answered their question. "I want to stay in the Bay Area so I might want to go to SFSU." I gave a weak smile as I waited for their response.

"Oh, that's a good school!" Breanna said joyfully. That was the end of the conversation.

I didn't understand why I felt so annoyed by talking about college and what I planned to do after high school. Maybe because I was so fed up with school (staying up late, waking up early, falling asleep in class, and homework piling up every day) that whenever they would talk about it, it agitated me. Don't get me wrong, I wanted to go to a four-year university but I didn't feel like it was for me. I didn't feel like it was as important to me as it was for my family and other people.

I was born and raised in San Francisco and I love my city with all of my heart that I don't think I could ever leave for a long period of time. San Francisco is a place that will make you feel at home, but it's also a place where it's fun to be a tourist. Twin Peaks, Crissy Field, Pier 39, the Castro District, the Haight, and many more are unique places that make up my hometown. The smell of the hotdogs and kettle corn while I'm walking on the streets of downtown, the people on the streets trying to sell their mixtapes, the sound of the waves banging against each other as I'm sitting on a blanket with my toes in the sand at Ocean Beach, the seals singing and the street performers at Pier 39, and the diversity of people who sit on the bright green grass at Dolores Park on a bright sunny day, are all reasons why I love my city and it will always have a place in my heart.

Being with my family is also a reason why I love being in San Francisco because all of my immediate family is close and whenever we all get together, it's nothing but laughs and silly jokes. We sometimes play *Cards Against Humanity, Apples to Apples, Monopoly,* or *Mancala,* but it just feels good to have people I love and care about around. There's always the warm, fresh smell of a home-cooked meal that is either cooked by my grandma or mom around the house, and the cozy feeling I get when I'm home—these are some things that I don't want to miss. My closest friends and family live in San Francisco and being away from them would make my heart sad and weak.

August 15, 2016 was the first day of my senior year and that meant a lot of things were going to happen: SATs, college applications, prom, graduation, etc. I was looking forward to all of those things but at the same time, I wasn't.

After realizing that I wasn't too thrilled about all of these things I had to do to get into a good college, I started to think about my future more than I have before. I started to think about what colleges to apply to and what I had to do to get accepted, but I also started asking myself if I even wanted to go straight into college after I graduate high school. All·of this overwhelmed me and stressed me out. I wanted to make my parents proud but I also wanted to follow my own path. This point in my life was very stressful. I was stuck and didn't know what to do. I felt as if I was at a dead end.

Another moment that made me feel trapped or stuck was when my mom asked me one day in the car while we were going home, "So what colleges are you thinking about applying to?"

I froze. There was a long pause before I answered her question that felt like we were stuck in Los Angeles traffic. Then I finally answered, "I was thinking about going to S.F. State."

"Oh, that's a good school. When are you going to apply?"

"Whenever applications are available," I said quietly.

To be honest, I wasn't ready for college and I didn't even know if I was going to get into a four-year university because I didn't take my SAT and that was simply because I didn't want to. I kind of regretted not taking the test, but at the same time, I didn't really regret anything because I had an alternative plan. My alternative plan would make a lot of things easier for my parents and me. I decided I want to be a registered nurse when I got older because I wanted to help people and let them know that everything will be okay. I specifically wanted to work with kids because I'm great with them, but I wasn't really sure how to get into a nursing program and I didn't know which schools ran nursing programs in the Bay Area.

One day, some people from City College of San Francisco and Skyline College came to my school and they talked to us about what programs they have and what they offer. I attended the Skyline meeting, which helped me think about what colleges I wanted to go to. Unfortunately, Skyline didn't have a nursing program but City College did. That automatically became my first option, but I wasn't sure about it because it was far from my house and I wasn't sure how I would get there. The good thing about City College was that I knew my way around and I knew a lot of people attending that school and future students of City College.

The more I thought about where I wanted to go, it started to stress me out because I wasn't sure where exactly I wanted to attend. I was afraid that if I were to tell people what I wanted to do, I would get more judgement because back when I was a freshman and a sophomore, people thought just because I was a bit more loud and energetic than I am in senior year, that I had bad grades and I was a bad student. I was afraid that people would still think of me in that way because of what I planned to do. I was also afraid of what my family would think of me. But after a while, I realized that it was normal for people to go to a community college for their first couple of years of college. Knowing that I wasn't the only one with that plan, I felt relief and it made me feel like less of an outcast.

A couple of months after the meeting, I finally made my decision. I wanted to go to CCSF my first couple of years of college. It wasn't as good as getting into a UC or a CSU but at least I was going to college and I actually had a plan. I knew what I wanted to do. I walked into my mom's room while she was doing her makeup to let her know that I made my choice.

"Mom, I know what college I want to go to for sure." I waited for her answer with anticipation.

"Where? I hope it's not far because I want you to stay close to us," she said while looking at herself in the mirror and filling in her eyebrows.

When I heard her say that, I felt relief because CCSF wasn't hard to get to and she wanted me to stay here in the Bay Area.

"I think I want to go to City College," I said quietly. "They have a nursing program there and that's what I want to be when I grow up."

"Oh okay, do your application soon then!" She smiled at me and continued to do her makeup, and that was my cue to go.

After that conversation, I felt relief because I thought it wouldn't go as smoothly as it did, but she made it really easy and she didn't seem to have a problem with what I chose to do. She seemed to be more proud and excited about the fact that I actually wanted to go to college right after high school. That's exactly what I wanted—to make my parents proud.

IT'S CALLED SPANISH

◆

STACEY R.

is a seventeen-year-old senior at Burton High School. She is originally from Los Angeles, but moved up to San Francisco by the age of five. She enjoys spending time with her family, especially going on vacations. Her favorite was going to El Salvador. Her other hobbies include listening to music, especially Reggaeton.

Since ninth grade, people are always assuming I am Mexican. This misunderstanding makes me feel mad because not all Latinos are Mexican. People assume the only Spanish speaking country is Mexico. However, if you are looking at a Central American map, you will see more countries on the map, not only Mexico. For example, other Spanish speaking countries include Cuba, Puerto Rico, El Salvador, Guatemala, and many more if you look at the map closely. It is not all about Mexico.

This assumption has impacted me since ninth grade and it still continues. The fact that they, people who are not Latino or my age, don't get it that Mexican is not a language and continue to make it a joke, don't understand that they are not only offending me, but other people in the Latin community.

This incident happened at the start of the fall semester of 2016 of my senior year, when I was heading to my English and European Literature class from JROTC (Junior Reserve Officers' Training Corps). I was speaking Spanish with a couple of classmates who were also Spanish speakers, when a teacher walked up to us and said, "Stop speaking Mexican." Mind you, there was only one Mexican person and the other two were from El Salvador and Guatemala. This was when I started to get frustrated. So, I told him, "Mexican is not a language—it's called Spanish!"

"Oh, chill you guys. I'm only joking," he laughed. "Don't take it seriously." And even though he tried to make it funny, he didn't realize that it was offensive to my classmates and me. Instead of sounding cool, it just came off as ignorant and hurtful.

After that, my frustration got the best of me. It escalated to the point of me yelling at the teacher and telling him, "There's no such thing as speaking Mexican!" And so, I asked him, "Do I look Mexican?"

He replied, "Most of you do."

I think he's never been to Mexico or any part of Central America because he can't tell the difference between Latin and Mexican. Some Mexicans look like white people, some look dark, and some other Mexicans look light. Not all Latinos or Mexicans look alike. Some Mexicans speak another language, not only Spanish. There are indigenous languages such as Nahuatl, Yucatec, Maya, and Mixtec. These are only a few languages that our great-great-grandparents knew and spoke.

I felt like he was trying to act funny and just make it seem cool to play around by saying it like that. We don't even sound Mexican or have Mexican accents. I am not Mexican. I am just a Latina whose parents come from different places—El Salvador and Puerto Rico. Spanish is a very important language for me because it is something that allows me to speak with my family and be able to communicate with my grandparents. It is also very nice that we're able to speak this language because we have the advantage to speak with our Latin community. Also, it helps a lot once you have a job if they know that you're bilingual.

The reason I am talking about this topic is because it made me mad; the fact that some people don't understand that there are many beautiful countries in Central America, that it is not always about Mexico, and that there is no such thing as speaking Mexican. As many times as you tell people it's called Spanish, nothing changes—they still think that Mexican is a language. And it makes me mad because I'm not even Mexican. This is important because people, especially Latin people, are not always Mexican. There are so many more cultures, countries, and people in Central America.

I want my Latino community to be recognized for the fact that not all Latin people are from Mexico. And there is nothing bad about being from Mexico, just don't mix up the Latino community with Mexico. I also want people to acknowledge and take other languages seriously, and be mature about it. Recognize that Mexican is not a language, it's called Spanish.

FORCED TO CHANGE

RAUL C.

is seventeen years old. He loves to play sports,
like football and soccer. Raul lives with his mom and dad.
He plans to join the Army after high school.

Whether I am going to school or taking the bus to practice, every morning I wake up to get ready and start my day. I don't get home until around 8:00 p.m. and then I rush to do homework. In a way, I really don't have time for others; only for that one person who knows who I am and the type of person I am: me.

Have you ever been misunderstood for wrong reasons—just because of the way you look, walk, or talk? It happens all around you, even when you don't notice it. It can happen anywhere at any time. I'm not the type of guy that would fight if I didn't have to, but I've been mistaken for someone else and it almost got me killed. At that moment, it made me realize that it wasn't safe in my own city. Yeah, I know I'm brown and we all look alike, but they don't know my name nor my story.

It's five in the morning. It's not my first time being a top five thrower in track but it is my first time being ranked number one in the city. I'm just focusing on what I have to do to take it all. So, I do what I do best, just slap on some earphones and shut everything else out. As I'm leaving my house to catch the 29 bus, I see this older woman looking at me with a dead-on look like I was going to hurt her for some reason, or like I did something wrong. But after I get to the bus stop I see her walk across the street like she's running away from me. Now at first I don't really catch on, but after thinking about it I know she's scared of me. Is it because I was wearing a black hoodie and Adidas sweats? Maybe my skin color doesn't help either. After the bus finally comes, the woman crosses the street again and gets on the same bus I was waiting for, or should I say "we" were waiting for. It's not the greatest feeling at first—having her cross the street away from me. It makes me think about how people in my neighborhood see me. Not only do I have to deal with being misunderstood at stores, but even in my community where I grew up. Where is it safe for me to be myself?

Don't you have that one place where you feel safe to be yourself or run away to? Well, this city is my home, it's where I was raised. It made me the person who I am today and gave my family a place to live, to work, and to be happy. I won't ever forget what it gave me. But it's not perfect. At times, it can be really scary to live here, with all this media in the U.S. going around about laws of banning Muslims. It really makes me wonder if my family could be next. Not only is it tearing up a family, but a city that was built by so many immigrants. At times, I don't feel safe. As a teenager, I can see what's going on in this city. I see a lot of drugs, gangs, wealth, and poverty, and these things affect us all. As I see all the people around me fall for them I ask myself, *is this a place where I want to raise my kid?* I can't say how many things, but I've been through a lot in this city. It not only keeps teaching me lessons but it has taught me how to survive. We have the choice of making our home safe and it depends on the person you are. I feel like I'm living in a city that is forcing me to change.

ALL FOR THE BEST

VONNIE K.

was born in San Francisco and is seventeen years old.
She loves South Korean culture. She wants to travel the world.
Vonnie also wants to study abroad in college. She loves
being able to create new opportunities for herself.

JULY 6, 2017

Dear Ayla,

    You may be miles and miles from home right now. Despite the wall that you have put up between yourself and mom and dad, I hope you know you'll survive. I get it, mom and dad are the types of parents who never change their mind once it's set. They should've at least mentioned the whole "marriage" thing to you and put yours and Talon's feelings into consideration. You didn't even know the guy in the first place and they were going to force you into a marriage you had no idea about. You and Talon had been together for four years! That has to at least say something to them, right? Or so you thought.

    Even though you and Talon had your ups and downs, everyone understood your love for one another. Growing up, you've been through a lot. Raised in poverty, mom and dad always trying to make the money stretch for the next bill. They were always trying to keep food on the table. Which, when you actually think about it, is probably the reason why they did what they did. At least try to see where they're coming from. Can you imagine trying to give your child the world when you can only afford a spec of it? Never once did mom and dad tell you no, or that you can't have anything because they always wanted you to have everything. They wanted the best for you and for you to have everything you needed. I guess they only felt that way because of all the things they thought they failed to give you. I don't know how long it'll take for you to realize this and you're probably really angry reading this. When I tell you that mom and dad really did only want nothing but the best for you, believe me. If that meant marrying you off to a rich man then so be it. Just try and humble yourself and remember that family will always be there for you through the good and the bad.

Love, Ayla

NOVEMBER 22, 2000

"Hurry up, Talon! The last episode of *The Walking Dead* is going to be on in three minutes!" I exclaim to my boyfriend who not only is built like an ox but moves as slow as one, too.

"Ugh, alright-alright, fats!" he says with annoyance.

I laugh and wait for him to open the door to my small apartment. It's 8:57 p.m. and it's already so dark outside that the stars are acting as if they were nightlights in an empty pitch-black room. I live on the east side of San Francisco where there aren't usually a lot of tour buses to show tourists around the neighborhood. The Hard Knox soul food restaurant floods the streets with the smell of their delicious cornbread and their Cajun meatloaf. There's always an *elote* man at the corner of every block selling either his corn or the *mangonadas* that everyone's in a rush to buy. The houses are bright yellow, sky blue, and neon green, so vibrant that it almost hurts to look at them. The neighborhood is so alive during the day but at night it's as if there's a crime scene from another episode of *Law and Order*. There are gang bangers, dressed in clothing as dark as the Moroccan desert night sky, that fill every corner. The crack heads that hang out on every block look as if they've been worshiping Satan all their lives, rolling around the floor talking and sometimes even screaming to themselves as if they were possessed. Stranded dogs and cats roam around at night scavenging for food, knowing that there's nothing but lost dreams and rubbish in the trash bins.

"Hurry, hurry, hurry!! You move like a freakin' turtle!" I say frantically, rushing to try and grab the keys out of his Adidas sweatpants pocket.

He chuckles and smirks at me while opening the front door. I mug at him while entering through the door. Even though I'm 5'3½" and he's 6'0", I'm not afraid to put my hands on him. I noticed my apartment seemed livelier and lifted, as if there was

was a parade of happiness that ran through. The grey walls have family photos hung on them and all the lights in the house are on.

"Mom! Pops! I hope you know the electricity bill is going to be off the charts with all these lights on," I yell, hoping my voice travels through the walls and vents to wherever they are in the house.

"Hey, I'm going to head upstairs and start the show," Talon tells me.

I nod in return and find myself walking toward the kitchen. As I get closer, I hear laughter but it almost seems as it was being forced. I barge through the door.

"Hey, guys. . . what's so f-f-funny?" I stutter.

I stop dead in my tracks and the room is filled with silence. The light in the kitchen began to flicker as a tall muscular figure starts making its way toward me. Slowly, I notice what he's wearing: a black suit and the newest LV dress shoes. His wristwatch shines in the light, making it seem like it cost an arm and a leg.

"Hello, Ayla," he says with a bright smile, and projects his hand out for me to shake.

"Umm, hi?" I reply with my eyebrows furrowed, confusion plastered on my face. I place my hand in his and am startled when he brings his lips to the back of my hand.

"Ayla, this is Theo Lansting, you know from the famous Lansting corporation known for their models of the new Grape phones," my dad says with a small smile and a hint of an apologetic look on his face.

I look at my mom and she can already tell by the expression on my face that I am still confused as to why Theo is here in the first place. Luckily since my mom and I are super close, and sometimes have this secret code talk we do with our eyes, she understands that I am confused.

"Honey, we meant to tell you earlier, but you weren't answering your phone so we figured we'd just let you know later when you came home," my mom said with sorrow in her eyes, trying to force a smile on her face at the same time.

"Well I'm here now. . . what's so urgent that you tried to get a hold of me for?" I ask, eyeing the mysterious man up and down with a smirk of distaste appearing on my lips.

"Ayla, where are your manners? You need to address your new fiancé with a little more respect," my dad's voice booming with anger, his face as red as tomatoes, and his tone stern.

Shock runs through every nerve and fiber in my body, followed by anger and confusion.

My mom rushes toward me and grabs my hands before I speak, "Listen to us Ayla, we were going to tell you but. . . "

"BUT WHAT! YOU WERE GOING TO MARRY ME OFF FIRST?" I scream at the top of my lungs, fairly convinced smoke was coming out of both ears.

"No, listen, sit down and let's talk about this, yeah?" my mom says in a whisper.

"There's nothing to talk about. I'm not getting married to this man even if you pay me one million dollars!" I respond, beginning to walk toward the stairs to go to my room.

"AYLA, GET BACK HERE RIGHT NOW," my dad screams.

As I stomp my way upstairs, Talon walks toward me from the top of the staircase. His eyes are lit in fury and he, too, seems confused.

I reach toward him.

"Talon, I . . . " I try to say, but he pushes past me and storms off into the kitchen. I follow quickly behind him and I already know what's about to go down. I rush in front of him and try to block his way. We stand in the doorway of the kitchen and the living room. I try to shove him back in the direction we just came from.

"ARE YOU GUYS KIDDING ME? TRYING TO MARRY HER OFF? YOUR OWN DAUGHTER? WHAT KIND OF PARENTS ARE YOU TWO?" screams Talon, his voice dripping with venom.

My head snaps up at him and at my parents and Theo, but this time Theo cuts off my parents and responds.

"Ah, I see. You're either the brother or the big-headed boyfriend who doesn't seem to understand simple good manners," Theo says with a smirk on his face and his voice challenging my boyfriend.

"Excuse me? Are you the man that they're trying to marry her off to?" Talon scoffs. "Unbelievable. Hey, Mr. and Mrs. Alofa, a piece of advice: if you want your daughter to be married to a complete stranger, at least make sure it's someone she'll actually have common interests with. Not some snotty rich kid from the suburbs," Talon says with actual disgust dripping in every word he speaks.

"Talon, listen. We're very thankful for everything you've done for Ayla but this is something that will be the best for her," my dad says very calmly as if he's not trying to marry me off in that moment.

"Yeah city boy, just go back from where you came from and let me escort my future wife to some dinner at D'Angelo's," Theo butts in, sounding like he thinks he's won this battle.

"Theo, don't you think you're being a little harsh?" my mom asks raising an eyebrow.

"With all due respect, Mrs. Alofa, you shouldn't let him come in between me and Ayla. It's obvious he doesn't even have enough money for him to take proper care of her anyways," Theo says with confidence.

"Now it's my turn to butt in." First, there is no you and I, there never was, and there never will be. Secondly, no one ever disrespects my boyfriend except for me. Why don't you take your big-headed self out of here and go back to wherever YOU came from?"

"Oh, Ayla you just don't get it, do you? YOU'RE MINE. Whether you like it or not," Theo says with a big smirk on his face.

CRACCCCK.

The sound of Theo's nose breaking filled the room and my mom and dad looked at Talon in shock.

"Jerk," Theo says holding his nose.

CRAAACK.

Another blow from Talon now to Theo's jaw.

Next thing I know Theo charges at Talon and they are throwing punches left and right while my mom and dad are trying to stop them.

I try to jump in the middle but my dad intervenes, "AYLA, STOP BEFORE YOU GET HURT AS WELL!" he scolds.

I back off and watch in horror, and more body parts between the two boys break. The entire situation begins to dawn on me that the reason for this was because of me. My parents want me to be married off with some stranger, and my boyfriend is in a full-on brawl, all because of me.

While the fight continues, I run past them, upstairs to my bedroom and I begin to pack. I pack anything that my eyes catch first and throw it in my suitcase. When I'm done, I leave a note saying, *"don't come looking for me."*

With that I run out of the house. With all the commotion going on they don't notice me leaving. I run down the street and never turn back leaving the chaos behind me and hoping for a better life for my loved ones.

DECEMBER 9, 2002

Light floods through my bathroom window as I stare in the mirror, my fingers lingering over the aged features of my face. Only two years have passed but it feels like an eternity. I began to notice a drop in my weight due to all the stress of what happened that fateful night at my parents' broken-down home. I'm now living in Southern California in Bakersfield. I have my own studio apartment, it's small but it's breathable. I work in a nearby cafe named Fates Cafe. I make a pretty good amount of money; it's enough to pay the bills. Talon and I aren't together anymore; we broke up after the multiple times he cheated on me.

I make my way back to my cave of a bedroom, which is covered in piles of clothes and pieces of paper with my resume written on them. I close my eyes and thrust my hand in the mountain of stuffed animals and pillows covering my unmade bed, feeling for my phone. My heart starts to beat faster and faster because I can't find it. Frustrated, I stand on top of my bed and scan my entire room.

"Wow," I say, as I see my phone on top of my nightstand, still charging where I left it the night before. "Good job, Ayla."

I turn on my phone and am immediately hit with multiple texts, notifications, and emails from Eva. Eva was like a sister to me back home. She lived across the street from me and our parents were very good friends as well.

What the heck, I think to myself, *I haven't spoken to her in over a year. What does she want?*

Curiosity gets the best of me, and I decide to call her back. The phone rings and rings, and as I'm about to give up, she finally answers.

"Hello?" Eva asks, her voice hoarse and dry, sounding very unlike her usual loud and happy self. That makes me concerned.

"Eva, it's me, Ayla. I got your millions of texts and calls. What's up?"

"OMG, Ayla. We've been trying to get a hold of you for the past year. Why haven't you answered any of my texts and emails?" Eva asked, her angry voice now booming over the speaker of the phone.

"I've been busy. I got your *emergency* text. I figured, since I didn't respond to any of the other ones, I would to this one. What's up?" I repeat, aggravated that Eva wouldn't get to the point.

"Ayla, what I'm about to tell you is going to be really hard. I want you to know that I'm here for you every step of the way."

"Eva, what are you talking about? Did you and Brian break up or something? Is that what this is about?" I ask, now feeling a little more concerned.

"No... what? Brian and I are fine. No, this is about your mom. Ayla, your mom..." Eva's voice begins to crack as she pauses. I can hear her sniffling in the background. "Your mom has lung cancer. Stage four. The doctors said she only has a few weeks left."

I don't say anything back... I can't, so I hang up. I can feel my knees begin to tremble beneath me and my arms go numb. I drop my phone, which now feels like a boulder between my fingers. My room falls as silent as an abandoned asylum, so quiet that I can hear my own heart shatter. I slide down the wall, broken, as tears begin to trickle down my face. Faintly, I can hear my phone begin to ring again and I don't need to check the screen to know who it is. I pick up the phone buzzing loudly on the sturdy ground, and I throw it across the room against the wall and watch the pieces fall apart.

I manage to crawl toward the edge of my bed directly across from me; I don't even shudder when I feel the cold concrete floor beneath me. I haul myself onto my bed as if I was an infiri, like the ones from *Harry Potter*, plop my face deep into my pillow and cry.

I cry until I feel all the water in my body has dried up like the Sahara Desert. My throat feels so sore, like cats have been scratching at it for hours, and my eyes are so swollen I look like I'm allergic to just blinking. My mom, my best friend, my rock and world, has cancer.

It's been a month. An entire month since I found out the only person in my life that seemed to know how to always make me smile and annoy me at the same time, has cancer. It's been a month but I still remember the phone call as if it were yesterday. I continuously replay that moment like a broken record in the back of my head,

Your mom has lung cancer. Eva's words haunting me. I kept telling that old lady to quit smoking cigarettes and now look at the predicament she's in.

I decide to try and distract myself the same way I've been doing for the past four weeks: binge watch *The Walking Dead* and drown myself in Ben and Jerry's ice cream. I walk over to my MacBook that I utilize as both my computer and TV and turn it on. I'm welcomed by an old picture of my mom, dad, and me. I smile at the old photo of us at California's Great America, but my smile begins to fade as I notice the tool bar flashing red next to the email logo. I click on it confused since no one had my new email address.

My eyes widen when I see who the email is from.

"Dearest Ayla," my dad writes in the subject line. Sorrow sweeps through me as I continue to read further down his email.

I hope that you have been well and that you have been eating all of your meals. I hope that you have a place to stay and you aren't roaming the streets homeless, in search of food and shelter. I pray that you are healthy and taking very good care of yourself. We all miss and love you so much. We know that Eva reached out to you months ago and informed you that mommy has stage four lung cancer. I don't want you to worry anymore and just know that your mother and I love you so much. She sent her love and asked me to let you know that her funeral will be next week, Thursday, the twenty-first of September. She wished she could have seen you before her passing but she will always be there for you in spirit. This past month she spoke of old memories that you two shared, from the time you shaved your eyebrows off when you were five, to the time she caught you using her makeup when you were eight. Just know that our intentions weren't as bad as they seemed. It was only because we wanted a secure and set life for you. Again, the family and I wish and hope to see you next week, hon.

Lots of love,
Dad

As I read the last sentence, tears stain my cheek and I feel a hole form in my chest. I reach out and close my laptop with shaking hands. I lay my head on the desk and think, *What now?*

DECEMBER 18, 2017

Dearest Ayla,

How you holding up? I'm guessing you either just found out that mom has cancer or just died and now you're debating going to the funeral or not, huh? I feel for you, trust me. When mom died, it felt like my whole world came crashing down. Satan himself couldn't make me feel the pain and regret I felt at that time. During that time, I remember waking up and moping around the house thinking to myself, "Wow, I really took her for granted and now she's left me." I know you're feeling anger as well because you don't want to admit you were wrong.

Well, you need to let it go. You need to forgive yourself and you need to forgive mom and dad. You should have cherished them when you had them. You could have never known that mom was going to be diagnosed with cancer, and that isn't your fault. You had no control over that. What you do have control over though, is deciding on whether or not to go to the funeral. I'm telling you right now it'll be worth your while. It'll fill the void that you've been feeling for the past couple of months. Mom is in a far better place now. I'm sure she remembers and cherishes every second she spent with you. As for dad, you still have time to make up the lost relationship you two once had. His famous cream of mushroom meatloaf is still as bomb as ever by the way. Don't be too hard on yourself, okay? Stop feeling so remorseful.

Love,

Ayla

P.S. The next time dad tries to marry you off (which I'm letting you know right now he will, more than once, too) just talk it out with him and show him you can support and take great care of yourself.

SOLITARIO

◆

GISELLE M.

*was born in Mexico and she likes to read. She will be the first
one in her family to graduate from high school. She also
likes to learn new things. She hopes to go to college after a
one year break and be a cosmetologist.*

OCTOBER 4, 4018

Hugo and his family were saying their last goodbyes to their city, Los Angeles. They were all moving to a small island named Las Cuevas. There were a lot of people living there for a small island. Hugo had his mother, stepfather, and two stepbrothers. Kevin and Trigo didn't get along with Hugo because he was very different from them; he was into science and they thought he was out of this world because he was always trying out new experiments. He was also very different from everyone in school. He couldn't make friends so he passed his time studying animals and cells. Hugo always had this idea of creating something that would keep him company. He was very confident aside from what everyone called him, a weird kid.

They arrived at Las Cuevas and it was a stormy day. The waves were furious and splashing onto the forest. Hugo's mom, Esperanza, was very scared and thought it was a bad idea to move away from the city. His father, Tony, thought it was just a new challenge for the family, and a good experience. Hugo, Kevin, and Trigo were excited to start a new chapter in their lives away from the city. They all arrived at their new home. It was a nice home. It had glass windows, two floors, a view of the ocean, and a big yard. It was their dream home.

Their new home had a basement that Hugo was going to use as his lab. He was very organized and careful when it came to his experiments. Hugo was a germaphobe, so his lab was very organized. All his utensils, plants, animals, and liquids were in an incubator, keeping them warm and alive. His lab was also very bright, which was perfect to do all his experiments. There was a very special box he had that he cared for as much as his own life. This box contained a human brain that he was working on, so it was also placed in an incubator attached to a bunch of wires and liquids to keep it alive. It was slimy, pumping just like a heart. His ultimate purpose for this brain was to implant it into his favorite animal, the red fox, so he would be able to talk to someone and keep him company since he didn't have a real friend to hang out with.

A week had passed since they moved into their new home and the rain finally went away. Hugo's father had planned a trip for their family to go and explore the forest. He met a friend that was going to take them. They packed food, sunscreen, bug spray, and left for their adventure. Hugo was going to find his red fox to take home. It wasn't easy, the weather was so humid. The walk was very long and suddenly they heard yelling.

"Ewww!" Esperanza yelled. She had stepped on a blob of poop.

"Honey, it's okay just wipe it off," Tony said. They found a small abandoned cabin where they went inside to eat.

"There's a tale about this cabin," said the guide.

"Is it about *la llorona*?" asked Trigo.

"No, actually it's about one of his sons. He used to do evil experiments here. People say they used to see shooting lights of different colors burst out into the sky like fireworks at night and during the day, when people came hiking here, they found debris and slimy green stuff," the guide said.

"And what happened to all of that?" Kevin asked.

"No one knows. That's a tale that no one has ever really found out about." They ate their food and before going back to exploring the forest, Kevin, Hugo, and Trigo all went further into the cabin to see what they could find. They all went into different rooms of the cabin and what they found was scary, something they had never ever seen: scratched walls with hateful words, like evil, dead, and loner written on them. Everything was so destroyed.

Hugo went into a room where there were animals and he loved it, but there was something strange, because even though they were alive they wouldn't move. It was as if they were paralyzed.

"Everyone please come here, hurry!" he yelled with desperation. They all ran to where he was and they all helped him release those animals back into the forest. One more cage was left behind, though. It was very unusual. It was covered with a towel and this animal moved. Everyone stepped back as Hugo was getting ready to uncover it. It was a red fox. He was so astonished and happy he had finally found it, so he took it with him back home. This was not a good idea to do. It was getting really late, so they took the trail back home.

"Mom, can I please keep him? I need him, please," Hugo pleaded to his mom.

"Fine, but I don't want him inside the house. Take him to your lab or something."

"Yes! Thank you, Mom." He then hurriedly went to his lab and placed the cage on his table. He didn't know what to do. He wanted to start his project but knew he needed a plan so everything would turn out good.

Three months had passed and Hugo was finally ready. He made a decision and he was going for it. He was going to implant the brain he had prepared into him. He worked day and night with the red fox, getting him ready for surgery. Hugo was very scared and excited at the same time. The red fox was bad news, though. He already had evilness in him because of where he was locked up. Hugo finished his surgery after about five hours and was patiently waiting for the fox to wake up.

"What is this?" a screechy voice said. The fox had woken up and he talked. Hugo was so happy everything had turned out so good that he ran around the room with excitement.

"What are you doing?" the fox asked.

"Oh, don't get scared, I'm your friend and I will care for you," Hugo responded.

Months passed by and they turned out to be really good friends. Hugo only took him out when his family wasn't around the house though because he wasn't allowed. Hugo had to go run errands one morning and he had left the fox locked in his lab. While he was gone, Kevin and Trigo went into Hugo's lab and they unlocked the cage where the fox was. Why did they do this? The fox was not allowed to be out, but Kevin and Trigo didn't like Hugo because their parents showed more care and priority to him because he was well educated and liked to study.

When Hugo was back he noticed what had happened and he started to panic.

"Mom! Who came in here? My fox is gone!" he yelled.

"Hugo calm down, we'll find it, don't worry," she tried to calm him down.

They searched everywhere for it and had no clue where he could have run. Days had passed and there was no sign of him. Suddenly something very strange was happening. Everyone was becoming distant and no one really talked to anyone anymore. Why was this?

"Mom, what's going on? Why aren't you talking to Dad anymore?" Hugo asked.

"It's just that he didn't turn out to be the person he told me he was. He was hiding a lot of secrets."

While eating breakfast the next morning, they were watching TV and noticed that

"He was very confident aside from what everyone called him, a weird kid."

not only were his mom and dad not talking, but other people, too. Everyone's secrets were being let out. Hugo had a bad feeling about this. He knew that he had given the fox the power to understand and speak every language. His brain also allowed him to read everyone's mind. He had to find that fox as soon as possible, so he came up with an idea. He went into the forest and started placing crackers, the fox's favorite snack, all over. With this, he was hoping the fox would come back to him. It was just a waiting game. Hugo even slept in the forest in a tent, kind of like camping, hoping the fox would come back.

Three weeks later he heard some noises outside his tent at night. He peeked out: *it was the fox*. He slowly went out of his tent with a blanket and threw it on top of the fox.

"What do you think you're doing?" asked the angry fox.

"That is a question I should be asking you. Don't you think I know it's you who has been separating families and friends? Why are you doing that?" Hugo asked.

"Let me finish my snack, dude," said the fox.

"Why are you being so rude, Fox?"

"Because everyone else is rude with each other!" he said.

Everyone knew there had to be something done about the problem. They all thought the same, everyone wanted to go back to normal but couldn't. How could they if all their secrets were out, all their lies? Hugo and the fox went back home.

They had a plan.

"Everyone please come here! I found him," Hugo said as soon as they got home.

"Hi everyone," the fox said. They all got scared and backed away from them.

"Hugo Armando Gonzalez de la Vega, what is this?" Esperanza asked, scared.

"I can explain," the fox tried to say.

"Shut up, you talking animal!" Tony yelled. Kevin and Trigo were there in shock, not saying anything. Hugo then explained to them what had happened and they were disappointed.

"I don't know what you're going to do about it but you're not allowed to come out until you figure something out and lock that thing up," Esperanza demanded. Hugo and the fox then went down to the lab. He was going to make a serum that he would inject into the fox that would make his brain grow and send a radar around the whole world so everyone could become close again.

It took him about three days to finish. It was a Tuesday, February 21, at 12:00 p.m. He was getting ready to inject the serum into the fox. They were both scared but ready to do it.

"Okay, go ahead," the fox said nervously.

"One, two, three."

His brain grew up to the size of a soccer ball. Hugo and the fox both went on top of the roof and the fox started sending a signal that would get to everyone in the world. Everyone fell under a type of hypnotizing effect. It was even on the news that everyone was back to normal, although the fox still had a soccer ball-shaped head. Hugo did everything to try to get it back to normal but nothing worked.

Two weeks later, the fox became so weak that he died. Hugo was so hurt he got rid of everything. He got rid of his experiments, utensils, animals, plants, everything. He never again did another experiment in his life. He was so hurt that by just wanting company, he caused chaos and he didn't want to be the one to cause another problem again. He didn't want anyone to be isolated because he knew what that felt like, so he decided to go on and make friends.

LETTER TO MY YOUNGER SELF

DONTAE S.

*was born in beautiful San Francisco and is seventeen
years old. He loves to play basketball. He lives with his
grandmother and sister in a small house right next to
Glen Park. He is going to college at either Cal State
East Bay or Alabama State University.*

Dear Dontae,

You've come a long way. I am proud of you. Through those late nights staying up till 2:00 a.m. doing notes and homework knowing you had to wake up at 6:00 a.m. to those days trying to keep your eyes open in the classes, pushing through the pain of your eyelids feeling like one hundred pounds. You managed to push through it. Those AP classes that you struggled with in high school now look easy in college. You really learned from your experience and came out on top even though you did not see it at first.

I remember those times when your sister, Nikki, would push you into taking those AP classes. She would say "Dontae, you need to take these classes so your transcript looks good for college," and you would say, "It's kind of late and I'm not ready for the challenge." You were tired of your friends in class distracting you and getting you lost in your studies so you wanted a different atmosphere. You were so nervous, sweating about making the big decision to do it or not. You decided to go with it and not look back.

You were three weeks into your junior year when you got the news. You were called down to the counselor's office feeling nervous and worried that something wrong had happened. When you got down there you felt something in your gut drop and your legs began to lightly shake. The counselor began by saying "Congratulations Dontae. . . " at that point you knew what was happening and your mood completely changed from nervous to excited. She finished saying, "Your schedule is changed because you got into both the AP classes you asked for." You welcomed the challenge and at that point your whole life changed academically. The next day was your first AP class right at first period. You noticed right away that there were only two other African American students and three Latino students; the rest were Asian.

As time went by, your school year was going great! Your hard work and dedication to the basketball team was paying off and we had a good record of 14–2. We were so excited you won our final playoff game to put us in the final championship game. Also, your semester report card was great: two Bs in your AP classes, a B in Honors Pre-Calculus, and the rest were As. You were doing a good job managing your basketball time with your school work and being with your friends, and even though you were stressed, you could still see the results of progress.

I remember you were so excited for the big game. The championship: this game was going to be the biggest game you ever played. We were nervous but determined to win. As hard as you all played, it just was not enough that night. There was a minute left in the fourth quarter and you looked up at the score and noticed that we were down twenty points and there was not enough time left for a comeback. You lost the game by a terrifying score, and then everything went downhill.

The next day at school the atmosphere felt different. People in the hallways stared but didn't say a word. AP U.S. History class got more advanced and you started to fail the quizzes and get lower scores on your assignments. AP English started to feel more difficult and you started to struggle. Your self-determination started to fade and you were losing focus. When it was time to take the big exams, you let your nerves get to you and after taking them you were worried if you passed or not.

When the College Board email came telling you that you did not pass, you were so mad, and you lost your drive to improve. Stressed out and scared to tell your family about the exam scores, thinking they would yell at you and be mad about all the hard work you did and still didn't pass, you didn't believe in yourself anymore.

"It's time to focus on your future and where you want to be for the next four years of your life," your sister would say at that time. She would make you stay in on weekends when you wanted to go out with your friends and work on applications and the FAFSA.

I remember she told you "Financial Aid is very important because the college will help you pay for what you need and you have to renew it every year you return." You sister was the key to why you are at the college that you love because she made sure you got all the work done before the deadlines. She would always remind you, "Make sure you're finished with the application this week" and "Send in your test scores tonight." She made you do all of this early so that you would not have to stress about it close to the deadline like some of your friends did.

Looking back at the impact she made and what she meant, I can now say she was right. Although you did not get the college credits, you realized you had to move forward and get prepared for college and scholarships. You knew you couldn't lay around and take a pause with life but that you had to use this push back as fuel to continue to move forward.

Everything seemed to be going right and smoothly. You had finished your college applications and there were still people working on theirs. Your FAFSA was completed early and scholarships were the only thing you had to work on. You were less worried about failure because it seemed as if at this point, you could not fail. Everything you were doing fell into place perfectly like pieces in a puzzle.

When the time finally came to make the decision on where I would be for the next four years, I was so excited for my future. I knew I was ready because I took a challenge and failed, I didn't get the college credits I wanted but I learned so much from taking the classes. I don't know the challenges I will face moving forward, but I do know that I'll be ready to face them from the experiences I faced. Taking the AP classes helped me realize that when things do not go the way you would like them to happen, you still have to continue to move forward from the experience.

Sincerely,
Dontae

WHO I AM

—◆—

NATALIE P.

was born in San Francisco and is seventeen years old.
She loves to spend time with her family and play sports,
for example, volleyball. She lives with her mother and older
brother. After high school, she plans on going to community
college to study physics or chemistry.

𝕴 come from a family where we revolve around athletics. My dad played college football at the University of Southern California (USC) and is now the head coach for their football team, while my older brother, Tyson, plays for him in his second year. My mom also played college volleyball and became a physical therapist. And then there's me, Nevaeh, the youngest of the family.

You can say there's lots of pressure on me to actually play in college. Because of that, my parents thought it would be perfect for me to play high school volleyball and get scouted for colleges, whether it was USC or not. Every little thing my family did— playing in college, winning championships, doing big things—set the bar for me, and to them, it's my job to reach it.

Our last home game for volleyball is senior night. All five of the seniors are called out one by one before the game starts, and we walk out alongside our families. Everyone else went up before I did, and every single one of them teared up.

When it was my turn, I walked down the court with my family, who were holding balloons, posters, and flowers. "Head captain, Nevaeh Jones!" Coach Kate says into the mic. Cheers come from the bleachers, the sidelines, and the team. As emotional as it was, I didn't feel an ounce of emotion come out, while the others had a spill of emotion. All I felt was a sigh of relief that the season was coming to end.

We come to the end of the court and toward the photographer to take a picture. Squished in together, we take one picture with all smiles, and another showing the goofiness that we all share. I feel no emotion about ending the season, just a weight off my shoulders. Volleyball was forced upon me by my family. It was really not something I truly loved.

We all get home after a win with all the posters, flowers, and balloons given to me by family and friends. I get to my room and throw all the things into the corner near my closet with all the others I have received. As I'm doing so, I see four envelopes laying on my desk, labeled with college logos: USC, University of Kentucky, Michigan State, and Duke. I know these are recruiting letters to play volleyball for them, but if playing volleyball in high school was forced on me, I don't know how I'm going to handle playing in college.

"Vaeh!" my mom says as she opens my door. "Did you see the letters I put on your desk? Must be more recruitments, right?"

"Yeah, nothing new," I say with no enthusiasm. She walks over to me.

"Wait, what's wrong Vaeh? Aren't you happy?" she asks me. We take a seat on the side of my bed.

"Yeah, of course I'm happy, mom. It's four more colleges that I get to pick from. And they're amazing colleges."

"Oh, my God! My last baby is going to college," she sobs while giving me a hug.

"Mom, I'm going to get ready for bed," I pull away from her hug.

"Alright, hon. Good night."

"Night, Mom," she walks out through the door and closes it. I get to my feet and put the new letters in my junk drawer, along with the other letters. As flattered as I am to be picked to go to these colleges, I'm only looking for one letter—Juilliard. That letter will tell me if they like my audition tape and will consider me.

Ever since I've heard about Juilliard, it's been my dream to go there and dance. I never told my family about dancing; it was always volleyball over everything. Telling them that I wanted to dance and not play volleyball would make them so disappointed in me. I throw myself onto my bed in defeat to sleep off the thought that I'll never get a call from Juilliard again, and I'll have to go to one of these colleges recruiting me.

Saturday mornings after volleyball season are dedicated to my dancing, but no one knows that. I've worked with this dance teacher who volunteers at the gym for almost three years. And to this day, no one knows.

I wake up early in the morning and get ready for the day at the "gym." The gym has a dance studio that no one uses, so it makes it the perfect getaway. I pack my duffel bag with a volleyball to seem like I am training to deceive everyone.

"Mom! Dad! I'm going to the gym for training!" I scream to wherever they are in the house, but I hear no reply. "HELLO?" I scream again as I walk down the stairs to the front door. "Well, if no one is going to hear me, I'll just take the car then," taking the keys from the key dish in the kitchen, I grab and run to the door, so I don't get caught. But the stack of mail catches my eye, and I wonder if my Juilliard letter is in the pile.

Out of curiosity, I look through it, even though I doubt it'll be there. "Cable bill, nope. Water bill, nope. Letter from grandma in France, I'll keep that for later. Phone bill, yikes," I nearly give up looking for the letter, but just when I'm about to throw the mail back onto the counter, the last letter I see is from Juilliard. I pick it out of the pile and throw every other piece of mail out of my hands and roughly open the letter open with the keys. I open it and unfold the letter, and it reads:

Dear Nevaeh Jones,

Thank you for your audition submission. Although you do not have much experience dancing and performing, your dancing was amazing and your dance coach put in a good word for you, where she was a Juilliard alumni. Thanks to her, we are considering you for our final audition. Your audition piece must be received within thirty days of this letter's date. Once again, thank you for your submission and we look forward to your next tape.

Juilliard Admissions

I gasp. I cover my mouth to avoid screaming aloud and waking up the rest of the family. Trying to be quiet, I jump in silence and shout into my hand to muffle the noise. I look up at the date and the letter was written—almost two weeks ago—meaning that I have a week to make another dance piece because it'll take another week just for it to get to Juilliard.

What doesn't come to mind is how am I going to tell everyone about this. I want to go to Juilliard, but I'm scared. Not about leaving or whether or not I'll get accepted, but about if this will be okay with my parents. Dancing? It's not what they really want for their daughter. It's always about sports.

I hear my parents' door open and I quickly shove the letter into the pocket of my duffel bag. "Dad?" I scream out. "I'm going to the gym. Bye!"

"Bye, be safe!" he's walking down the stairs, groaning, waiting for his morning coffee.

"Bye." I walk out and lock the door. Running inside the car, I throw my stuff into the backseat and scream to let out all the emotions; I am happy, yet I don't want to tell anyone about this.

Once I arrive at the gym, I head straight to the dance studio. Luckily for me, the whole studio was vacant. The whole back wall of the studio is one big mirror. And all I see is my reflection. All I see is me. The person who is hiding inside of me, waiting to come out and be who she wants to be. But, you can tell by the look in her eyes that she's scared to come up to the surface and be who she really is.

I walk over and connect my phone to the speaker. I put the song that I am planning to dance to for my second audition tape on replay and start dancing. My body flows with the music, as if the music is telling me how to move.

A little over an hour later, after the song replays a few dozen times, I gathered enough moves to make one piece. I take my phone and place it on a high chair with a bottle behind it to stand it up and record it for the audition tape.

As I dance in front of the camera, I see a body looking into the room through the clear walls. It catches me off guard and suddenly, I stop dancing and turn my head slowly to the person. He's walking to the door and I gather up all my things, thinking I may have been in here too long and people are waiting for me to finish up.

"Sorry, I've been here since they opened. You must have been waiting a long time. It's just that I have to finish this audition piece for. . ." I babble on and on and he cuts me off.

"Juilliard?" I recognize that voice. It strongly resembles my dad's voice. I pick my head up from stuffing my phone and bottle into my bag.

"Yeah, how did you. . ." Right then and there I realize, not only was my dad watching me the whole time, he also has the Juilliard letter in his hand. "Dad?"

"Hey, Vaeh," he says with his hands in his jacket pocket. "I didn't know you dance. All of it was beautiful." I walk up to him.

"What are you doing here?"

"Just checking in on you, making sure you're not over-training for the college scouts. Looks like something different."

"Look, Dad, I can explain. Don't be mad, or sad, or disappointed. Just hear me out, please?" I tell him.

"Nevaeh, you don't need to explain. I've never seen you so passionate about something." he looks at me, but I lose eye contact with him.

"I'm sorry, Dad. I've been meaning to tell you about it. I was going to tell you when I get accepted, but I haven't yet. I still have to send in my second tape."

"Why did you have to hide this from me?" We walk over to the bench against the side of the room and sit down.

"I don't know. I just didn't want you and Mom to be disappointed in me. I don't really want to play volleyball in college. I barely wanted to play in high school. It was only because of you guys and Tyson that I felt like I had to play volleyball like mom. It was always sports and nothing else. You guys pushed it on me."

"If sports weren't your thing, you could have just told us Vaeh. Your mom and I would have understood."

"Really?"

"Of course! If dancing is what you love to do, then you do it. Don't rely on us to plan out your life. We were only guiding you to be dedicated to something. And it looks like you were dedicated to dancing, not playing volleyball."

"So, you're okay with it? With me applying to Juilliard without telling you?"

"One hundred percent okay. You know, we all knew that you weren't so into volleyball. You always had that look like you were being forced to play, but you're phenomenal at it." We both share a laugh. ". . . for a dancer, that is."

"Ha, ha, funny," I sarcastically say to him. "So, if I get into Juilliard, are—" He cuts me off.

"You mean *when* you get into Juilliard."

"Oh, yeah," I chuckle. "When I get into Juilliard, are you going to be okay with me going there?" He puts his arm over my shoulder and my head fits perfectly in between his arm.

"As long as you're happy, I am perfectly fine with it," he says and places a gentle kiss on my forehead. "Your college savings account should be more than enough for Juilliard. And maybe you can use a little from your grandparents' trust fund, too. Come on, let's get home and tell your mom all about this."

"As long as you tell her everything. I used the emergency credit card she gave me to pay for the application and the shipping for my first audition tape."

"So that it's even, I'll tell her the Juilliard story, and you can tell her the credit card story."

"Fine," we both laugh as we walk out of the studio.

I realized that I didn't have to pretend to love something because of what my family wanted for me. As long as it made me happy, it's what was best. Since I started high school, I was scared to tell my family what I actually wanted to do. I was scared to tell them who I wanted to be—not an athlete, but a dancer. I should have known that they're my family, and they'll accept me for my decisions and be there through every step of the way. After I told them that I wanted to be a dancer, I can now be who I am.

THE DAY THE INTERNET WENT BLACK

KUN H.

*is a senior at Burton High School. He was made in China
then grew up in San Francisco. Out of his seventeen years
of life, he has spent twelve years in PC gaming. He's looking
forward to having a family in Canada or Taiwan. He dreams
of a simple life with no trouble or accidents.*

𝕴 spend my time on the computer more than anything else. My computer means everything to me. These are my teenage years, and I'm a computer addict. The internet is used broadly in today's world. It is one of the most important inventions in human history. The internet provides communication, business, opportunities, and entertainment. Computers are the technology that allows people to get work done efficiently. In the United States, most people have access to the internet. Of course, I was no exception.

As a senior in high school, I rely on the computer to do everything—my homework, my projects, labs—and I am taking AP computer science programming and Arts, Media, Education Broadcast, which are two classes that require computers the entire time. I look forward to becoming an expert in computers for my career, most likely as an information technologist because it pays well and it would also be fun if I could work with computers as a job. The last week of November, I was assigned a fall semester final project, which included two computer classes. I had two weeks to finish the project. It wasn't due until mid-December, which is when fall semester is over and winter break begins. Since I had two weeks, I didn't have to rush it.

A week passed and my projects were due in just one week. I was still playing video games, and decided to work on my projects the next day. I wasn't worried because as long as I had access to the internet, I knew it would take no longer than a day to finish it. At two in the morning, I was struggling. Should I play another game before I go to sleep? The game I play is very addictive and time consuming. One round takes around thirty to forty-five minutes, battling in player vs. player mode. When I decided to play one last game, my internet crashed, so I thought it was a sign that I should sleep instead of playing another round. I felt relieved because I wouldn't have to struggle late at night. Maybe it was the wind that blew the wires and it would be fixed the next day.

The following day I got out of school, rushed home and planned to play a round before starting to work on my project. When I turned on my PC, I saw that I was still disconnected from Wi-Fi. I checked my router and found that I was cut from service. I began to worry about it a little, but I still had one week to work on the projects, so I let it slip out of my mind. Since I can't get anything done without the internet, I decided to sleep on it. I woke up at 9:00 p.m. I hadn't had any good sleep in so long because I stay up late playing games at night. I checked my router again, but service was still off, so I went back to bed. I was a little worried about the situation, so I left the window next to my bed open widely, so the cold air could blow in and calm me down from this eagerness. The next day, I woke up at 6:00 a.m. It was earlier than I had ever woken up. I didn't know what to do before going to school, so I sat in my bed and waited it out. I thought about it and I felt that I needed something in life that can fill in during the blackout of the internet, or else I would be bored to death.

I found a close friend of mine playing basketball at the court behind school. It was a dusty ground because of the construction on the building near the court. From what I observed, he was having so much fun. That motivated me to try it out and so I joined him. He knows me so well that I believe he noticed that I was acting different from usual. He probably thought something went wrong in my life or else I wouldn't have been spending two hours playing basketball, but he didn't say anything about it. Over the two hours, I felt that he went easy on me. He could have won the game playing against me because he used to be on the school team and I was just a PC nerd knowing little of basketball. On my way home, I was exhausted, but it was true that I had fun playing basketball. After that day, I started playing basketball regularly and I finished my final project at my friend's house. With his help, I did not receive any late deductions on my final projects.

Over winter break, I played basketball with my friends repeatedly. Every day I just waited for their call to show up. The break was over shortly. I went back to school and was assigned two assignments that required computers on the first day after winter break was over. From that moment, I knew that it was inevitable—it would be nearly impossible to pass those classes without the internet. I also learned that I can't get anywhere in life without my computer. It isn't replaceable in life. Over this incident, even if I am powerless when I lose the internet, there will always be a way out.

THAT'S NOT
FOR GIRLS

KAYLA MAE A.

is a senior attending Burton High School.
Her favorite subject is English and she loves to write.
She is a firm believer in equal rights.

"That's not for girls," was something I never heard growing up. I was taught that everyone is equal, whether it be between race or gender, though I soon learned that everyone was not treated equally. Growing up, I saw stereotypes between the genders everywhere. When I say everywhere I mean in everyday life. I would be watching TV and a cleaning commercial would come on, and it would always be a woman who was doing the cleaning. The woman would have a big enthusiastic smile and would be prancing around like she was so happy to be cleaning. I would also see commercials where a woman would be in the kitchen cooking for her family or husband. As for men, I would see commercials about being strong and tough. There would always be some kind of muscular guy promoting colognes or construction. I wondered why the media would have a boxed interpretation for the roles of men or women. In my family, cooking, cleaning, or fixing things were equal things between my parents. It was never a set job for either of my parents. My parents never said how things were or were not supposed to be. My parents were open-minded and I got that same attitude from them which allowed me to not be restricted with things in life.

With the open mindset I had growing up, I never listened to society's "perfect" norms. I was into playing sports and getting messy. I loved to play basketball, kickball, and soccer. In my after-school program I would always try to convince my teachers to let us play some one of those sports. When we would play games, a majority of the team would be boys except my best friend Jennifer and myself. Playing sports was just one of the things I did that went against society's norms. Although I was so used to breaking society's norms, there was a time I broke them without even knowing.

I was in the living room with my sister Krista when my aunt arrived at my house. My aunt was from Fremont and she rarely came to San Francisco because she was a busy nurse. She had one child, a boy, my cousin Ryan. Aunt Susan and Ryan were coming over to celebrate New Year's with the rest of my family. As a six-year-old, I was excited about celebrating New Year's because it meant staying up past my bedtime and being up at midnight. I was even more excited to see my cousin because he was one of my favorite cousins on my mother's side. We usually went all out with New Year's decorations such as crowns, leis, and horns. This year my aunt provided party hats for my sisters, my cousin, and me. The hat was oversized, cone-shaped with "Happy New Year" written in cursive in the middle, and shimmery trimmings on the bottom. There were three hats: a bright pink one, a royal blue one, and an emerald green one. My favorite color was blue and had always been blue, so I instantly chose the blue hat. It was then my aunt said something completely unexpected.

"Kayla, what are you doing?" she asked.

"I'm getting a hat!" I grinned.

"Okay, but don't you want the pink hat?"

I glared at the pink hat. It looked like the nasty Pepto Bismol my mother would make me take when I was sick. There was no way I wanted to wear that hat.

"No. I want the blue hat. Blue is my favorite color."

"Blue is for boys. Pink is for girls. You can have the pink hat and I'll give the blue hat to Ryan."

In that moment, I felt completely devastated. I felt like someone had punched me in the stomach. I had never been denied something so simple as a colored hat. I wanted to throw a tantrum and scream at the top of my lungs. All I wanted was my favorite colored hat, but I was denied that by my own family member because the color was not "for" my gender. From that moment on I despised the color pink. I hated the fact that a specific color was associated with girls. I despised the gender norms that society had. As I grew up, I realized other people were not raised in the same mindset my parents had for me.

One day in my tenth-grade English class, we had a discussion about society's

"Growing up, I saw stereotypes between the genders everywhere."

expectations for men and women. I was excited to talk about this topic because I think it's important for everyone to understand that we are no different from each other when it comes down to gender. We started off the discussion about what differentiated the genders from each other and then what similarities there were.

"See the only thing that makes us different is our biological features," my teacher said.

"Yes, but there are specific things that women and men should and should not do," a male student said.

When I heard someone say this I knew they meant it in a negative way.

"What do you mean by that?" I snapped.

"I mean women are supposed to stay home, cook, clean, and watch the kids. Men are supposed to do all the hard work," he casually stated.

"Well, you clearly don't know what you're talking about. This isn't the 1950s. Women have equal rights, we're more than just doing housework. We can do anything a man can do," I said combatively.

"That's my personal opinion, you don't have to listen or agree."

This infuriated me more, all I could think was how can someone be so little-minded that they would say something so appalling. By this point, I was furious and I couldn't let him get away with saying those things.

"Well, obviously, I do have to listen since you were arrogant enough to say that out loud in our classroom discussion. How would your mother or any woman in your family feel if they heard you say that? Your mother birthed you and took care of you. A woman giving birth to a child itself is another example of how strong women are. There is something really wrong with you if you think it's okay to talk about women like that. Women have been patronized and have been fighting for the same equal rights as men for so long, and you are disrespecting that."

After I said that, there was complete silence in the room. All eyes were on me. I did not know what else to do or say because he did not respond to me either. My teacher eventually broke the silence, but in that moment, I felt strong and empowered for standing up to him.

Dealing with the conflicts of the hat and the disagreement I had in class were small parts of what I have experienced overall. I have been in more situations just like those, but I would like to think that every situation has made me stronger. I have learned to speak up for what's right and not be a quiet bystander. It is important to me that women everywhere have the same equal rights as men.

Everyone is different based on their personalities and how they were raised. Although we are all different and special in our own ways, our genders do not define us. You should not look at someone and make a judgement based on appearance. That is one of the reasons why men and women are so misunderstood. Society teaches young girls and young boys the way they are "supposed" to act. Young girls are supposed to play with dolls and kitchenettes growing up. They are taught to wear pink, wear dresses, and to be gentle and passive. Young girls are not encouraged to participate in any rough or messy activities. Young boys are taught to be tough, never show emotions, and most importantly, not to cry. They are taught to wear blue and play multiple sports. These social norms mold these adolescents into thinking there is a set expectation for each gender. This is not how we should be teaching young kids. We should not be limiting kids to what they can and cannot do. We should be teaching them they can do whatever they desire. We should encourage young girls to participate in sports. Young boys should be told that it is okay to cry and to express their emotions. If we keep teaching young boys and girls how to act, then we are putting them into a box, limiting their abilities to achieve success. Instead of doing that, we should tell them to disregard society's norms and to reach for whatever they want to achieve. That is what's going to make these children happy in life.

THE WORST DAY TO COME TO WORK

BING L.

*was born in Guangdong, China, and is
seventeen years old. He loves to sleep. He is planning
on going to City College of San Francisco.*

𝕴t was a Saturday afternoon when Daniel's boss called in on him. Daniel was at home enjoying his first day off as a software engineer; he was watching a movie until his cell phone rang. He slowly walked to his desk and picked up the phone. "Hello?" he answered. Daniel waited for a few seconds before hanging up until. . . "Sorry about that, been busy with signing the papers. . . can you come in and fix a bug for MangaZone, one of our contractors? They have been experiencing data loss. . . as I was saying, please fix this ASAP. I have to go right now, I have a meeting I've got to attend!" he said rushing out of the room before ending the call.

He was disturbed by the news, but agreed to it and said with a deep hollow voice, "Sure thing Bob, I'll be there by 6:00." He slowly got up and walked to his room until he felt a strong wind blowing onto him. As he walked closer to the window, the wind started blowing harder than before, blowing his short and military style haircut backward. The closer he got toward the wind, the harder the wind blew. By the point he reached the window, Daniel was already soaking wet from the wind blowing rain toward him. The floor and wall were wet from the constant gust of wind from before, but Daniel had no time to clean it. He then slowly made his way to his bedroom, started to undress and headed to take a shower. Soon after, Daniel started to dress up and walked down to his phone, grabbing it and setting an alarm for 6:00 p.m. He took a nap for a few minutes before the phone started ringing. Loud sounds started coming from outside causing him to make a face full of fear. One that he would not forget had he looked in the mirror, like a ghost who got spooked after seeing himself. He rushed outside with an umbrella and got into his car. It took a few minutes for him since he had to heat the car up but as soon as the car was able to start running, he drove it off at sixty miles per hour. The scenery was a blur both due to the speed he was driving at and the weather. It was a destination which should've taken him thirty minutes, he made it in twenty due to his fast and reckless driving. Daniel stepped out of his car, and ran toward the building hoping that his umbrella would shield most of the rain off of him, but sadly his entire bottom half was all wet since the only part that the umbrella shielded was his top half. He made his way to the dressing room, changing his pants, and went toward his office.

The moment he turned on the computer, loud noises came from the outside causing a blackout. He was scared and afraid, but he knew that the only one in the office was him. Daniel slowly made his way toward the power room. Something on the ground made him trip, causing a cup of water to splash onto him. "One of the best days I've ever had!" He exaggerated. When he opened the door, a strong wind gusted out causing him to shiver; the power room looked like one that a crazy scientist would use to test his experiments. Now with his clothes wet, he was about to pull the lever, until another loud threatening sound came from the outside. But this time, thunder hit the building and made its way to the power room. The moment Daniel turned that lever, the flow of electricity transferred onto him, causing a blackout upon himself as his crispy body fell onto the ground.

Time passed by and soon Daniel started to regain consciousness. He woke up shaking his head rapidly from the pain he was feeling, got up, and looked around. He was in horror as he was looking around since he knew that he wasn't in his company building or in the hospital. He was in the middle of a forest, and he didn't even know how he got there. Faced with fear, he crouched down and put his hand on his head and kept repeating, "No, No, No, No." Full with fear and confusion, he stood up and looked around once again. Now filled with little confidence, Daniel started walking around the forest; it was like a maze for him since he didn't know where he was going or even what time it was. What felt like a few hours for him were only a few minutes. He walked and walked until he heard something from afar. He ran toward it hoping to find someone or something since he had been starving since he woke up. To his surprise, three green, short, ugly creatures were eating the living flesh of an animal which he could not identify due to the gruesome scene he witnessed; the smell of blood was all around the air. As Daniel quietly walked backward, trying not to get caught, he was whispering to himself, "No way. . . " The three creatures were finished eating and were about to walk away until they heard noises coming from the direction Daniel was in. It seemed like Daniel accidently stepped on a twig, and as of now he was running for his life screaming,"NO!" He ran at top speed for ten minutes straight, (which he was not aware of) a record for his fastest mile run in ten years.

As he was slowing down, due to lack of oxygen, he tripped on something, causing him to fall down, spraining his feet. He looked behind him, but they were nowhere to be found, not until a few seconds passed. They were rushing toward him and grinning; their grins, full of wickedness and their lips bloody red from the animal they just ate. Daniel panicked but noticed that he tripped on a rusty sword, talk about luck. He pulled the sword off the ground, but tripped backward. The first creature jumped onto him, but that was a dumb mistake since Daniel accidently stabbed it to death. The sword, now with a dead body on top of it, broke in half due to how rusty and old it was and also because of the weight it was holding. Luckily for Daniel, the creature he killed dropped its weapon. He picked up the small tiny knife and pointed it toward the other two creatures as he tried to get up. Due to the death of their comrade, the other two ran away due to the fear inflicted by Daniel.

Daniel was both happy and scared at the same time, and before he knew it, he blacked out for a few minutes before gaining consciousness; probably from the hunger and growling coming from his stomach. He walked in a random direction for a while before stumbling upon an apple tree. Since he was hungry, he tried saving up stamina, but the moment he saw the fruits, he suddenly sprinted at full speed toward the tree, trying to fill himself up. Two hours passed and the forest's light was fading, almost complete darkness. Weird sounds started to come from different directions, spooking Daniel and forcing him to make a run for it. He ran for a few minutes before stopping and noticing that he was lost. Luckily for him, there was light coming from his right. As he walked toward that direction, the weird sounds started to get louder and louder, echoing in his ears, traumatizing him later on.

He finally got out of the forest and looked around, observing the scenery and scouting to see if there was a place for him to camp. He was still wondering where he was since he knew that this was not his country. As the sun was going down, Daniel walked to a small village that he saw when he was standing atop of the cliff next to the entrance/exit of the forest. The strange thing was that the horrible sound he kept hearing when he was inside the forest stopped the moment he stepped outside the boundaries of the forest. He was now at the entrance of the village. As he surveyed the village, he noticed that the village was like a wasteland, bone dry, and the house was almost about to collapse. As he walked inside, an old man popped out of nowhere, causing him to jump back. The old man greeted him kindly, "Hello young adventurer. May I know your name?"

". . .My name is Daniel, and you are?" Daniel said in a confused voice.

He replied in a loud but jester-like tone, "Ah la, I am the one and only, Gilfrid the Chief of this village! May I ask why you come to this old and broken-down village?"

Daniel looked around, and started to notice that there were people coming out of hiding—some were kids, while others were old men and women. He answered as he walked around the area to keep surveying the village. "I came to. . . I came to this village because it was close and I needed a place to stay." He looked at the Chief; the Chief looked like he was in his sixties and smelled like someone that hadn't taken a shower for a week, causing Daniel to step back a little the moment Gilfrid stepped a little closer. He didn't dare to call him out on it since there might be consequences to his action; he was the village Chief after all.

"No worries young adventurer, we welcome you with our open hand! But there is one condition," he said in a serious tone.

Daniel thought for a moment, thinking of the possible outcome, "It depends on what the condition is."

Gilfrid replied, "It isn't much. We are having problems with food shortage and we suspect that the thieving mice from the cave near our village are coming out and stealing our supplies of food. We would like you to enter the dungeon and retrieve the stolen food for us."

Daniel didn't want to take the risk and was about to decline the offer, but the Chief saw through his hesitation and tried to tempt him into accepting the request. "We shall cover your stay here and shall give you whatever you desire, even our young maidens! That is only if you were to accept the request from this old fool." Gilfrid threw in the bait, now waiting for Daniel's answer, but all was clear to him since the face Daniel saw was a lecherous man lusting for the love a female companion. His face was all red, and who knows what was happening inside his mind, but one thing was clear and that was him accepting the request of Gilfrid. It was getting dark so Gilfrid led Daniel to his room. "Here is your room. It may be old but still usable. Even though the furniture is old and the bed is worn out, it is still a livable room." Daniel had been wondering why they would give him such a huge reward to just retrieve their food supply, but he didn't doubt much of the old man and the villagers, never did he know that he was about to fall into a horrible trap set up by the townspeople and the Chief himself. He slept heavily like he had been awake for twenty-four hours working nonstop and was now finally getting some sleep, unable to wake up until the sun was almost about to set. The Chief rushed into the room, followed by several villagers with pitchforks and an unburned torch in their hands. "Adventurer, we cannot wait any longer, those thieving rats stole all our supply while we were asleep, and we need to take action!" yelled Gilfrid and the villagers.

Daniel now fully awake was confused, since he couldn't hear what they were saying. He got up and went to the bathroom with some clothes that Gilfrid had given him last night. The moment he got out of the bathroom, the villagers dragged him outside, and gave him the necessary tools to venture into the cave. He was given some food, water, and a dull sword. The villagers gave him enough time to eat before venturing toward the cave with Gilfrid as their lead. "Why are you guys following? This is very fishy. . . " he said, but it was too late as the villagers started to walk toward him, their eyes, full of pure darkness as they smiled at him.

Before he knew it, someone smacked him on the head causing a blackout once again. He fell onto the ground next to the cave with Gilfrid in front of him. The villagers tied up Daniel and carried him inside the deep dark cavern. Noises started to echo from the depth of the cavern, probably from the water dripping down from the ceiling, or from the footsteps of the villagers. They lit their torches as they went down deeper. When Daniel started to regain consciousness and looked next to him, he saw carvings of stick figures. What he saw was a creature with wings; he probably thought it was a dragon and saw the people bringing a sacrifice to it. He was screaming so loud, knowing that he was the sacrifice to the dragon. His screaming was echoing through the entire cavern, causing the eardrums of the villagers to rupture. Gilfrid was so angry that his face turned red as he used his cane to whack Daniel on the neck, knocking him out once again. "What an annoying person, had he been any louder, he would've woken up our god and we will be the one to face the punishment," said Gilfrid. "We must make haste, before the dragon god wakes up." In a few minutes' time, they were at the deepest part of the cavern, where their god resides. The villagers threw Daniel's body on the ground next to the dragon and left in a hurry. Gilfrid was still there praying to the dragon before leaving. He whispered, "I'm really sorry." before leaving the huge room.

The giant creature woke up; there were large scars all over its body. As the mystical beast roared, rocks on top of Daniel started to fall due to the vibration sent from the loud roar. The dragon started breathing fire like it was going crazy; had Daniel not stood behind a fallen rock, he would've been roasted. He looked back and saw words carved onto the rocks of the cave warning those who read the message.

To the fellow adventurers who have come this far, I send a warning to those who were foolish enough to be tricked by the villagers. Do not believe them, they are full of wicked intentions; they are the minions of the dragon and will do what the dragon bids. Maybe this message is the last you will see, but I wish you luck.

—Gilfrid Woodsman

Daniel turned his head, but only to see the insides of the beast's mouth. In a split second, the head of Daniel and his body disconnected.

What's left of him was nothing but the bones of what the dragon spit out after its meal. The life of Daniel Martez had ended in this world, but not in the other one. He jumped up screaming with his eyes shut with bandages covering his entire body. Doctors and nurses ran into the room to see what was happening. They were shocked since they didn't expect the patient to wake up after being hit by the lightning. He was in a coma for almost six months already and the doctor expected that he would be in a coma until the day he was on his deathbed. Daniel started to unravel the bandages on his body and face, only to know that his entire body was full of burn marks. He stared at the mirror to see what happened to his face, but only to see the face of Freddy Krueger.

REVENGE OF THE HUSBAND

ERICKA S.

*was born in San Francisco. She likes watching comedy
and cooking shows, playing softball, and experimenting
in the kitchen. One day she would like to work
as a nurse and travel the world.*

"Why did she do this to me? She made me look like an idiot!" exclaims Charles, running his hand through his hair. "Does she know that I am hurt right now? I loved her!"

He elbows his phone, causing it to clatter on the basement floor. "What if I tell her how I feel?" He leans forward to pick up his phone. "Never mind, I do not want to seem weak," he thinks to himself, shaking his head.

Charles is fixing up his phone, trying to get all the chips inside. "How can I make her feel what I'm feeling right now?" He sits there looking at his phone, feeling like he is about to explode.

It has been two months since Charles and Laura's separation and he still feels the pain of the event. Every day, Charles hides in the basement of his suburban home in Silicon Valley, trying to plot the perfect revenge for Laura. After Charles comes home from work, he goes downstairs in his basement where he has all his office gadgets with three computers, security camera, and all his tech equipment. It is his lab, a dark place where he is the only one who can access it. He created a super sensitive passcode to gain access.

"I am so ready to get revenge!" he says while logging on his computer. He jumps on his computer with a big grin of his face. "I wish I could see her face when she receives it." He starts by logging into the hacking system. "I haven't done this in a while, so hopefully I can get this to work. . . yes, I am on." Charles starts inputting this long code, 10011101010111, and it goes on and on with the code. "Why didn't I think of this sooner?" he mumbles. The clock strikes midnight and Charles is finishing up. "I am almost done here." He inputs the last digits of the code and one moment later, he is finally done. "Oh, my God! I did it." He checks the clock. "When she wakes up, she is going to be shocked," he says, laughing. "It's time for me to sleep. I'm going to sleep like a baby tonight," he thinks excitedly, walking upstairs.

The next morning, Laura wakes up at her home in Wamawho, California, where the sun looks really bright and happy. "I want some coffee," she yawns. She runs down the stairs of her condo, goes to the kitchen, and picks up a mug. "Mhm, I want decaf," she says while putting a K-cup into her Keurig. She picks up her cup of coffee, goes to her granite countertop, and logs onto her computer. *Boom!* Her cup slips from her hand and shatters on the floor. "Oh, no! What happened to all my emails and all my accounts?! They were all important!" She tries logging onto Facebook and her bank account, but the passwords don't work. "My money disappeared! How could this have happened?! I am totally broke!" She pounds her hand onto the counter with a fury in her eyes. "Arghh!"

Meanwhile, Charles sits in his bedroom, snorting with laughter. "I wish I could see her face right now. I bet she is miserable," Charles laughs for the next five minutes, just thinking about her reaction.

Laura decides that she needs her best friend, Tiffany, to help her out. She fumingly storms out of the condominium, hops in her Smart car, and drives a few miles to her best friend's house. She arrives, hops out of the car, and bangs on the door.

"Tiffany, I need you right now! Something really bad happened!"

"What happened?!"

"Everything is gone!" weeps Laura.

"Come in, and tell me everything that happened!"

Laura sits on her friend's couch and begins the story.

"So, I woke up, had my morning coffee and when I went to check my email, bank account and all my other social media accounts, they were all gone! I think they were all hacked!"

"Really? Wow, that's a real bummer," said Tiffany.

"Yeah, and now I can't do anything. I can't buy any clothes, make-up, food, or anything else!" yells Laura, breathing through her nose deeply, her face reddening.

"Who could have done this to me? Did I accidently put all my passwords out there? Did someone want to just delete my whole life? I don't deserve this! This is bad! Why is this happening? I just got a divorce and now this?"

Meanwhile, Charles walks to the kitchen to look in the refrigerator to see what he can cook for breakfast. "Huh. I am craving some French toast right now." His stomach starts to growl just thinking about it. Looking into the fridge, he notices that his fridge is empty. "Oh, no. I need to go grocery shopping today. I don't have eggs, butter, or bread for my French toast." Charles closes the fridge. He walks toward the door, grabs his keys, and slips on a pair of sneakers. "I need to hurry up! I am very hungry right now." His stomach starts to growl again. He pats his stomach and says, "Yeah buddy, I know you need some food right now, just wait." He walks outside and goes into his MINI Cooper.

"Did the marriage end badly?"

"It was not that bad. I was the one that wanted to split up. I didn't want to but I wasn't feeling it anymore as a relationship. Charles was also getting a little aggressive, too. He would get angry easily and I didn't like that." explains Laura.

"Who do you think could have done this to you? Who would hate you this much?" says Tiffany.

"Huh, let me think, uh, my neighbor doesn't like me but I doubt he would do this. Maybe it was one of my co-workers. I'm pretty sure that they are jealous of me being better at coding than they are."

"Maybe it is your co-workers, then."

"Yeah, it would make sense since someone that could have done this would have needed to be good at coding and hacking and stuff. And they would also have some type of anger toward me."

"Yeah, that makes total sense."

And then Laura realized who perfectly fit that description.

"Hold on Tiffany, I think know who it was!"

Charles arrives at his local grocery store. He grabs a cart and walks into the store. *Ding dong.* "Hi, Good Morning," says George, a cashier of the store. "Good Morning," says Charles. *Where are the eggs?* he thinks to himself while pushing the cart around the aisle. He continues shopping around until he has all the food he needs to fill up his fridge. Twenty minutes later, Charles finishes and goes to the cashier to pay. He puts all his groceries on the conveyer belt. "My fridge was empty. I needed to fill it up."

Beep, beep. "Your total is $75.85," says George. "Cash or card?"

"Card," says Charles.

"Okay, just swipe."

Charles swipes his card and enters his pin number.

"Sir, I'm sorry, but your card got declined."

"Wait, What? What do you mean it got declined?"

"It means that you don't have money on your card."

"That can't be happening; I am rich, I have a lot of money! You are wrong," yells Charles.

"I'm sorry sir, but I guess you need to check the problem in the bank."

"Are kidding me right now? Alright fine!"

Charles leaves his cart at the register. He walks out of the store stomping his feet with a frown on his face. "This better be a joke because if I don't have any money, I don't know what to do." He starts driving to the nearest bank. He slams his steering wheel. *Pound. Pound. Pound.* "This is so dumb."

"Who is it? Tell me now. I want to know." says Tiffany.

"Charles!"

"Your ex, Charles?"

"Yes, who else. Who else knows how to hack other than the people I work with? And who is the one that is angry toward me since I was the one who filed for divorce. He must be furious that I did this to him." And suddenly something pops up in her mind. "Wait, so if my bank account has no more money because of the hacking, then does that mean he doesn't have money either?"

"What do you mean?"

"I mean, married couples have their bank accounts joined together. We had our joint accounts together when we were married. And we haven't separated yet. If I don't have money, he doesn't have any either."

"Ha-ha, what a big mistake that is on his part!"

Meanwhile, Charles arrives at the bank. "Can someone please help me!" he yells out while he was entering at the door.

"What's happening, sir?" says the banker.

"I don't have any money!"

"Have a seat over here. I'll check out the problem here."

"What is your account number and name, sir?"

"My name is Charles McGee and my account number is 01375975426."

"Okay, so I am looking at your account right now and it seems like you don't have money in it."

"No, no, no! That's impossible."

"It says here that the last time you had money in this account was actually at midnight. And do you know that you have a joint account with a woman named Laura McGee?"

"Yes, that is my ex-wife but I forgot that our accounts were joined together."

"Have you talked to her recently because she might have withdrawn all the money."

"No, I haven't talked to her recently since the divorce."

"Ahh, I see, I don't think we can help you with this, sorry."

Charles stands up from his chair and yells out, "Thank you for nothing!"

Charles furiously walks back to his car thinking about why his money's all gone. He starts to drive and when he is at the stoplight, he remembers something familiar about what the banker says. "Wait, did the banker say that my money was all gone at midnight? That's when I hacked into Laura's accounts." And then suddenly it hits him. "Wait. Oh no, I think when I was hacking her accounts, her bank account was also hacked and erased all the money which is also my money. Oh no, this cannot be happening. This is all my fault. . . " The light turns green and while he is driving back home, he is banging his forehead on the wheel. "I am broke now because of what I did. How could I be so dumb? I didn't know it would affect me." He starts to cry and laugh at the same time. As he arrives home, he goes to bed and starts thinking about how he ruined his life by trying to ruin someone else's life. He feels devastated. His actions went back to bite him in the butt. "What was I thinking? I shouldn't have done this!" Charles is having all this regret in his mind. "How can I fix this?"

"I hate how he did this to me. I should call him to confront him about it," says Laura.

"If you think it's the right thing, then go ahead," says Tiffany.

Laura grabs her phone and starts calling Charles. Charles answers.

"Charles!"

"Hey Laura," says Charles

"I know what you did. And why did you do it? That is just messed up. Do you know how angry I am right now! You better fix this, or I'm going to call the police on you!"

"I know, I know! Let me explain and please don't call the police on me."

"Explain what? That you made all my stuff disappear and that I don't have any money left? Is that what you are going to explain about?"

I was angry. Okay Laura? I was devastated that you wanted to have a divorce. You were an amazing person. I just wanted you to feel how I felt. It really hurts."

Laura was speechless.

"I know that I messed up because it also affected me, because now I don't have any money."

"Well, your fault. If you didn't have this crazy idea to go to my accounts and erase them all. Like who does that? Oh, I know, a lunatic."

"Come on, you don't have to be like that."

"Are you really surprised that I'm this mad?"

"No, but you don't have to react like this. We were married for ten years, Laura. You were my first love. And how can I forget that? When you told me that you wanted a divorce, how do you think that made me feel? I didn't want to be away from you. And when we separated, I died a little on the inside, Laura. I got lonely and didn't have anyone to talk to. I just wanted you to feel the pain of losing something important."

"Oh, I didn't know you felt that way."

"You didn't even bother to call to check up on me."

"I'm sorry."

Laura and Charles became friends for a while but eventually drifted apart. Laura couldn't forget about what Charles had done to her. Charles started to look for other people to meet to forget about Laura. Charles realized that revenge wasn't the key to his problems, and that what goes around comes around.

THE SILVER LINING

Embracing, Accepting

SPECTRUM

—◆—

VICKY L.

*was born in China and is eighteen years old. She loves to play
badminton and shop. She loves the weather and diversity in
San Francisco. She hopes to go to college in the University of
California system and obtain a bachelor's degree in business.
Her dream is to open her own business and benefit society.*

I feel lost. As I wander around the building, I see students walking quickly like they are in a train station in New York City. This is my first day of school since I moved to San Francisco and I have never been so nervous in my life. I cannot find my first period classroom, but I am afraid to ask for directions. Ten minutes after the bell, I finally find my class and walk in from the back door. I intentionally close the door silently, but the slight noise is enough to catch the attention of the class. The students turn around and stare at me with suspicion and the teacher insists that I sit at the empty seat in the back of the room. I remain quiet for the entire period and the lesson flies through my mind without being processed.

Students rush out of the classroom and head in different directions in the building. I hardly manage to squeeze my tiny figure between people and make my way to the next class. I sit in the back of the room in all of my classes and I feel invisible. The classes are long and it feels like a seventy-two-hour day. School is torture to me and I really miss my friends back in Portland.

On the second day, I become more familiar with the school building, but my classmates are still a group of strangers to me. I try to avoid eye contact with teachers in class and hope not to be called on to answer questions. At lunch time, I pick up school lunch and sit at a table alone. I feel isolated when I see groups of students sitting together and I know I will never fit in.

"Hey, get up." Someone taps on my shoulder and I turn around. A group of senior guys are staring at me and they look irritated. I ignore them and continue to eat my lunch.

"This is our table," says the guy with thick eyebrows. I am afraid to look at them but I pretend to be calm and keep eating my food. The guy walks up to me and throws my food on the floor. I kneel down and try to clean up the food, but they start kicking me from behind. I feel the pain in my back and I cannot get up.

"What are you guys doing?!" yells the Dean. The guys run away while I lie on the cool, hard floor.

One of my classmates from math comes over and helps me get up. "Are you okay?" he asks. I look at him, then look down at the floor again. "I am Peter. You are Tommy, right?" He looks at my bruised face with sympathy. I feel embarrassed and want to dig a hole in the ground and hide myself. I let go of his hand and run away from the crowd.

Since the day I was beaten at the cafeteria, I have become one of the biggest targets of the "gangs" at school. They push me in the hallways and trash my backpack with crumpled homework and gum wrappers. Peter always tries to help me, but I feel awkward and try to avoid him. I am scared to go to school every morning and I want to get away from this dangerous place.

On a rainy day, I walk out of school and get on the bus. My cuffed jeans are soaked with water and my backpack is completely wet. On the bus, I hear people talking about virtual reality games and how realistic they are. It reminds me of the virtual reality headsets my mother gifted me last Christmas.

The rain is pouring down like beans and I run home after I get off the bus. Despite how much I hate school, I hate being home alone even more. I hate this grey, old, small house with the smell of loneliness and mess. The sun never visits our house and my room is always dark.

I dig under my bed to look for my headset after changing into dry clothes. I find it in a brown box where I store all of my old books. I download a virtual reality game from my phone and connect the phone to the headset. I am excited to try out the game and escape reality temporarily.

Walking down Mission Street, I see colorful graffiti on the sides of the buildings and each of them tells a different story that represents the uniqueness of the neighborhood.

Many bikes are parked in front of coffee shops with vintage interiors. I can smell the smokiness of the coffee in the air mixed with the smell of fresh made tacos from the small delis. The neighborhood is old, but charming in its own way.

"Hey!" says a guy who's in his twenties, wearing a beige, oversized hoodie and ripped jeans. I stare at him with confusion.

"There's a party down the street. Come with me!" he smiles.

I follow him without overthinking it and we arrive at a huge, fancy apartment at the corner of the street. There are giant LED lights shooting out from the wooden roof and the furniture is modern and colorful. There's a big crowd of young people at the party, dancing and socializing with each other. Someone hands me a blue drink in a glass and I take a sip of it.

I wake up in a garage with five other teenage boys. My head is hurting so much and my vision is blurry. The garage is dark and wet and I feel scared. A tall, tough looking man, who's wearing all black walks toward me and examines my body with his deadly stare. "Is he the new kid?" he asks.

"Yes, he came yesterday," the shorter guy next to him answers.

They drag me out of the garage as I scream helplessly. "You, go steal a phone and come back here by 8:00," he says emotionlessly.

I am very confused, but I automatically follow his command. I walk down the street and stand behind the bus stop. The wind is freezing cold and I feel pain in the gap between my bones. I observe for hours and watch people come and go, but I am afraid to act. The sun is setting and it's getting darker and colder. I am scared to disobey and decide to steal and make it back to the apartment before 8:00.

I notice an older lady, who has been standing at the bus stop for a while, and I take a step closer behind her. When I am about to steal from her, my head starts hurting. It's like the evil and good inside me are having a cold war. I take a step closer quietly and reach my hand into her bag without looking. I take out her phone quickly and run away.

I come back to the garage at the apartment and give them the phone. They insist that I sit down and I see the other boy getting beat up because he failed his "mission." My inner-self is telling me to help the boy, but I remain silent to protect myself.

After that day, there's a party every night and different people join the gang. The purpose of the party is for people to trade illegal things secretly and I am only a tiny part of this world. I continue to steal every day and I feel like my body is out of my control. I realize that they are taking advantage of me and I am terrified.

At night, I decide that I have to escape from this place while everyone is asleep. I carefully pass people sleeping on the floor and walk toward the window. When I open the window, it makes a squeaky noise and everyone wakes up.

"What the hell are you doing?!" the head of the gang yells angrily. I try to climb up the window frame without shaking and I jump down to the alleyway. I don't have shoes on and I run as fast as I can on the freezing, wet streets. Three guys are chasing after me with guns in their hands. I am running out of breath and I am probably going to die tonight.

"Ouch!" I run into someone at the corner of the street and I fall on the ground. I look up and see Peter standing in front of me.

"Tommy, what are you doing?" Peter grabs my arm and helps me get up.

"Help, Peter! They will kill me!" I said breathlessly.

He helps me escape and we hide under the highway. This space is pitch black and it is a shelter for homeless people. The ground is wet and the air smells coppery. Peter stares at me strangely for a moment and he asks, "Tommy, did you forget this is a game?"

"A game?" I am confused.

"This is virtual reality. Have you forgotten? You need to stop this game immediately! Just take off your headset!" he exclaims.

I feel like a meteoroid just hit my brain and I realize why I am in this strange place alone. I hesitate for a moment and say, "No one cares about me in reality and I feel like trash. Maybe I should stay."

Peter exhales deeply and looks at my eyes sincerely. "I care, Tommy. Trust me. We should go back together and I promise I will help you at school."

Peter gives me strength and I decide that I have to go back. His kindness reminds me of my friends back in Portland. I really miss my father and he must be worried about me. After taking a deep breath, I take off my headsets slowly with my eyes closed.

"Wake up, Tommy!" The world appears to be all white and my vision and colors are slowly coming back. I see my father standing on the side of my bed and he looks like he has not shaved his face for a week. "It's already 9:00 and you are late to school. I am so sorry I did not wake you up this morning. I made breakfast for you. Get dressed, Tommy."

Tears rush out from my eyes and slip down my hot cheeks. I realize how much I miss him. I hug him tight and say, "I love you, Dad."

He smiles and pats me on the back like I am a little child. "I love you too, Tommy."

My dad drives me to school today and the fresh air smells so good after a rainy day. The sun is warm and comforting and I feel a sense of relief. While I am walking into school, I notice the smiles on students' faces and their laughter makes the school come alive. The classrooms and the hallways look extra colorful today. I am ready to start over.

THE ICE CREAM STORM

JOHNNY L.

was born in San Francisco. He is seventeen years old and enjoys an occasional game of basketball. Video games are also an enjoyable pastime as well as hangouts with his friends. In the later years, he hopes to step into the field of technology, but is still unsure about a specific career.

It was another typical morning in the city of Kyanite. Several early birds began their days checking their journals to see what lay ahead of them while others basked in the sun without a single bit of fear in the world. One of these larks included Jake, equipped with a snazzy, red jacket, white collar shirt, lime-green tie, and a set of leather shoes, while living in a moderately-sized log cabin down by the shore. As Jake stepped outside, he noticed some ominous dark clouds moving in toward the city. He ran closer and closer to this mysterious source only to hear the sounds of buildings collapsing, citizens screaming, and the dying tune of several ice cream trucks. A mixture of fear and confusion built up in the minds of others watching this from afar.

It was another case of *here we go again* coming from Jake's face because this was something he had seen before. As he overlooked the crumbling city, clutching his fists and letting out a heavy sigh, it was about time that Jake put an end to this nonsense. In a matter of seconds, he ran back home. With a snap of his fingers, he summoned a tall

"Anyone can start over and begin a new journey in their life."

and skinny player outfitted with a set of ripped, raven-colored jeans and hoodie. Phil, as he was called, began to wave his hands around when a small grey cloud appeared inside the cabin and an ice cream truck smashed right on top of Jake's elegant coffee table. Phil looked around to see various parts of the truck scattered across the room. Jake was not pleased at all.

"Oh dear, I am truly sorry for the mess I caused here, Jake," said Phil. "I will try my best to get this cleaned up so you can get back to whatever you were doing."

"Stop with the nonsense and cut to the chase, Phil, what is the point of this?" asked Jake.

Jake directed Phil's attention to the dying tune of the destroyed ice cream truck.

Phil gave a little chuckle. Jake rolled his eyes; he'd had enough of Phil's childlike personality.

"I was just looking for some 'fun' in this world. It's not like there is anything entertaining going on around here."

Phil walked around Jake's office and stumbled across a gigantic bookshelf. With a stunned look, he went up to grab a novel only to cause a waterfall of books to tumble down onto the ground. Phil looked at Jake's even more irritated expression.

"Well couldn't you find some other means of entertainment around here? This *IS* a place of fantasy, after all. Anyone can start over and begin a new journey in their lives."

"I do find this type of entertainment enjoyable, it fits my personality extremely well."

"Entertainment shouldn't cause any harm to others because that's not how anyone should be treated around here. How would you like it if you had to go through years and years of pain?"

"I would know because I *have* dealt with years of suffering!"

Jake did know about Phil's past. It was about four years ago when Jake first met Phil. It was around the same time Jake had brought this virtual world for thousands to discover. For many, it was a way for troublemakers like Phil to escape their awful realities and begin new lives. Phil's life was just like the rest: alcoholic parents, bullies at school, depression, and a dangerous neighborhood. Jake wanted to help Phil as much as he could by bringing him into his world, but Phil was not as cooperative as he expected. Phil was an intelligent person, but due to his past, he craved attention. He found multiple ways to manipulate the world for his own amusement. There were rampaging dinosaurs, year-long thunderstorms, and occasional days where everyone transformed into frogs. Jake was able to fix these problems, but he couldn't change Phil.

"It's been so long since I first met you; I deal with so many troublemakers just like you that it can be tough to remember everyone's case."

"Well I'm sorry you've had to deal with so many awful people and I apologize for what I've caused here; you're doing an amazing job, Jake."

Phil went over to give Jake a big hug. Jake honestly thought Phil had come to his senses. Perhaps they finally found something in common and now they could start a new relationship.

MISUNDERSTOOD TEEN

———◆———

DAMAREA' D.

is an eighteen-year-old senior at Burton High School. He is
hoping to go to a four-year university to study music.

𝔐y name is Damarea' and this is the story of my life, or part of the story at least. But before we get started, let's get something straight: I'm not a broken or even damaged person. I don't hold grudges over any of the events that occurred in my past. I like to think of myself as resilient and the issues that occur are just stepping stones of my many life lessons. So, to begin, I'm going to describe myself, to give you a better visual representation of me (wink, wink!). I'm of African descent. I am, in my opinion, very attractive, and I've always been very mature and reserved for my age. And did I mention I'm 6'3"? Most people, when they see me, quickly come up with their own opinions of me. . . which I guess is normal. I mean, after all it's part of human nature, isn't it? Everyone jumps to conclusions when they meet someone new. It's what makes the world turn 'round. But of course, there are no actual facts behind their judgments, just stereotypes and inferences based on first impressions. People's impressions of me are always the same.

"His face isn't showing much emotion; he must be angry. He's also tall so he must either be a bully or a basketball player. He's black so he's obviously a thug, a womanizer, a player. Obviously doesn't have a father."

But I'm not any of those things. All of my life I've been misunderstood. Misunderstood by my race, sexuality, and personality, all because I don't fit into the spectrum of an African American male. In addition, I'm okay with that because I love myself and there's no need to conform to something others consider "normal."

When I was young, I knew that there was something different about me from the other guys, but I didn't pay it any attention, I appreciated that I was unique. Middle school was an excruciatingly tough time for me. I hated sixth grade. New school, new faces, new vibes, new teachers you had never met before. In middle school, I sort of lost that affiliation of uniqueness and considered myself "different." Eventually at the end of middle school I regained that thought of being unique and didn't consider myself out of the ordinary. In high school, I had to constantly remind myself. In connection with the male species, it became clear to me that I was a creative individual. I was a piece of art.

One by one, different issues started to occur in my life. For one, in middle school I was always accused of being gay by my male peers. I was "gay" because I didn't want to be in a relationship. I felt like I was young and there would always be time for relationships later on in my life. It's not that I don't want to be in a relationship, I actually wouldn't mind being in one. It's just that I know what I'm looking for and I can't see why should I settle for someone who can't add something valuable to my life. I feel like I shouldn't rush into these situations. I was always told by my parents "books before girls," and I knew that deep down if I did happen to be in a relationship unexpectedly, that would be something that just happens. But, because I am attractive, there was a various number of girls who had crushes on me. I didn't try to get with any of them. I must've been "gay" according to the other males (*Ugh!*). I mean is it just me, or does that sound a bit ignorant? People can be so close-minded at times and they assume before even asking. But, like I said, that's just life. (*Smiles*) For the record, I am heterosexual if you're confused. I just have a mind of my own. I was constantly harassed for my choices. There were always rumors, and questions, and taunting. In these cases, I couldn't control myself and reacted to the energy they were giving. (*Sigh*) But hey! I had to stand my ground, right?

This all left a mark on me when I graduated from middle school and went to high school. I noticed that I was upset at everything. The world was really getting to me and I was starting to hate it. I couldn't understand. Why me? I don't bother anyone. I'm a good person. But my thoughts were getting the upper hand. I was losing myself entirely. I couldn't complete any task without disturbing thoughts interrupting me. This one time I happened to be washing the dishes. I was listening to music that was quite depressing in the hope of it making me feel better. It expressed all that I was feeling. It took my mind off of it for a while because I got lost in the song, focused on the words which reminded me of my pain. I scrubbed various plates and bowls and utensils. Then I came across a butcher's knife. I wiped the bubbles from the knife and looked at the reflection of myself. Something about my reflection was unrecognizable, unpleasant. Watching myself fight back tears, I thought of committing suicide. I held the knife up to my neck, wondering what it would feel like to end it all. It could all be over with a slight movement of a blade. It was cold as ice. I imaged what would happen to my body after my sin was complete. Would I fall to floor? Would someone find my corpse in a matter of minutes? This haunting image brought me to tears, just thinking about what could happen to me. Although, I knew from the beginning I wasn't going to kill myself; I didn't have enough courage to do so. Also, I knew that if I ever did commit suicide, I'd never figure out my purpose or why I was chosen to be put on this earth. The thought was satisfying, yet terrifying enough for me to come to my senses. I couldn't do this anymore. I made a promise to myself that I would no longer tolerate all of these issues that cause me pain. Life is a movie and I'm the director of my life and I get the final say so in who I let stay in my life. It was time to take matters into my own hands. If the issues wouldn't go away themselves, I would make them. I needed to free myself somehow.

The knife experience was very eye opening. I decided it was time for me to make a change. I needed to take time to accept and appreciate myself for all that I have done and will do. I've come far and there's still more to go. So, I taught myself how to love me again. I spent a lot of time being by myself, alone in the dark. It gave me time to think, because you see. . . I'm a night owl and I feel at peace in the dark. The darkness gives me comfort in a sense. I learned that I'm more outgoing and more energetic at night, which my mom hates. But that time to myself helped me rediscover the person who I am today, all due to giving a little attention to myself. I was happier on the inside. On the outside the world was still as ignorant as before, which I can't really change, but I could change how the world affected me. Whenever a bad incident occurred I'd tell myself, *it's okay, D. . . just let it go. . . it's in the past now and tomorrow's a new day. Just smile.* This for the most part worked, until I discovered that I could learn to understand why people act the way that they do. And it's because they're curious and don't understand. Once I knew this I figured that I could change the way that people think by answering their questions and starting conversations with them about why they think what they think—so I did. Turns out talking resolved lots of my issues that could've been avoided if those who were curious just asked me first before assuming. I believe that I learned to deal with these situations in a productive way, if I must say so myself. It made life easier once people understood my way of thought and it even strengthened a few relationships with people I thought I'd never be cordial with.

I had to grow mentally to resolve my issues. It was a very effective way of improving my self-esteem all on my own. I am now very confident in myself, I honestly couldn't care less what people think of me. When I do hear what others say about me it doesn't even affect me. I actually find it funny now, like, "Who said what about me? Ha-ha! I never knew that about myself."

I taught myself that I'm me and there's nothing anyone can change about it. If they don't like it, I don't let it get to me. As for future situations, once I'm in college I'll continue to feel as I do now with, of course, more assertiveness to change the way that people think on a daily basis. I may continue to be misunderstood and I may have to deal with racism, stereotypes, and homophobes in the future, but I won't let that get to me. I'll handle it one step at a time with my mentality.

BLANK MIND

—◆—

CLARICE A.

*was born in the Philippines. She moved to San Francisco when
she was twelve years old. She lives with her mom, dad, brother,
and sister. She likes to read personal fiction. She hopes to go to
Skyline College, but has not decided what to study yet.*

Have you ever thought that you depend on your parents too much? I have. I want to be independent, I want to lessen their worries. That's why I decided to get a job. Nina, the sponsor of Burton High's *La Raza Unidas* club, introduced me to someone who could help me to find a job. After we set an appointment, I felt like I could do anything. My mind was full with possibilities.

I arrived at the interview ten minutes early at their office in Japantown. That ten-minute wait felt brutal because it made me think of all that could go wrong. All the courage I gathered was gone. Waiting is the worst when it comes to this situation. It was my first time having a job interview and I wanted to get it over with. It made me feel like if I messed this one up, I would mess everything up.

When they called my name, my heart was beating so fast that I thought I was having a heart attack. I forced myself to walk into their office. As soon as I got in the office, the first thing I noticed was how empty the walls were. There were no posters, or pictures whatsoever. The second thing I noticed was the man sitting in front of the table. As soon as he saw me he stood up and introduced himself. I introduced myself too. I forgot his name as soon as we sat down and began talking.

He asked, "What are you interested in? Do you have any preferences?" He threw all these questions at me, but my mind was blank at that time.

I tried to respond, "Uh, I'd like to work in retail and stuff." I couldn't focus on what he was saying. I tried to look around and calm myself down, but the empty, lonely walls stared at me.

At one point he said, "How about this? Let's do a practice interview from here on out." It caught me off guard. I didn't know what to do, I could feel my heart beating even faster than before. I wondered if he could hear it from where he was sitting. I tried to answer him, but I felt like there was a heavy lump stuck in my throat that stopped me from talking. Now, I knew he'd help me to find a job, but I didn't expect him to help me with interviewing. Practicing with him required a lot of talking, which I'm not really good at. I couldn't refuse him because I didn't want to leave a bad impression. When we started practicing, he asked me to describe myself.

I know it's just a simple question, but at that time my brain stopped functioning. It's a very vague question, so I was not sure what he wanted to know. I didn't want to say anything irrelevant. In the end, I told him, "My name is Clarice, I'm seventeen years old. I'm a junior in Burton High School. I was born and raised in Philippines. Tagalog is my native language and my family and I moved to the United States when I was twelve years old."

When answering his question, I could hear the shakiness of my voice like I was running out of air to finish. After I answered him, he told me I did good, but I know for a fact that I did horribly. He could tell that I didn't believe him. At the end of the day, he helped me sign up for SF Youthworks, an internship program that helps young people build job skills. We had workshops every Wednesday for eight months. My mentor, the other interns, and I discussed various ways to save our money, and talked about our community, but mostly we built relationships with each other.

Joining that program helped me a lot, not only to find a job or prepare for an interview, but it also helped me to gain self-confidence. They made me feel like my opinion matters, and it made me think that I should start voicing my opinion, not only during workshops, but also at school. At first I was scared of voicing my opinions, but life is all about taking risks. You have to go through some obstacles first before you get to the finish line.

MY SIDE OF THE STORY

NARELIN M.

*better known as N.K., was born in the Philippines and is
seventeen years old. He loves to play football and
is an Oakland Raiders fan. N.K. lives in San Francisco
and played AAU basketball.*

Dear Basketball,

I've been playing your game since I was a kid at the park. I created so many memories with other people through you, and they affect my life today. The lessons I learned on the court taught me more about life than school ever did.

My earliest memory of you is from the sixth-grade schoolyard when I played a game of "HORSE" with my friends, Russell and Dontae. I would get competitive with them to the point where we would fight over you. That's how serious it was.

Well. . . it was a whole other level of seriousness in my eighth-grade year. I was in the counseling office looking at flyers and I saw one about trying out for a basketball team in the Catholic Youth Organization (CYO) league. CYO is for kids under fourteen who want to play ball. I wanted to try out for the Epiphany Eagles. The thing was that it was a three-day tryout, and I had already missed two days. I decided to go to the third tryout anyway, and for a kid who has not played organized basketball before, I did pretty good. I ended up making the team. The coach of the team was Coach Rich, a good guy. He taught me the basic fundamentals of your game, things like the two-three zone defense and boxing out.

That summer, I had a lot of fun and I did pretty well in the CYO league, so I decided to try out for the Junior Varsity (JV) team at Burton High School. High school ball was way more competitive than the CYO league. In high school, you have to win every game to be good and to be noticed, unlike in the CYO league, where your record doesn't really matter because you are going to play no matter what.

I did make the JV team, though. The coach was Coach D. He was this big dude, about 250 pounds, and he loved you, too. I liked Coach D. because every time he talked about you, anybody could see his passion about your game, and I started feeling the way he did about you, too.

I was the starting point guard for the pre-season, until I hurt my knee. I couldn't play as well as I wanted to the rest of the season. The team made playoffs, but then we lost to Washington High in the first round. I think they ended up winning the championship.

At the end of the season, Coach D. asked me if I wanted to play Amateur Athletic Union (AAU) Basketball. AAU is Big League—I got to travel and play in tournaments. The team got to travel all over, to places like Los Angeles and Las Vegas. One time I looked up in the stands and saw LeBron James with Chris Paul. Another time, my teammates and I were in a mall in Vegas and we saw the Washington Wizards point guard, John Wall, coming up the escalator just as we were about to go down. I thought *what is he doing here? Where's his security?* He gave us high-fives. It made me realize that he is just a regular guy like me, and that he loved you as much as I did.

So, back to AAU. It's mostly for high school students. I spent 90 percent of the summer playing you my freshman year. One thing I learned that from you was that "if your brother fights, you have to fight with him." This is something I believe in—a core value. This was taught and preached to me by Coach D. I did not understand it at first, but he grew up in a tough society where nothing was achieved alone—you need your brothers to have your back in order to survive. He also taught me that if you don't treat your teammates like your brothers, it would be hard to win games.

The last two years I've been more distant from you, since Coach D. left Burton. I didn't want to play you as much when there were other coaches, and I played football for two years instead.

Flash forward to my senior year: my first game back for the basketball season. I was nervous when I stepped on the court for the first time in a while. I knew my mechanics and reflexes were a little off, considering I had just finished four months of strictly football.

It was the pre-season and we were going up against Gateway High School. Looking at their players and statistics throughout the week, we were expected to blow them out. That was definitely not the case. They kept up with us throughout the entire game, which surprised me because their best players had graduated the year before. Also, we had the home court advantage. In the first half, I played terribly—I had turnovers and I committed silly fouls. I guess my reflexes were still football reflexes. I'm just glad my teammates were there to pick up my slack. Thanks to Russell and Dontae, my childhood friends, we didn't get demolished.

The second half was more intense. I was guarding this guy on the other team, number seven. They made a fast break off an outlet pass to him, and I was hustling back to cut him off. He went for a lay-up, and so did I; I ended up hitting him in the face and landing on him on the ground. He missed the lay-up, but there was no foul called. As I was running down court for offense, Gateway's coach was screaming at the referee about why there was no foul on the play.

I guess number seven was highly upset with me, because a couple of plays later he tried to get me back on my drive to the hoop. He started talking more trash. He said things that I could not take seriously, things like, "Why are you even playing basketball, you're weak!" I mean, he did have a point, since I'd only scored six points the whole game and four of them were from free throws. Shockingly, Gateway ended up winning the game by five.

I was highly upset with my performance. I felt like I played the worst game of my life. I remember looking at my teammates' faces and I saw how disappointed they were. They didn't even look me in the face. Seeing that made me even more upset.

After the final buzzer rang, my team and Gateway's team lined up at the half court line to shake hands and say "good game." I stayed in the back of the line because I was embarrassed that we had lost to a team we were supposed to have destroyed.

As I was shaking hands with the players on the other team, one of them said something to me. Guess who it was? It was number seven. I was cool with it at first because he had the right to talk mess after beating us. But he kept talking more and more, like a fly you can't kill. I tried to ignore it, but then he took it too far.

"You and your team are so weak!" he said.

I looked at him, shook my head, and headed toward the locker room. Number seven followed me and still kept talking mess. Then he said something to Dontae. I'm not sure what he said but I knew it wasn't good. I snapped. I turned around and pushed him. The referees were blowing their whistles and from the corner of my eye I could see fans running down the bleachers toward us. My teammates and some fans tried to grab me away, but I still tried to get him. They ended up grabbing my arms and I was so tired I couldn't really throw a punch, but number seven was close enough so I could head-butt him. He head-butted me back. Then more people came to stop us before it escalated even more. They steered me to the locker room where my coach had retreated after the disappointing loss.

I looked at him and I could tell he was upset. He had two looks: one where he's upset about basketball, and another where he's upset about something else. In this case, he was upset about me.

"What did you do?!" he yelled.

Before I could give my response, he told me I was off the team.

After that, I didn't hear anything else he said. I felt numb and confused, kind of that feeling you get when your dog gets put to sleep. I think my brain was having trouble processing the fact that my high school basketball career was over. This upset me so much, because I have been playing you for as long as I can remember.

While I was taking my jersey off, I could hear coach yelling at my teammates. I didn't know what he was saying. It felt like I was listening to some weird white noise. While I was getting dressed, I couldn't think straight and kept trying to think. I still could not process the fact that I was not on the team anymore. I knew how much I would miss playing you.

I walked out of the locker room and people were asking me what happened. I ignored them and I was still trying to think but I couldn't. Later on, I spoke to Dontae and he asked me what coach had said, and I told him. He said that wasn't right, because I was defending the team. After he said that, I was able to think a little more clearly because I realized that what I did was the right thing to do in my opinion.

Some people might disagree and say, "Violence is never the answer!" and my response to that is, "How else did we achieve peace?" I think the thing that bugged me the most was that coach did not let me tell my side of the story.

Today, my friend and teammate, Russell, still tells me that coach did not mean what he said and that he was just upset at the time. I just laugh. He also asked me, if I had the chance to do that whole day over, would I? Looking back at it now, my answer would be no, because I feel like I did the right thing in protecting my brothers, even though coach will never know that.

Even though there were negative things resulting from my love for you—injuries, misunderstandings—I have no regrets. I am thankful that I met you because there were days I had problems at home or with school, and instead of doing drugs or other things like that, I played you to clear my head. I think that was the best part of my relationship with you.

Sincerely,
N.K.

JUDGE ME BY PERSONALITY, NOT BY APPEARANCES

DONNA F.

was born in Pago Pago, American Samoa. She likes to play
volleyball and spend time with family and friends. She hopes
to go to college to study psychology. She loves food.

𝕴 woke up really early that day. The sun was shining through my room window like the moon in the sky at night. I got up, fixed my bed, and went to the bathroom to wash off. It was our first day back to school from a long and cold winter break. It was my last year as an eighth grader at Waterfalls Middle School. After I washed up, I put on my new blue jeans with cut-out spots on the knees, and my nice, white top with Marilyn Monroe's face in black and white on the front. My aunty got them for me on Christmas, and I really loved the textures. I walked downstairs to see my mom in the kitchen cooking breakfast.

"Morning, Mom!" I said with a bright smile as I walked to the dining table.

"Morning, sweetie!"

On the table, I only picked bacon and two pancakes to eat because I wasn't really hungry. I said my goodbyes to my mom and off to school I went.

In the car, I kept thinking about what my best friend said about this girl named Taumeasina at school, and how she kept discriminating against me and my best friend on social media. I felt anger inside of me like fire boiling up my blood with so much steam. I hopped out of the car. Alice was running toward me with a big smile on her face. She hugged me.

"I missed you! I get to see you every day now that school has started again, because girl talking on the phone was so not the business," she said laughing loudly.

"I missed you more best friend," I said toward her with a little frown on my face. Students started passing by us staring at me and mumbling something under their breath.

"Girl? Don't mind them, they just believe whatever they see on social media," she said.

"I don't care about them, I just want to know where the girl who was talking smack about me is at right now!" I told her, clenched my fist, and walked toward the gate.

We entered and passed by this group of boys.

"Hey Lani! You available tonight? I heard you don't have only one boyfriend because you have a lot. Want to add one more to your list?" a boy in a red sweater said.

I got even angrier. Not only was I angry, I was embarrassed. But I let anger take over. I stood there for a while not knowing that Alice was right next to me talking. I couldn't hear her. Everything around me went in slow motion, all I could see was those boys laughing at me in a mocking way.

I came to my senses to my cousin Christian standing in front of me with worry in his eyes.

"Sis, what's wrong?"

"It's a long story. . . it's nothing," I said, turning to walk away.

Before I could walk, I heard Alice telling him about what's going on, from social media to the boys. I felt weak in my stomach. I turned back and before I could stand straight, I saw my cousin walk toward the boy that called out to me and smack him across the face.

"Talk like that to my sister again and that's going to be the last thing coming out of your mouth ever again," he said with so much anger. The boy held his face with his right hand and just walked around. I walked inside the school.

As I was walking down the hallway, I saw Taumeasina standing next to a group of girls. I thought to myself that maybe if I just ignored her she would stop talking behind my back and on social media. I passed by her and she started mumbling some words to the group of girls and they started laughing toward me. I thought to myself, *no way, I'm going to finish this right here right now*. I turned back and walked straight in front of her. I was only inches away from her. I could smell her Victoria's Secret perfume reeking from her clothes. Her long black hair with brown tips was pulled back in a ponytail. She was wearing white jeans with a red sweater with "Stanford" printed in white on the front.

She looked at me in surprise as if she got hit by a ball on her face. I got her attention by asking her again.

"Why were you talking smack about me?" She stuttered for a second saying "I. . . I. . . I wasn't." In my head, I told myself, *Good Job, Donna!*

But as soon as kids started coming and surrounding us, her expression turned into a serious look on her face. I stood there waiting for what she was going to do next. Kids around us were standing there amused by what was going on. Of course! Who wouldn't love to watch two girls standing in the middle of a hallway arguing.

I looked at Taumeasina and she said, "Ain't nobody talking smack about you!" loudly. My entire body felt on fire starting from my toes all the way up to my head. I was angry. I held my fist like a ball, getting ready to smack her across her face. But before I could do that she swung at me with so much force. I could tell by her body movement it was coming hard. Luckily, I came back to my senses and dodged her hand. I stood up straight and before she could come back from that last punch, I straight up smacked her in her face. She bumped into the lockers on the wall and fell on the floor. She got back up and we started going at it. She pulled my hair and dragged me on the floor. My hair was now in my face which made it impossible to see, but I never gave up. I pushed her toward the locker and started swinging upward, aiming for her face. I grabbed hold of her hair and pulled her down onto the floor. I stood on the top of her smacking her while she did the same thing back. My one last punch to her face made her let go of my hair and right when I stood straight back up, I smacked her across the face so hard.

The kids started booing her. She stood back up with her head down. I looked at her face. She turned and I saw that the spot where I hit her on her face, my handprints were printed in dark red marks on her cheek where I had hit her. We were both panting, fighting to get some air. It felt like we just finished running a mile on the track.

All of a sudden, a tall person stood in a perfect black suit, his hair well combed back. I stared at him for at least a minute; he looked like he was in his twenties. My best friend Alice smacked me out of my senses. I glared at her and she gave me an evil smirk. I looked back toward this boy in between me and Taumeasina. I noticed he was one of the tutors that always volunteered after school. He stood there looking back and forth toward me and Taumeasina with worry in his eyes.

"What is going on here?" he said. His voice sounded so low.

The crowd around us got silent as if someone had run around and duct-taped their mouths.

"Nothing!" I said loudly.

Anger began to boil up again in my body like fire being ignited. He grabbed both me and Taumeasina by our arms and walked us downstairs to the main office. On our way, Mr. Tall and Handsome told us that fighting is never the answer.

We wasn't fighting. Well, maybe a little! That's what she gets for talking about people behind their backs, I said to myself in my head.

We entered the principal's office. We both sat in the chairs in front of her desk. The principal's name was Ms. Zelda. She looked at both of us with anger and curiosity in her eyes. She especially was giving me the death stare because she knew that I was never like this. I was always the one making peace, but now I was in her office.

"Okay, ladies! Explain! What happened?" she said.

Me and Taumeasina didn't say anything, but just stared at our laps. Ms. Zelda was not going to deal with us today.

"If you don't tell me what happened, you two are going to get suspended for one week," she said.

I looked at her and said, "Okay, so over the break, my best friend Alice texted me the day before Christmas that Taumeasina has been talking smack about me on social media." I looked at Taumeasina and she was still staring at her lap. "I didn't believe it at first," I continued, "but then, I looked on her Facebook page, and there it was. All the negativity about me was on there from post to post. I felt sad because I didn't do anything to her for her to be spreading rumors and posting stuff about me on the internet."

Ms. Zelda looked at Taumeasina and asked her if this was true. Taumeasina took a while to answer and then she finally said, "Yes, it's true." She looked toward me.

"Look, I'm sorry for posting all that stuff about you on social media, and for spreading rumors about you. I have no excuse for what I've done. But, I'm really sorry and it won't happen again," she said with sincerity in her voice.

I told her that I forgave her, and asked her to promise to never do that again, not only to me but also to other students. Because I know how it feels like and it's not a good feeling. Being a victim of bullying is a really devastating experience. You have all these people looking at you, making false accusations, assuming that you are a kind of person who you are not. And it makes you feel really sad, people judging you for someone you are not. And the bad thing about it is that you don't even know half of the kids who are looking at you as that person. Kids nowadays are so quick to go where drama is. They don't come up with a solution for it; instead they take videos and make fun of the drama that is right in front of them. They don't want to make peace.

Ever since that day Taumeasina and I have never had a problem again. We say hi to each other in the hallways. Whatever she and I had is now in the past. And I actually love it that way.

FRACTURED FUTURE

———◆———

DANIEL G.

*was born in 1998. Growing up, he always had
a knack for rebellion which would lead him to many
problems in school as a young boy. This would mean he
was always in the office, getting a phone call home,
or getting in trouble for many other mischievous activities.*

Growing up as a carefree, rebellious child, I always thought I was indestructible because I would pretty much be able to get away with anything. I was always doing something mischievous or rebellious growing up, with no real motive other than the fact that I just found it fun to do for the thrill of it. This behavior carried on into school and resulted in me getting in trouble, not doing any work whatsoever, always being in the office, getting a phone call at home, and all the other troublesome things a kid like me would get into. Again, thinking I could get away with anything, I felt all of this wouldn't matter. So why care about it at all? Am I right?

Wrong. Unfortunately, all this fun and careless behavior came to a quick halt in the eighth grade and I was met with a huge reality check. It was parent-teacher conference week and kids would usually have either one or two teachers talk to the parent, with the child present, and discuss their behavior, grades, and all that school stuff. Well, for me I had a mandatory conference with all seven of my teachers, and both my parents needed

"It's okay to be worried about the future, but do not let that get in the way of the present."

to be there. It felt like I was having an intervention. And it sort of was like that, but even more awkward. All seven teachers teamed up against me, while my parents had to hear it all. There was nothing I could really do but sit there and wonder when it would be over. During the conference, my history teacher at the time, Ms. Arney, brought up how all this would affect my future, and that I need to take things like this seriously.

Now, at first this confused me because I thought to myself, *this is what every teacher says. Why should I care?* So, at the moment, that whole conference meant nothing to me. But as soon as I got home, I started thinking what she meant by "affecting me in the long run." And this got me thinking about the future, which led to extreme overthinking and birthed this fear of the future that I still have. Now, at first this was weird to me. Never in my life have I experienced a fear that was emotional instead of a fear of something scary, like monsters or movies. I didn't really know how to handle that, which only led to more fear.

So, throughout the rest of the year, I pushed this little fly of fear into the back of my head to avoid thinking too much about it. But every now and then, whenever the topic of the future would come up, it triggered fear, and I'd just be out of it for a while. The fear became a reality when, in that same year, our class submitted their high school applications. Everyone wanted to apply to Lowell and Balboa. For those who don't know, Lowell High School is a top-notch school that is very privileged and is known for having very smart kids that have a lot of homework. I just wanted to go there because it is near the Stonestown Mall and has off-campus lunch. So, I was just going to be snacking on food during the lunch break. Unfortunately, I was not even close to meeting the acceptance requirements for Lowell. This upset me. It's basically like having someone tell you you're not good enough to go to this school, which sucks a lot. Looking back now, I'm happy I didn't get into Lowell. That school is hard, and I would not have met the wonderful people here at Burton High.

Going on to high school, I was still a little mischievous brat, getting into trouble a lot, and not doing work. You know, the usual. My fear of the future was still there throughout high school. It came out every time we talked about colleges, job interests, classes I want to take, and stuff like that. It wasn't until senior year when I finally realized that all my actions did, in fact, have consequences. It was that time of year when seniors apply to college, and everyone's academic hard work and achievements are shown. Since I had not done that well in school, I could not boast of much academic success.

But I did get involved with a bunch of extracurricular activities throughout my high school years: football, track, Reserve Officers Training Corps (regretted that one), two jobs. And I did all these things while still balancing a high school education. So, in my college applications, I wrote about all I had experienced, learning about responsibility, social skills, and many other things. Sadly, I do not think that colleges look for these kinds of skills in their scholars, so there is little chance that I will get into a top-tier college. But I'm okay with that. I don't need to go to a fancy college to be happy and receive a good education.

After learning many life lessons trying to overcome my fear of the future, the fear has slowly faded away. It's okay to be worried about the future, but do not let that get in the way of the present. If you are happy right now, keep it that way to have a happy future. Live in the now.

PRIDE GOETH
BEFORE A FALL

—◆—

LOUISE MARIE M.

was born in the Philippines and is seventeen years old.
She loves to shop and play sports and make people laugh.
She lives with her mom and dad. She plans to
go to college after high school and become a nurse.
She enjoys reading and writing.

Dear Marie,

I'm writing eight months after leaving AP Calculus. Those were some tough times, huh? Two months before the end of junior year, my Pre-Calculus Honors teacher, Mr. Chui, began to discuss with his students which math class they plan to take next year. During this time, I was still unsure about which class I wanted to take. I began to ask my friends which class they picked and a majority of them chose AP Calculus. When the teacher called me up to his desk, he asked, "So Marie, which math class do you plan on taking?"

"I honestly don't know, Mr. C.," I replied, "What options do I have?"

"Well, since you are in a math honors class, your options are to take either Advanced Math or AP Calculus," he responded. I didn't know which one to choose. In my heart, I just wanted have as many classes with my friends as possible in senior year. So, I replied that I wanted to get into AP Calculus.

"Are you sure, Marie?" Mr. C. asked repeatedly. I began to feel offended and aggravated. *Why does he keep asking me the same question?* I asked myself, *does he believe that I don't have the potential to take the class?*

Finally, I said, "Yes, Mr. C., I'm sure that I want to take AP Calculus next year."

He sighed, but agreed to sign me up for the class. When I returned to my seat, my mind overflowed with sad and angry thoughts. *Of course he doesn't believe in you. You're not good at math,* I said to myself. *You're one of the students who always gets the lowest grades on tests, stares blankly at the board, and asks your friends for help every day.*

In my many years of attending school, this was the first time that I had ever felt belittled and discouraged by a teacher. I held the tears back and tried to endure the last few minutes of class. I began to think Mr. C. was rude for encouraging everybody else to join AP Calculus except me. I felt dumb, slow, and as if I had no potential to get through challenges.

On the first day of AP Calculus class, I sat next to my friends, Lesly and Zabrina. When the class was settled down and the late bell rang, Mr. Y. said, "I expect a lot from you all." And he meant it!

For the next few weeks, the homework, classwork, and lectures were overwhelming. Every day, we would get a new homework sheet and classwork that was unfamiliar to me. We were required to show all of our work and when I would ask Mr. Y. for help, he did not give me enough attention or time to understand the lesson. I'd seek help from my tablemates, who just frowned and ignored me. I felt like I'd been dropped in the middle of the ocean. From then on, I had second thoughts about my decision to stay in the class.

One night, I was doing my homework on limits and notations. I was so confused and frustrated because I couldn't find a helpful YouTube video that would explain how to solve the problems. I was determined to finish my homework, so I stayed up late. My mom came to check on me and asked, "Why are you still awake?"

"I'm not done with my AP Calculus homework," I replied.

Since I'm an only child, my parents are very focused on me, and my mom worried about the consistent sleepless nights I'd been having. I decided to transfer out of the class.

The next day during lunch, I rushed to talk to my counselor, Ms. Hidalgo. When I arrived at the counseling office, there was a line in front of her door. I impatiently waited for my turn to talk to her, my stomach growling. I started to feel lightheaded. By the time it was my turn, the bell rang. I let out a really loud sigh.

"I'm sorry, Marie, can you talk to me after school?" she asked. "I don't want you to be late to class." I nodded and left her office.

As I walked down the stairs to my Physiology class, my friend asked, "What's wrong, Marie?"

"I waited in the counseling office and missed my lunch for nothing!" I responded furiously. "I thought that I would get rid of my AP Calculus class."

After school, I went to Ms. H.'s office again. Luckily, I was the first one there.

"Hello again, Marie," she greeted me cheerfully, "Now, how may I help you today?

"Hey, Ms. H.," I replied. "You see, I have AP Calculus with Mr. Y., and now I totally regret my decision to take the class. I'm really having a hard time catching up to the lessons and barely get any sleep. I was wondering if I could transfer out of that class back to Advanced Math."

"Well, I think you should keep trying," Ms. H. said, "but you can leave AP Calculus if both Mr. Y. and Ms. M., the head of the math department, agree to sign your pink transfer sheet."

When I went back to Mr. Y., he said, "I believe you have the potential to continue taking this class."

He didn't sign the transfer slip. Two more weeks passed. I grew impatient and decided to talk to my mom about my problem. However, before I could even talk to her, she saw my grade in that class and scolded me.

"Why do you have a C- in your AP Calculus class?!" she exclaimed. "That's a borderline D!"

I tried to calm her down.

"Listen Mom, I can explain," I said. "Please sit." She sat down and relaxed. I tried to collect my thoughts for this difficult discussion. I took a deep breath.

"Mom, you know math is not my strongest academic subject," I said calmly. "I've been having a hard time in AP Calculus. I've tried to convince my counselor and my AP Calculus teacher to let me transfer out. My teacher refuses to sign off to let me transfer out. I'm getting really desperate and just want to get out of there."

"He can't do that!" she exclaimed. "If he won't let you transfer out by this week, I'll have to walk up to your school and talk to him myself!"

Chills traveled through my body. My mother is the type of person who does what she says.

Since I didn't want my mom to embarrass me, I made sure to talk to Mr. Y. the next day, after school "Mr. Y., I spoke to my mother about leaving AP Calculus, and she said if you don't let me out of this class by the end of the week, she will have to talk to you personally."

And that did it! He signed my pink transfer sheet.

After school, I ran to Ms. M. to have her sign it. Since I was late to volleyball practice, I texted my coach: "Hey Coach! Sorry but I will be late due to a very important matter. Don't worry, I'll run on the track to make up for the warm up."

I was so relieved to get her signature, but I didn't realize the consequences of my determination to drop AP Calculus. Then my counselor informed me that in order to switch my math classes, I'd have to switch my fifth period Physiology to fourth period, which meant I'd lose my favorite class, Ethnic Studies.

"Is there any way I can keep Ethnic Studies?" I pleaded.

"I'm sorry, but it's not possible."

Ethnic Studies was a class that targeted Filipino history, culture, and language. Since I am of Filipino heritage, I was very interested in these issues. We regularly discussed real world problems such as discrimination and racism. For the first few classes, we had to each present PowerPoint introductions to tell the class about ourselves and did an icebreaker that made us all comfortable with each other. That class had given me a safe place to temporarily distance myself from required courses. Although it was heartbreaking to leave the class, I had no choice.

Now I'm in Advanced Math class, which is a better class where I get the support I need to improve my skills. But I still miss Ethnic Studies. Now I understand if I don't analyze my decisions, I have to learn my lesson the hard way. Instead of accepting my deficits, I chose to push myself past my limit. Then, I had to struggle to get myself out of that situation, and I lost my favorite class.

The lesson today is not to take things so personally and not let pride interfere with my choices. Pride got in the way of making a good decision for classes in senior year. To this day, when I bump into the Ethnic Studies teachers, I feel a little pinch of regret. Thinking back to the day that Mr. C. hinted that I wasn't ready for AP Calculus, I knew in my heart that he was right. But I was offended and thought he meant that I wasn't smart.

However, I learned a lot about myself and so, it was a valuable lesson. But I also know I should not emotionally abuse myself over past mistakes. Instead of dwelling on the negative, I will use the mistake as a lesson to help guide me in the future.

Lovingly,
Marie

FIRST TIME BEING JUDGED

◆

DONTEZ G.

was born in San Francisco at Kaiser Hospital. He is eighteen years of age. He likes to build Radio Control cars. He wants to learn how to be a better engineer in life but he also loves to hang out with his family and friends in his free time. He was M.V.P. on Burton's football team.

𝕴t was my first time going into the nail shop down the street from my school. I usually don't go to different nail shops, but this time I didn't have a choice because it was the day of my trip to Ghana and I was in a rush. So, I parked the car, got out, then proceeded into the shop around 10:45 a.m. As I was walked in, the lady greeted me. I said, "Hi, I would like a pedicure." So, she warmed up the hot water in the tub. As she was doing that, I started looking around. Most nail shops have interesting items. This nail shop had some pictures of butterflies, flowers, client's nails, and family photos. She also had a nice collection of Buddha statues and jades. Once the tub was at the right temperature for me, she poured some oil in the water that filled the shop with a magnificent, flowery fog.

The reason why I get my feet done is because it helps me relax and I'm into good grooming. It also just feels good for someone else to rub your feet. The first time I got my feet done was with my mom. She kind of tricked me into getting my feet done, because she knows I don't like being tickled or having my feet played with. It was pretty weird to me having someone touching my feet, but it felt so good. They soaked, massaged, and trimmed my nails. After a while it just felt normal to me. I wasn't embarrassed to walk into the nail salon.

Twenty minutes into the foot massage, the lady asked me, "Would you like to pick a color for your feet now?" I was kind of puzzled that she would ask me if I would like to pick a color for my toes. I was totally numb to the fact that it was happening to me. I felt like she was trying to judge me because of what I got, making it seem like it wasn't manly and that it's only meant for girls. Some people shouldn't jump to conclusions about what people want in life. I was too shocked to be mad.

Forty-eight hours later, I landed in Ghana with a group of students from different schools around San Francisco. When we got off the plane, it was very humid. I was wearing slippers and a white T-shirt. Africa was not what it seemed like on TV. The city kind of looked like Mexico with a lot of simple buildings, tall trees, and street vendors. Most people spoke English or French. As I was walking into the building to get my visa, one security guard looked down at my feet and started laughing. He asked another guard to come look at my feet. The other guard asked me, "Why do you get your feet done? That's for gay people." I told him, "Because it feels good. You should try it someday. You'll like it too." He laughed again and left.

I wanted to slap the life out of him, but I knew if I did I would have been going to jail. So, I held back my frustration. I walked away to try and find a place to sit down and gather up my thoughts. I told myself, *"You can't get mad at people that don't know you, so chill out."* I'm a person that takes my health seriously. I love to play sports like football and baseball. I also box. I should not get judged for what I do in my free time. My manliness should not be defined by people who aren't curious about themselves.

Walking away from the guards told me a lot about myself. Being the bigger person taught me that some things, like other people's opinions about who you are, are not that important in life and you should not be blinded by social norms. While you worry about me, I'll be somewhere getting my feet done, feeling relaxed.

UNITED

DEMESHA B.

*was born in San Francisco and is seventeen years old. She
likes to play basketball with her friends and meet new people.
She wants to attend Skyline College to become a respiratory
care therapist. She also likes to travel and has
two brothers, one younger and one older.*

Being misunderstood makes people wonder whether or not they did something wrong to cause judgment. Usually, when people are misunderstood or judged, they think of stereotypes, sexism, or racism. It makes people feel out of place sometimes. When a person is judged or misunderstood, it gives them a different interpretation of life or of themselves. For example, in this story, Demesha figures she has done something wrong to have someone think of her in a certain way.

Demesha worked for Green Park Services in mid-2014 with her uncle Rob. Rob was in his forties, tall with a somewhat muscular build, black slick hair with a milk chocolate skin tone. He was known as a ladies' man by everyone and his booming laugh brightened up any room as his eyes filled with tears of joy. Demesha, a short yet athletic teenager at fourteen years old with nice brown poofy hair and beautiful brown eyes, saw herself as a talented and well-educated young woman. She knows that she is capable of doing anything she has her mind set out to if she works hard enough because nothing is impossible. She knew this because there had been times before where she had felt that there was an obstacle in her way and it pushed her to do more.

Normally she would express herself and speak up when something did not feel right to her, until one fateful day.

On a cold and cloudy morning in May, Demesha woke up and had a big argument with her parents about responsibility and how she has not been involved with her family as much. This made Demesha upset because all she did was try to talk to her family, but no matter what she said, they never listened to her, so she just left for work. When she got to work that morning, she was still upset until she saw her uncle Rob. Knowing Rob, with his full laughter and constant jokes, would cheer her up, her mood instantly changed from slightly irritated to *okay now I'm ready, let's do this*, when she heard his booming voice.

Green Park was full of bright green grass and the minty cold smell that instantly wakes up your nose. The blooming trees and plants surrounded the edges of the park. The sun hid behind the clouds as it was just beginning to brighten up the day, but the clouds were somewhat dark and glossy with a nice blue sky. The air was squeezing my nose like a tight mask. The cry of birds chirping was soothing and, to Demesha, was a sign that it was time to get the day started. "Hey how's my big head niece doing?" Rob said jokingly. Demesha laughed at the joke and gave Rob a big hug. After all the giggles between Demesha and Rob, Rob brought up that he needed a few workers to help remove some brush from a nearby road. Since there weren't as many people in for work that day, he figured he would not have everyone do as much today and let everyone go home early. Usually the brush are solid rock-like branches and stumps, cut up in sections, so it's easier to pick up in a truck. Demesha never turned down a challenge, so she volunteered. Rob called one of his main workers named Bill so he could bring up his workers to help him out for the day. Bill was about six feet tall, his bald head was as shiny as a diamond in the light. He wore a grey-ish gold tee with white streaks. Bill also had a large beer belly that sat low below his belt. Not to mention, he smelled of a large ashtray with a hint of mud.

A few moments later, Bill arrived in an immense pickup truck to take the workers to the location, and suddenly paused in his tracks when he saw Demesha about to board the truck. Bill got out of the truck and went to speak to Rob about his so-called problem. The whole time Demesha overheard the conversation and Bill kept repeating, "I need someone else, I can't take her, she is a kid and I need muscle." This made Demesha feel misunderstood and, most of all, judged. As a woman, people tend to think that we are not capable of much because of our feminine qualities, which is not true because a lot of women are capable of doing things that many men cannot do. For Bill to jump to assumptions let Demesha know that this guy was not educated enough or had not enough common sense to know not to judge a book by its cover, which is wrong.

After everything was discussed, Rob expressed to Bill that the behavior he was setting was not appropriate in a work environment and anyone is capable of anything, plus it was unnecessary. Bill suggested that the level of authority he had over Demesha allowed him to say or do anything he wanted. "She is just a kid," Bill said. "If she is just a kid then why try and act as if she is a grown up and put her in a situation like this?" Rob said, angrily.

Bill sat there thinking about how he could have reworded his comments to make them sound a little less harsh than they did, considering that he did not know Demesha was Rob's niece. Demesha sat and watched everything happen and felt that Rob defending her made her feel protected, that he was doing the right thing.

While Rob and Bill argued their points, Demesha realized she did nothing wrong.

"I am a good kid, maybe he doesn't know a good kid when he sees one. I have done this before without his help, and I know I am capable of way more than just lifting twigs and branches off the ground, but I decided to be helpful and all I got was a rude bubble gut guy," Demesha thought to herself.

As she was giving herself a wake-up call, she overheard Rob yelling at Bill.

"Get in my office now!" he yelled.

Bill slowly moved to Rob's office and started expressing his apologies to Rob.

"I am sorry, I did not know. I misjudged her, Sir, and I should have known better. I am not focused today and I'm having a bad day," Bill said.

Rob sent Bill home and thanked Demesha for keeping her composure while he handled things.

"I got your back, niecey," Rob said. "Let's go finish this job."

After that day, Demesha never doubted her abilities. She told herself every now and then that nobody knew her like she knew herself. *There may be people out there that know of me. . .* she thought, *but there are lot of people that don't really know me or my story. This is one of the many obstacles to overcome in life and I am glad I overcame this with no regrets at all with my decisions. With more and more confidence comes greater outcomes.*

MY LIFE AS SHORT, BUT MOSTLY TALL

AMBER B.

*is focusing on her education and well-being. She enjoys
quality time with her friends and family. She plans to
travel the world one day and explore different opportunities
powered by her imagination.*

As I looked up, I watched the clouds forming. I felt the wind blow upon my skin, which gave me goosebumps as we walked into the entrance of the carnival. It was loud. I heard people yelling from rides, kids laughing at clowns, and the carnival music playing. My two friends wanted to start small. We went onto carousels, laughing and eating ice cream.

I wanted to get on a large ride with a long line. I didn't see the sign that said, "You must be fifteen years old or this tall to ride this ride."

Excitedly, I got to the front when suddenly, one worker exclaims, "You can't get on the ride, you don't meet the height requirements."

"But I'm seventeen and I've been waiting in this long line and it's freezing!" I said, upset. "It's park policy."

He responded carelessly, instructing me out to the exit stairway. My disappointment and embarrassment rang out like a bell. My cheeks were burning red and my nose was pale from the freezing air. I watched my friends go on the ride. They didn't get out of line with me, they just stood there listening to me getting kicked out. I walked down the stairway, exiting the ride and I heard boys in the crowd giggling, "Ha-ha, you can't get on the ride 'cause you're a midget!"

A few days later, back at school in history class, the teacher told us to choose groups. Once the students heard 'groups,' they were speeding across the classroom racing to choose their best friends and leaving a whole gap of desks empty. I was left among the unwanted. And in that group of misfits, they gave me the smallest part. They talked out the project to themselves, but didn't include me. I tried to mention different ideas for the project but they would just giggle and turn away.

"Can I help with something at least?" I asked.

"Yeah, do your part, write down what we say and anything extra."

Another said, "I don't ever hear you talk and you don't seem like you have ideas, so we got this."

I sat there in silence, listening. My thoughts were filled with many ideas, creatively swimming in my head. After some time passed, and my group was still ignoring me, talking among themselves, I walked away.

"Can I work by myself?" I asked the teacher awkwardly. "My group doesn't listen to me." The teacher agreed since everyone already had groups and there was no one left. I walked to one corner of the class with a dimmed light and started to do the project which was to write a diary of someone living in the era of World War II. I came up with many ideas such as being a soldier on a side of a war being injured, a woman with no rights looking for a job to support her family, a child watching their parents struggle, etc. I chose being a soldier in the war and being injured in combat. I wrote about him being lonely and missing his family, how he has to walk miles and miles to get to a campground with many groups of men, and also about the way he starved and felt unsanitary.

As I finished the project, I realized I didn't *need* anyone to count on. I watched different groups struggle with misunderstandings, and I was relieved. I like being independent and using only my thoughts. I get to be credited for the work I do and not others. Later, all the students shared their projects. The teacher picked his favorite student's project. He chose *my* work! Everyone was shocked and stood silently. I was even shocked. I felt like I could hear everyone's thoughts as the room stood blank.

How did the short, quiet girl do so well or better than me?

It's not fair, I should have won.

She doesn't look that smart, how could she have won?

I laughed thinking about their thoughts, about how they think I'm just a small girl with no brain or creativity, that I am quiet with no mouth and blind with no sense. But no one knows me, they don't try to know the funny, nice side of me. People just think and assume anything they want, see, or hear.

I was happy and proud of myself for winning on my own. I felt like I could do, or be anything and anyone I wanted without a care of what people would say. Since then, I have become more independent and I keep to myself. I got used to being by myself and being successful as a whole person. It made me feel relaxed and more confident. All my creativity was a gift to me and I knew not to worry about anyone. I look outside now and see the sun shining into my eyes even when it's not there.

Now I take responsibility for myself as a foster child. I got used to being unwanted, doubted, and left out. I realized day by day how my schedule would work out. I realized no one will do my school work or homework, only my brain. I learned how to protect myself and be independent. I don't, and won't, let anyone bring me down or make me feel an inch less. I don't care about what people say about me, because they haven't walked in my shoes. I've had my battles just like anyone has. My views have changed. I have changed. Now, I just focus on me and my goals, and use those negativities as background music to me crossing the finish line to success.

ASSUMPTIONS

◆

ABRIL T.

was born in Mexico and is eighteen years old.
She moved to San Francisco when she was three. Abril
loves to read and write. When she graduates, she wants to
continue school, and make her family proud.

𝕭eing misunderstood is one of the worst feelings ever, but there is always a way to prove people wrong. My teacher saw me as a timid, shy Latina who wasn't confident enough to speak up. Graduating from elementary school happened in a blink of an eye. Now I'm in middle school. I was worried that I would be too shy to talk to my new teachers. Now having seven new teachers was challenging, because I used to have two and I would be really close them. Being the eldest child to go to middle school was basically an experiment; I was the first one to go. My parents and I had no idea how it would work out. We attended orientations to make sure we knew what would happen. They explained the basics for a "middle school life," but they never explained what my teachers would expect of me. Meeting seven new teachers was nerve-wracking. I met my teachers during lunch so I would know what to expect. After we talked and had a few lunches together we had a close bond. In my opinion, I was a great student with good grades—responsible, careful, and respectful. Knowing that made me feel good about myself.

Almost half of the year was gone, and the parent-teacher conferences were just around the corner. I wasn't worried about anything; I was confident that my teachers would have positive feedback to tell my parents. To this day, I remember the exact day and what happened. The conference was after a school dance. My ears were still buzzing from the loud music inside and I was hot and sweaty from dancing. Walking down to the classroom the temperature dropped dramatically. I had my teacher's voice in my head. "Abril is such a wonderful student, she has good grades, she turns in all her homework. There is really nothing to worry about." I was so happy, and hyper just a second ago and things were going really smooth. My teacher was recommending me to the best high school in the whole state. This is when suddenly I got a punch to the face.

"The only thing I'm worried about is. . . " When he said that my feelings started drifting down hill. ". . .Is that Abril is really timid, and shy." At this point I was lost. I had no idea what to say or do. Of course, I knew that I was quiet at certain times, but I would speak up whenever it was the right moment. He had seen me participate in his classroom many times, so what was he telling my dad? The other thing that was running through my mind was that he probably confused me with someone else. There were certain times where he would call me other students' names. When I really thought about it, it was because they were Hispanic, too. We had the same skin color but different features. I had so much stuff on my mind I had no idea what to do. Even when the conference was done, I felt confused.

When I got home, I started thinking about it more. I started feeling angry not just at my teacher, but especially toward myself. Did he actually see me participate in his classes? Or was I the one not participating as much as I thought I was? Or was it my facial expression? Do I look like the "typical quiet Latina" who doesn't talk at all? All the comments he said would probably not have affected most people like it did me. Most people would brush it off. People had come up to me and told me I had a "resting mean face." What is that supposed to mean? People don't want to talk to me because of how I look?

My eighth-grade year I finally started taking bigger steps. I joined a club and started talking to teachers and different students more. Believe it or not the teachers in the club helped me. It was one of the best things that happened to me. I started noticing that people do change; it might be in the long run but change comes with a reward. Before graduating I went to talk to my sixth grade conference teacher and thanked him for his comments that changed me.

Now I am in high school. At first my teachers again saw me as the "quiet Latina," but it didn't make me sad or angry. Being a Latina can bring many challenges in life. I learned to always show my confidence and to always speak up. My dad always gives me the best of advice: "Keep your shoulders straight and your chin up high, don't show people your weakness. Always trust who you are and not how others judge you." Now that I'm finally graduating high school, I have to face the real world. I know going into college is a huge step and it will be one huge challenge. But what I have learned throughout the years is that you can prove people wrong. Even if people see me as that "shy, Latina girl" I know who I really am. I am strong and confident. I've learned to speak up for myself. I'm not the same girl who was in the conference.

THE IMPORTANCE OF FIRST AND LAST IMPRESSIONS

TREVOR S.

*was born in San Francisco and is seventeen years old.
He loves to create. He has an older brother and has always
had animals. He is planning to attend college and
explore the world after high school.*

"It's pretty simple, pretty obvious: that people's first impressions of people are really a big mistake."

—*Vincent D'Onofrio*

We think we can tell what kind of person someone is based on first impressions, but I have learned that we can never know a stranger. I have always been this unknown stranger, even at birth. If you ask my mom, she will tell you that she was expecting a normal baby, but got a newborn the size of a three-month-old. Not only was I large at birth, I have been large my whole life, towering over my entire class by at least six inches. This hasn't always been the best; I have had a hard time making friends. I learned that I am perceived as an intimidating individual, especially now that I am taller than most adults. However, this has led to some beneficial situations.

"We think we can tell what kind of person someone is based on first impressions, but I have learned that we can never know a stranger."

In my life, I have been an avid rider of public transportation. It has helped me get where I need to go, but riding the bus has had its fair share of problems. Like the time, I waited an hour in pouring rain, looking at the bus arrival time, which was at a constant "nine more minutes." I have also encountered some incredibly horrible people, people your mom tells you to stay away from, people even a hardened criminal wouldn't get near. This story is about my experience with one of these people.

Every so often I spend the night with a group of friends. We're a band of misfits, including important characters such as my best friend Carl, a girl, and Skipper, the only other girl. One night we decided to go out at 9:30 p.m. to catch a ten o'clock movie and roam around our usual haunts afterwards. To get there fast we had to catch a train from Balboa Park Station to Powell Street Station, a route that is filled with night crawlers and outcasts. With our fairly sizable group of six, we deemed ourselves invincible.

We got on the train and up to the 20th and Church Street stop, the Upper Dolores Park stop, without a hitch. Then, this unstable man steps on. He appears to be homeless. I normally help the homeless out every chance I can get: a dollar here, a half-sandwich there; but this scruffy-looking man was not looking for help, but instead for trouble. He was shouting at everyone who came within five feet of him, and hit on every woman that was in his sight. Normally I would try to ignore it, but he was harassing my friends.

He wasn't simply saying a couple of comments here or there, he was letting loose an onslaught of obscenities and cat-calls. I would not have considered myself a threatening individual before that day; but, when I stood up, he directed all of his fury and wrath at me. Unfazed, I looked down at him. I did not care about being called names. I went through most of elementary school being bullied and harassed. But when he was insulting my friends, I felt a need to help and protect them, almost a divine duty to fight back against this man. Towering over him, I felt as if I were eight feet tall. I mustered up all my courage and simply told him: "Get off."

What happened next is not for the squeamish. He ran out the train door, pulled down his pants and squatted. I started, unfinished, "Is he . . ."

Carl asked, "Is he what?"

Skipper continued, ". . .he is. . ."

Carl asked again, "What is he doing?"

There it was, he stood up and ran. He left a lasting impression.

I've also experienced some heartfelt moments, when I could take the time and get to know someone, or something. . .

On the Saturday after my mom's birthday, I had a rough start, getting yelled at until I was up and ready. (I vowed to never stay up late again, which I soon broke.) I was gathering clothes clean enough to wear, when I looked at the clock, which read 10:20 a.m. I was breaking a tradition my mom and I have, going to one of the spring farmer's markets. I was rushing the rest of my morning routine, skipping my normal Listerine rinse just for an extra thirty seconds, so I could do the ten-block walk and buy some fresh fruit. My brother was just getting up when I was stepping out of the bathroom. I quickly called to my mom, "Does T want to go with us?"

"Yes," my mom shouted back.

"But he takes forever. He won't be ready until at least noon, and by then the market will be closed."

"We still have another hour and a half until noon, he doesn't take that long."

"But mom, all the good food will be gone by the time he is ready. I don't want the worm-infested apples or the mushy pears."

"If you stop complaining, I'll get you something special other than fruit," my mom said, hinting toward a treat. That shut me up. I waited the extra twenty minutes and we finally left at 11:00 a.m. We took the ten-block walk and immediately I noticed that it was a different type of day. At the market, there was a dog rescue company. I shot over and lit up immensely. I tried to play with a dog, but none would come up to me.

After another twenty-minute stretch my mom was done shopping at the different stalls. I pestered her to get a new animal, but to no avail. I made stupid promises that I would easily break within the first week, like "I'll clean after it," or "I'll exercise them every day."

We left. After lunch, my mom came up to me and said, "Come on, we are going to the SPCA to look at cats."

My plan worked. I knew that whatever we looked at, we would almost certainly get one. On arrival, we were greeted with a sale: "Buy one cat or kitten, get one free," as there was an excess due to the birthing season.

We wandered aimlessly among the different cats, none really sparking an interest. We got to a room with four black kittens: Hurron, the smallest boy, Tangenika, the largest boy, Victoria, the only girl, and Cob. Cob had a different name, as he was from a different litter. He was the last of the bunch and no one wanted him, so they stuck him in a litter with kittens of similar color and birthday. We asked to get a closer look to see if we had any kitty chemistry. Upon entering the room, they scattered. They hid in their mini-tents and under the chairs. I felt defeated, an elephant among ants.

They must have felt that way because they came out to play with my mom and brother, while I sat in the corner. This went on for about five minutes before I saw a tiny head pop up above my knee. Hurron, the fearless, had approached this towering giant. It made my heart melt. He was playing with me, while the others were still intimidated. My brother ended up bonding with Cob, and later called him Smokey; and I bonded with Hurron, calling him, ironically, Montagne, French for Mountain, or Monty for short.

Most importantly, first and last impressions have been a big part of my life. I have learned that you can never guess at who someone is if you have never met them, and you have to get past that first impression. What you do will leave a lasting impression. Even now I am experiencing my own words; my cat, who at first seemed like a soft purr ball, has turned into a power-hungry rascal.

THE REBOUND

—◆—

MITCHELL C.

*is a local from San Francisco. His interests tend to be
surrounded by basketball and video. Later on, in the future,
he hopes to choose a career that fits his lifestyle.*

𝕀t has been a month since I played basketball and I am finally out of my summer class. All the classwork and quizzes every week kept me busy and stressed out, but despite my complaining, I passed my City College class.

My Broadcast class was something I didn't mind waking up to. Broadcasting is one of my career interests. Every high-schooler was given the opportunity to take a City College class for free so I thought, *since I'm already in the Academy of AME (Art, Media, and Entertainment), I might as well get a head start on everyone else.* It was a battle of love and hate since I took it during summer and I wanted that free time. Regardless, it was worth my time.

As I was heading back home all I could think about was the amount of free time I had! I never felt so much freedom to have time for myself and hang out with my friends, so I decided to call one of my best friends, Stanley.

Stanley is the tallest Asian guy in my group. You may think, "Tall guy on our team equals easy win, right?" In this case, that is the complete opposite. He is probably the worst center I have ever witnessed in my entire existence. For some reason, he struggles to grab *a rebound*. That's right, a rebound! It doesn't make any sense that smaller guys, like 5'8" or shorter, would out-rebound him. It's funny that I actually tested this myself by joining the enemy team. I intentionally matched up against him and guess what? I out-rebounded my clumsy friend. What's worse is that I am 5'6" and he is six feet tall! Try and process this situation. . . because it's that bad. To make it worse, he can't post anybody, and when I say anybody, I mean *anybody*. When he posts someone, it looks like a hopping crab is walking sideways on the beach in fast forward. It's probably the most unorthodox way to post someone that I've ever witnessed! Just thinking about how he plays is just bad in general. There are other problems about his game, but I'll just leave it at that.

As Stanley diligently picked up his phone, I could already hear the sound of cars passing by with a bunch of my other friends laughing in the background.

"Hey, babe!" said Stanley, with a tone so happy that I could already tell he missed me a lot.

"Yo, I'm finally out of my class! Let's ball tomorrow!" I stated loudly.

"Dude, you have no idea how much we miss you," he said.

"You're just saying that 'cause you guys be losing the majority of the time," I said with a smirk on my face.

"Psh, what you talking about!" he said, but I could easily tell they needed me that bad. "We don't need you that bad," lying behind his breath.

"Alright, I guess I'll just play by myself tomorrow since you guys don't need me," I said sluggishly while I played with his horrible bluff.

"No, we need you!" Stanley said, regretting what he said earlier.

"That's right!" I proudly said aloud. "Just what time you want to meet up?" I asked.

"The usual," he said.

"So, I'm assuming ten o'clock tomorrow at Saint Mary's Recreation Center," I said.

"Yeah, but we don't know what gyms are open tomorrow," he said hesitantly.

"Then call the gyms, if any of them are open," I spoke quickly.

As I said that I could hear the wind in the background like no one is on the line. His presence was wavering on the line and I knew exactly what he wanted me to say.

"Fine," I said in an annoyed tone. "I'll call all the gyms, as usual."

"Yes!" he said joyfully. "I'll let you know what time I'll be at your place."

"Alright, but who else is going?" I asked.

"Kevin and. . . Cody," he said disappointedly.

Kevin is a student at Galileo with Stanley. Kevin is very outgoing, chill, and obnoxiously loud. He says anything that comes to mind without hesitation. The side that I've never seen from him is his short temper. Sometimes when I eavesdrop on their conversations, his face turns bright red, as he's very heated at that moment. If I'm correct, even though he may be chill, there is still a chance he may fist fight later depending on how pissed off he gets. I just met this dude about three months ago. Hopefully nothing goes wrong between us.

Cody, on the other hand, has been my best friend since middle school. We carry many similarities such as our type of humor, interests, and topics of conversation. Cody and I look out for each other whether it's about minor issues or if we just need someone to talk to about personal problems. It's great to have a person like him around because it benefits both of us. We help improve each other by telling the truth, even if it hurts.

"That's cool, just let me know when you here," I said.

"Alright, I'll see you tomorrow," he replied eagerly.

"Yeah, you too," I said as we simultaneously hang up.

For the first time in months, I jumped out of my bed naturally. The sensation of an alarm being useless at this moment is amazing. The grogginess of just forcing yourself out of bed, ready for round two of knocking out again is dreadful for a high school student. Haven't felt this since the starting of summer and now I'm fully rested from my thirteen-hour sleep.

After an hour of my gorgeous morning, I finally get the call that all of them are at my place. Walking downstairs, all I saw were devilish smiles, teasing me about how many games they could've won if I had been there; we were messing with each other like we always do. Anyways, we figured out that Mission Recreation Center was the only gym open that day, so we took the bus there.

We started to talk to one another and soon after, we separated our conversations to our ideal high school friends. At this point, I realized what was wrong with our group.

You see, our group isn't as chill as you think it is. Think of it as a hidden grudge toward one person, but you keep it to yourself and others who carry it also. I knew right away it was about my friend Cody. Cody disrupts our team chemistry since he is real cocky on and off the court. He declares right off the spot that the opposing team is weak and we'll easily take the 'W.' It's bad enough he has a big mouth, but doesn't show it the majority of the time. When we start losing, he starts to be a ball hog and we can't do anything about it. He also doesn't know how to project his anger in a good way. He blames us for the loss instead of re-evaluating or communicating what to do during the game. This has been going on for a couple of months now, and it's on the verge of breaking us apart. Don't get me wrong, I agree with them because it gets me mad and heated as well, but I'm scared my relationship with my best friend would break if we all told him the truth.

After the long bus ride, we finally arrived at the basketball gym. As we were walking up the stairs, I could feel the adrenaline boiling throughout my body. I couldn't contain the excitement, my hands and legs twitching uncontrollably. Seeing people playing full court got me so psyched up to play next that I diligently put my full focus on how each player plays as I walked to the bench to change into my workout clothes.

Getting dressed up has never been more exciting than it was at this moment. I aggressively changed my clothes in a flash. As I tidied up, I grabbed my basketball and went straight to the hoops on the side to warm up.

I was really cocky as I let my instincts take control at the start. Shot after shot, it was going in like I'd never taken a break from basketball. The shots I took were all swishes that were wet like water. Not only did that boost my confidence, but winning a one-on-one against Stanley was a relief. In my opinion, I thought he would beat me since I hadn't played for a month, but somehow, I was still better than him. After a couple of minutes later, our group was called in for a four versus four full-court game.

At this moment, I was scared. I hadn't played a full court game since my eighth-grade basketball team days. Adjusting from half court games to an NBA game isn't easy at all. In a half-court game, you can take it easy once in a while, but during full court games you can't. Stamina is important to the game of basketball and I knew I didn't have it in me. A guy that hasn't touched a basketball in a month, including weight gain, isn't going to have fun. I knew how screwed I was, but I just had to suck it up and play as we were about to start our match.

Since the other team won, they had the ball first. As our game progressed, my group automatically knew we weren't ready for this. As soon as I thought I was tired, I looked at my friends and they were all huffing and puffing. They weren't as determined to run up and down the court and we were horrible competing against them. I was ticked off for thinking that they were in shape this whole time. With no one willing to take the leadership role, since Kevin was too exhausted to talk, I figured I had to lead my team. I never took a breather every time my body told me to slow down, which was my downfall. The energy I had earlier was now diminished. Without my ability to shoot well, run up and down the court, and dribble, I knew I was in for a long day.

Three exhausting hours had passed and we lost all of our games, as I anticipated. Sitting down on the red wooden bench, my mouth was dry but my gray T-shirt was soaked in my sweat. Deciding whether I should play more or not, I looked at my friends and they seemed worse off than me. Cody was knocked out sideways on the bench, Kevin was blankly staring at the dusty court, and Stanley, who recently broke his ankle, was desperately in front of my face begging to drink from my water bottle. At this point, I was ready to leave the hot gym without air conditioning on.

Forcing my sore body to take off my shoes, I see Cody walking up to me with his game face on.

"Yo, we up next," he said.

"What do you mean, we up next?" I said with a concerned face hoping that it was not what I thought it was.

"We playing against those guys over there," he said as I looked behind his shoulder, seeing four new people that haven't played a game yet.

"Dude, why didn't you reject their offer, you know we're going to lose," I said as my tone changed seriously.

"Well, I asked them myself and they said yeah. It's too late now to say we're not going to play them," he said.

"You know I have bad knees, right?" I said as my anger grew.

Little side note: I have a limit for how long I could play. I have a condition called "runner's knee," that gives a disadvantage to many athletes. To summarize what it is, I will experience pain or inflammation around both of my kneecaps when I exercise in an activity that involves running, jumping, squatting, or going up stairs. Basketball has many of those activities so that is what I have to look after. As my knee cries in pain, I can no longer run or jog due to the shock absorption my knee goes through, nor jump comfortably. With those conditions in mind, once my knee can no longer withstand the pain, I'm basically the most useless player on the court.

"I know, but it's too late," he said, as he shrugged his shoulder and turned around to get warmed up for our game.

Knowing that Cody knows about my condition got me riled up. This isn't his first time doing this to me. He never tells me about the game I've been put in until the last minute. He is used to doing this to me since I hide my true emotions a lot, but he really pushed my limits this time.

Showing my true emotions, I got up off the bench with my knees struggling to bend and limping my way to the game. As ticked off as I was, this is probably going to be the worst game I'll ever play in. Before starting the game, I asked Stanley how his ankle was. As soon as I asked him, he was mad, too, since Cody didn't ask him if he wanted to play or not. Basically, Stanley was also forced to play as well. This built up more of my anger toward Cody, more than ever before.

As our game started, I was already struggling to even calmly walk to the other side. My team was exhausted, so even an easy bucket was hard enough to score. This was our worst performance yet. But I forcefully played through the pain I was dealing with. I started to exert my frustrations as I tried to make jump shots that turned into air balls.

After a couple of air balls, I turned back to defense and saw Cody glaring at me. I was ready to fight my best friend. I couldn't handle any more of his abusive ways to bring me in a game when I'm in pain. Although I wanted to swing at him, I kept it inside, but started to talk to my team in a way I've never done before. As I inbounded the ball and passed it to Kevin, I insulted and cursed at him whispering as he walked down the court, which I dearly regret.

After our loss, I lost control of myself. I started to cuss out loud toward my friends, especially Cody, blaming them for what happened, and everyone in the gym looked at me as if a fight were going to happen. Starting off I let out my anger at Cody and aggressively insulted him about how selfish he is. Expecting a huge apology in an explaining way, all he said was, "Sorry," and just walked off like nothing happened. Hearing that from him got me more infuriated about who he was. I didn't have the guts to swing at him but just walked out of the gym to cuss out my feelings.

As I came back to the building, I was still mad at Cody, bloodthirsty to punch him as I sat down on the nearest bench. Trying to cool off, Kevin walked up to me. As I looked at his face, he was also pissed off at me.

"What's up with you?" I said fast, trying to initiate him to back off.

"Brah, why you mad at me, huh?" he said furiously.

"Aren't you with Cody, selfishly thinking for yourself instead of me and Stanley?" I said, jumping out of my seat staring at him dead in the eyes.

"What you talking about, I was forced to play with him also," he said looking at me in the eye.

"Don't mess with me," I said out loud echoing the gym.

"What would I be on Cody's side for?" he said, trying to be louder than me.

This continued on as people started to look at us. Both of our fists were clenched together, full of hatred toward each other. Both of us didn't back down from our argument as more anger was put into our fists. It was like a competition of who was going to swing first. We were both so heated that both of us didn't want to back down from our side of the story. Apologies were sent back and forth but never reached a sincere apology.

I couldn't deal with him anymore as I started to walk out of the gym again just putting my anger out on random objects. I cussed out even more as I let all my anger out. Feeling calmer but still a little hotheaded, I walked back to the gym and saw Kevin still mad at me. Walking toward him, Stanley pulls me aside away from Kevin, as if he was telling me to back away from him.

"Why you pull me over here?" I said, trying to cool my voice.

"You see that painting over there," he said, pointing at the brick wall.

"What about it?" I said, turning my head back to Stanley concerned.

"Well, if you see that little spot on it, Kevin made a dent on it," he said, pointing to where the dent was which was next to Kevin.

Realizing how much of a dent it was, I said, "No way man, you're lying!"

"You want proof? I Snapchatted the whole thing!" he said, popping out his phone from his pocket.

Watching the clip gave me goosebumps. Thinking that I was mad just made me think that I was too soft to even go against Kevin. Kevin, without hesitation, started to punch the brick walls in a blink of an eye. Every punch that was thrown at the wall I could picture my face getting swollen. The worst part is that he did this for a full ten seconds! After the video ended, I had to immediately walk up to him with sincere apologies.

Walking up to him was no easy task. Straight up nervous, and throat still dry as ever, it made my apology even harder. Just by looking at him in the distance, I could tell he was still ready to swing. My anger disappeared thinking that if our argument went any further, that dent on the wall could've been me.

After ten minutes of trying to talk my way through to him, we finally concluded our argument. As relieved as I was, I could still sense the frustration behind his breath. To this day, I'm cautious to avoid getting him mad again. Moral of the story: don't project your frustrations to your whole group before you argue with the wrong friend.

THE MAN BEHIND THE MASK

CELIN C.

is a first-generation San Franciscan from a large Salvadoran family. A lifelong soccer player, he believes the game is his best therapy. His goal is to go to college, serve as a role model for his siblings, and make his family proud.

One afternoon after school when I was in seventh grade, some friends and I decided to go to Walgreens. We were just looking to buy snacks. We walked about one block from our school, James Lick Middle School, to the Walgreens in Noe Valley. As we were about to enter, one of the employees stopped us. She was a blonde woman, about five feet tall, in her twenties, and wearing round black glasses. "Can y'all make a single-file line?" she asked. It felt like she was giving us orders for a reason I didn't understand. We did what she said, but didn't know exactly why this was happening. It made us feel like the Walgreens workers felt we were going to steal something.

As I got older, I began to understand that people judge others by their appearance. It's as if I have a mask that hides who I really am. People judge others by their race, sex, and even the way they dress. The Walgreens employee was judging us because we were Latino males and also because we were young teens.

This isn't the only time I've been misunderstood or judged by my appearance. It's happened to me a lot and also to my friends. It's the sort of thing that I personally have to deal with everywhere and all the time. This makes me feel like society in general sees me and other Latino teenagers as inferior to others, but in reality, we are the same.

Even in a place like school, where I should feel safe to be myself, other students still tend to judge me. I notice that people seem to care more about my ethnicity than the person that I really am. These other students tend to identify me by the crowd I hang out with rather than the person that I am. My friends and I have many similar interests and are very alike. We are all Latinos and we enjoy the same hobbies. For example, we enjoy playing soccer and video games. On the other hand, when it comes to school, some of my friends aren't as dedicated as I am, and tend not to take it as seriously as I do. Even though I'm a good, motivated student, people see me as a slacker because of the way I look and the people I hang out with.

One time that I really felt misunderstood was when I received a high score on a test and was accused of cheating. I wasn't accused by a teacher, but by another student. This student was one who was always on top of her stuff, used to getting the highest score, and she was proud of being an outstanding student. The teacher passed out the tests one by one. When she got hers, she looked angry, sad, and shocked.

When I got my test, I celebrated with a proud "Yes!" When she noticed this, she turned to me and asked, "What grade did you get?" I showed her my test, and she looked surprised. "No way. How did you get that score? You cheated," she said angrily. My test was only ten points higher than hers, and I didn't understand what the big deal was. It offended me because I had studied hard and it paid off, and here was some girl judging me for who she thought I was.

I didn't know exactly why she reacted the way she did, but to me it felt like it was because of the way I look and the people I hang out with. Instead of her judging me and assuming I am a bad student, I would have liked her to be more appreciative and congratulate me on my efforts. I wanted her to see me as a hard-working student. My emotions dramatically changed from excitement to anger, and I wondered why she reacted the way she did, and how many other people think of me in that same way. It's frustrating that people don't know the real me.

In my lifetime, I've been judged and misunderstood many times. Even though these experiences were frustrating at the time, in the long run they have shaped me by making me a more aware person. They have shown me that life isn't easy, and that I should work hard to prove the stereotypes wrong. I want to show people who misjudge me my true identity so they will see the true man behind the mask. These experiences have also made me realize that I shouldn't judge others by what they look like on the outside, but by who they really are.

SMELLS LIKE KIDS' SPIRIT

ERWIN G.

*was born in San Francisco and is eighteen years
old. He loves to play the guitar. This summer,
he plans to make music with his band.*

From all the years that passed in school, images change around me. Life can be highways with only one direction to go and not go back. It turns out to be a maze. School, outside of campus, hallways, everywhere I go all I hear is bad words, screaming, shouting, yelling, swearing, and people don't really look where they are going. Sometimes they don't look forward. I remember some things in middle school. I woke up at seven o'clock in the morning to get ready for school. It's always quiet in the morning. It feels nice when it's quiet, but at the same time, it feels like no one knows you're there. Maybe it's just me.

Once I'm ready, I prepare my breakfast. Every morning it's cereal. Sometimes it's more sugar or less sugar. Cinnamon Toast Crunch or Honey Nut Cheerios, back and forth it's always the same. After my breakfast, I brush my teeth, wash my hair and face. The water always starts off cold in the morning when the faucet is on hot. I look at the time and see that the school bus is about to arrive in the next five minutes. I'm barely drying my face so I still have time. I get my things ready and I'm off to the outside world.

When I stepped foot inside the middle school I'm going to, I started to have a weird feeling that I can't explain. It's a feeling that someone has put a curse inside you. Maybe there's some people who have the same feeling; your mind is blank, your body starts shaking, or your body just shuts down. We can all relate to that feeling from our first day of school. There are some days that can be okay when you don't have to worry about your surroundings, but the middle school I'm going to is a place that's far from my district.

My place is near the Mission District and the middle school I'm going to is close to Visitacion Valley. My mom told me it's a good school for me 'cause it's small and has a lot of programs and community service. She also told me bad things about the place. This middle school is close to Sunnydale and she told me it's dangerous.

I am headed to my fourth period class, the Band class. Seems dark inside but there's light in the next room. The door was locked and everyone stood there waiting for the teacher to come and open the door. Once the bell rang, the teacher walked toward the door and unlocked it.

"Sorry I left you guys outside like that," said the teacher. She told us to take a seat and listen. "Good morning class! My name is Ms. Lauren and I am going to be your music teacher." She seemed pretty nice. She had a lot of energy for her age, even for a teacher. I'm not saying she's old for her age to have this much energy. She's probably around the mid-twenties. Friendly, energetic, nice, and gentle. In my experience, mostly teachers are grumpy, selfish, bitter, unfair, angry, unfriendly, and boring. At that very moment, the teacher saw me spacing out. She asked what my name was.

I responded, "Erwin."

"Okay, just keep your mind in class, okay Erwin?" said Ms. Lauren.

She repeated herself saying that we're going to divide the room into people who know how to play an instrument and people who had never played any instruments. Once we were divided, Ms. Lauren asked us what instruments we want to play. Man, I had always dreamed of playing the guitar. I told her I want to learn how to play the guitar. Half of the students want to learn how to play the guitar and the other half wants to learn how to play the piano and the drums. Once Ms. Lauren knew her strategy, we went to the next room and got placed with an instrument. The first thing to happen was everyone trying to play the instrument, and boy did we sound awful. It felt like we were abusing the sounds of the instrument. Ms. Lauren immediately told us to stop because she was going to tell us something. "I'm going to start with the guitar players because it's easy to learn, so I'm going to go and teach the guitars while you guys, the piano players, get headphones and try to learn something."

After ten minutes, I'm starting to get the hang of playing the guitar. The only thing I'm having a hard time with is my pace and my finger movements on the guitar to which strings my fingers need to place next and the frets. It'll probably take a week for me to get the chords down. Right now, the tip of my three fingers on my left hands are blistered and red from all the finger pressure I need to play on every chord. I take a little break, then play it again. Ms. Lauren warned us that we had one minute before lunch starts. I'm a little nervous to go. I don't know any people around and this school makes me feel anxious and nervous. I have no other choice but to get myself some lunch 'cause I'm starving. Once the bell rang, I walked out of class and took my time to get to the cafeteria to get lunch. This school was standing for a while. Old lockers that they haven't used since the nineties or something. The floor was all cracked up, ceilings were missing, lights were blinking. It seems that they don't have the budget to replace new lights, floors, ceilings, and lockers. I don't blame them. After taking a slow walk, I saw the cafeteria. Filled with students. Leftovers everywhere that they left the trays there, students screaming and shouting, lines were long but kept moving. I went to go to the line to get my lunch. The line wasn't so bad. It feels boring when you have no one to talk to and when your friends from elementary don't go to the same school.

I got my lunch and now I'm heading out and eat. Many students were playing basketball, soccer, and golf. I noticed that my middle school has a golf course to play on and it's really small. I remember I was interested in playing golf but it looks boring. I'm mostly eating and watching people pass by sitting alone.

SUMMER ADVENTURE CAMP FOR PATIENCE

SHELLY L.

was born in San Francisco, California and is seventeen
years old. She loves to do arts and crafts, such as crocheting.
She is the oldest of the three kids in her family.
After high school, she plans to go to a four-year college
to earn a degree in child development. She will miss her
friends and teachers after graduating high school.

Last summer, I worked in a small summer camp called Summer Adventure Camp for Kids (a.k.a. SACK) at my old church in Chinatown across from Portsmouth Square Park. It was my fourth summer working at the camp and I finally got the senior counselor (SC) position. On the day of orientation, I met the group of counselors that I would be with for the next eight weeks. Most of them were new to the camp. I sat down next to Elizabeth, who was recently a camper, but this summer was working as a volunteer. I almost didn't recognize her with her short, frizzy hair and twinkling braces.

"Hi, Shelly," she greeted me.

"Hey, Elizabeth. When did you cut your hair?" I asked.

"About a month ago. I donated my hair to a place that makes wigs for cancer patients."

"Nice!" I looked around at the other counselors sitting in front of me and greeted them. We went around and introduced ourselves to each other. There was Wilson, my other volunteer, Angela, my junior counselor (JC), and Yvonne, my co-senior counselor. Because they were new to the camp, I broke down the camp rules and expectations for counselors and gave them a tour of the camp.

First, I showed the counselors the social hall where a lot of the big camp activities are mostly held because of its large space. Then I showed them the camp's kitchen where the lunch is prepared and the back of the kitchen where there is a door that leads to the stairs to the nursery, the room our group was assigned to. The counselors liked the nursery's span of windows, which gave a nice view of the sunlight shining through the skylight illuminating the sanctuary. We went down a flight of stairs and reached the lobby which displayed many pictures of the church members since 1978.

The first day of camp came and we greeted all of the incoming campers. Our group was called the Yellow Giraffes and we were responsible for the small, adorable second- and third-graders. During the first week of camp, I took the initiative to lead most of the activities for the group and had Elizabeth lead some as well because we were experienced. As the weeks went by, I gave the new counselors more responsibilities. Every day after camp, there would be a camp counselor meeting to talk about our group of kids and any problems that came up during the day. Sometimes we would do team-building exercises to get to know one another better. The counselors eventually caught onto the system of the camp. But as they grew closer to each other, the more they began to forget their responsibilities as counselors.

One day at camp, I noticed that one of my counselors was missing.

"Has anyone seen Angela?" I asked my group of counselors.

Yvonne looked up from working on an art activity with one of the kids. While adjusting her glasses, she said, "I think she went downstairs to get water for the group."

I was a little suspicious because she had been gone for a while. Then she entered the nursery with a pitcher and cups. I made eye contact with her and she immediately looked away. Right there and then I knew something was up. Later at lunch, someone tapped me on the shoulder. I turned to face furrowed brows and glaring eyes that belonged to my older cousin, Jo, who was an SC of blue group, the oldest age group.

"Can you put a leash on your counselor?" Jo asked furiously.

I was confused. "What do you mean?"

"Angela has been coming to my group recently and distracting my kids and counselors. Christian and Andy are especially distracted because they have a crush on her. I tell her to leave but she keeps coming back."

Suspicion confirmed. Angela left our group to hang out with another group. I had to talk to her. After our usual end-of-the-day counselor meeting, I told Angela to meet me in the nursery for a talk. When she arrived, she slowly opened the door and cautiously walked in. She grabbed a chair leaning against the wall and sat across the table from me. There was a short silence.

"Do you know why I called you up here?" I asked.

She shook her head. "Uhh. . . I'm not sure."

"You told Yvonne that you were grabbing water for the group but another counselor told me that you were hanging around blue group at the time. Neither one of us gave you permission to do that, so why did you do it?"

"I saw that they were doing a fun activity so I wanted to join them."

"As a counselor, you are supposed to stay with your group. You can't wander off to other groups without telling your senior counselors. Angela, you are a junior counselor. I've noticed that this isn't the first time you've acted inappropriately and this is also not the first complaint I've heard from another counselor. I have talked to the director already and we agreed that if you don't get your act together soon, I could demote you to a volunteer. Do you understand?" I saw her eyes widen when she heard "demote."

Almost immediately, Angela replied, "Yes, I totally understand. I'll make sure to do a better job as a junior counselor."

I dismissed her to finish cleaning the church sanctuary.

A few days later, I started to notice some counselors giving me weird looks. Whenever I passed by, they had raised brows and their lips were tightly closed with the red margins of the lips becoming narrower, and the lips becoming thinner. Some counselors would turn and whisper to each other or purposely bump into me. It made me feel uneasy. When I went down to the kitchen to prepare for lunch for the camp, the doors were closed. I lifted my hand to knock on the door when I heard my name on the other side.

"Why the heck is Shelly a senior counselor?" I heard one voice ask. I froze.

Then another voice said in reply, "I know, right. She abuses her authority and thinks that she can do whatever she wants."

The first voice spoke again. "Have you noticed how she treats Yvonne? Yvonne is a senior counselor too, but Shelly treats her like a junior counselor."

"Yeah, I've noticed that too. She's a horrible counselor. I'm glad I'm not in her group."

I didn't know what to do. I was angry and wanted to yell at them but I hesitated to open the door. Instead, I turned around and went to the bathroom. I walked into one of the stalls, shut the stall door, and sat on the toilet seat. I noticed that I was breathing heavily so I tried to calm myself. I was so shocked and overwhelmed that it took a while for me to calm down.

I could see where some of their criticism may have come from. I may have looked bossy when telling my counselors what to do, but I was just doing my best to help them become better counselors. And I could understand if Yvonne felt less than a senior counselor because I took on most of the responsibilities instead of sharing them with her. I wondered if I wasn't ready to be a senior counselor if this was how other counselors viewed me. Maybe I should have been more thoughtful and checked in more on my counselors. I should have asked them for feedback on my performance as their senior counselor. That way I would have known what I needed to do more work on.

However, this doesn't justify what those two counselors said about me back there. My anger then took over. *How could they talk like that behind my back?* I thought to myself. *If they had a problem with me, they should have confronted me.*

I looked at the time on my phone and noticed that I was late for lunch duty. Still angry, I stormed out of the bathroom and returned to the kitchen. The two counselors that were gossiping were starting to prepare for lunch. They saw me walk in and gave me the look that everyone else had been giving me all week. I didn't bother worrying about it and just did what I needed to do to get lunch ready. I was so done with the immaturity of the counselors at camp and just wanted to get the summer over with.

About a month later, after camp ended, I told Jo about what happened in the kitchen back home. She seemed very nonchalant after my rant to her. It didn't seem like her to act so calmly after hearing me rant. She would usually become angry too. So, I asked, "Is something wrong?"

"Oh, it's nothing." She hesitated and then sighed. "I would be a horrible person to keep this from you, but you should know that Yvonne confronted me a few days before camp ended. She told me that she felt like she didn't fit in and thought she was doing a bad job as a counselor after seeing how hard you were working."

So, it was true. Yvonne didn't feel like a senior counselor. I felt guilty for not talking to her earlier about this.

Jo continued to say, "Even though camp ended already, I think you guys should talk." She was right. Yvonne was one of the better counselors that actually took the camp seriously. I couldn't just leave her with bad thoughts about herself.

Fortunately, a few other counselors wanted to hang out one last time before school started. They organized the hangout to be at Japantown and I found out that Yvonne was invited. *This is the chance for us to talk out our unsettled problems from camp,* I thought to myself.

While the rest of the group went to the arcade, Yvonne and I sat outside. It was awkward at first, but I gathered up the courage to start the conversation.

I noticed earlier that she cut her long locks and now her hair just reached her shoulders. "I like your hair. It looks good on you."

She laughed. "I like it too. Short hair is so much easier to take care of compared to my long hair."

"I totally get it. Having long hair is a struggle." There was a pause. Then I said, "I'm really sorry for not treating you like a senior counselor."

She was taken aback by the blunt comment.

"I should have been more considerate of your position. I guess since I have worked at the camp for so long, I'm used to taking on a lot of the responsibilities and I didn't want you guys to be overwhelmed by the workload of this camp."

Yvonne said, "To be honest, I didn't really think much of it until Angela brought it up."

I was confused at first. *How did Angela get tangled up in all this?*

Yvonne continued. "Angela and I would talk a lot after camp just about what any girl would talk about. There was a day when she came to me after a meeting between you and her and she told me that you threatened to demote her to a volunteer. I was surprised when I heard that because in my opinion I thought that Angela was doing a great job as a junior counselor. Angela went on to say that I should stand up for myself and to tell you to stop treating me like a junior counselor. It was my first time hearing that, but when I told myself that I started to agree. That was when I first started to despise working with you."

After hearing Yvonne's side of the situation, I was speechless. It was Angela who started the rumors and gossip about me just because I threatened her position. I was upset with Angela, but I felt sympathy for Yvonne.

"I think I understand how you may have felt. I was in your position once when I first started working at the camp. I didn't do a lot my first summer working and received criticism from other counselors. I'm really sorry for making you feel that way most of the summer. I should have discussed with you first about Angela before bringing it up to the director."

"It's alright. I forgive you. It must have taken a lot of courage to talk to me about this. And, honestly, I didn't really like Angela. She was bad news to begin with. She gossiped and talked trash about everyone to everyone."

"Yeah. Thanks to her, she made my summer at camp miserable."

Knowing that Angela was the source of the rumors, I wasn't sorry for threatening her position. She had experience working at other summer camps, so if she had a problem with me, she should have approached this problem with a professional manner instead of spreading rumors. Just thinking about what happened made my blood boil.

The summer has passed now and I was not going to stress over what happened anymore. Although my experience at camp was dreadful, it was an experience that I could grow from. Angela was a toxic person and what she and some of the other counselors did was unacceptable. I realized that by stressing over that one situation in the summer I ruined my own experience at camp. In life, I am going to bump into a lot of Angelas and it will be challenging. But I'm not going to let them get ahold of me and drag me down. I have to face them head-on and approach these situations with an open mind and patience.

MY LIFE COMPLETELY CHANGED

SOFIA G.

is a senior at Burton. Next year, she will be going to Skyline College. She likes to sleep a lot and take walks in places like Golden Gate Park. She is a proud Latina.

I was four years old in 2004. This was the year that my life completely changed. I had the best family ever; it was my dad, my mom, and I. We were all happy. We would always go camping to the river to swim and it didn't matter if it was a school night or that they had to go to work the next day. My dad and I had a very strong bond, we were inseparable. It was something that felt like it was going to last forever, but every day was not rainbows and flowers. My father was an alcoholic. He would get drunk whenever he got the chance. He would waste all of our money and we never had much by the end of the week. When he was drunk, he would mistreat my mom, abuse her verbally, mentally, and physically. The worst part was witnessing him being someone who isn't himself. My dad on weekdays usually never drank, which were the days my mom could take a break from him being drunk. He would act like nothing ever happened, which would hurt my mom and she would become more frustrated. My mom was a very strong person at that moment. I've never seen anyone go through so much and still be there and not just for herself, but also for her daughter. She always thought of calling the police or leaving my dad, but she always stopped herself because she didn't want to hurt me.

The day my dad left was really emotional. I mean, obviously. I felt like everything was crumbling down upon me. I didn't know what to do or how to stop him from leaving. When he was packing the last of his luggage, I was packing my stuff as well. As I was crying I would pack my belongings in his luggage and as he was taking them out I would put more stuff inside of it. When he started to grab all his things and leave, I felt my tiny little heart just crumble into pieces. Just seeing him leave was really unbelievable. I told him to not leave me, that I wanted to go with him, and that my mom will come with us too, but he never responded back to me. It frustrated me how he could just leave his family like that. The only thing I saw in his eyes was how sorry he was and how he didn't want to go, but he had to. I wanted him to say something to me, to explain to me why he was really leaving. I wanted him to help me understand why he was doing that to us, but he didn't say anything. He finally left and I wondered to myself if he was ever going to come back. Every time somebody rang the doorbell I was hoping it was my dad. Sometimes I would just imagine him coming back and hugging me. I imagined what our lives would be like if he didn't leave.

As time passed, life was difficult for my mom. She took on more financial responsibilities because my dad was the person who took care of that. My mom started looking for a babysitter; she couldn't take care of me because she had to work. It was a really drastic change for me. Once she found a babysitter, she started working immediately. I was never apart from my mom, so I was scared of seeing someone else every day that wasn't her. This was just when my dad had left, and I remember asking my mom when she dropped me off at my babysitter's house, "You're not going to leave me, too, right?" When I told her that, it felt like I hurt her by still thinking about what happened. I don't remember the feeling after my dad left nor do I remember how my mom was acting and how she held it all together. All I remember is how we both stuck together and knew we had each other. Now my mom tells me that it was a good thing that I was born, because if my dad had left she would have never had me and she would be all alone. And now I am her companion for life.

THE
SILVER LINING

━◆━

HOI C.

*was born in a small city in China widely known as Hong
Kong. He has aspirations of putting 100 percent into his
work effort no matter what assignment is in his way. Despite
his work ethic in school, he learns that when showing up as
an individual, many aspects in life will not remain the same.*

𝕯ear Burton (past self),

How are you doing past self? I just wanted to give you a heads up that things won't always go your way and this is just a little word of advice. Somewhere out there is a saying known as "the silver lining." The saying goes on talking about no matter how gloomy a situation may be, there is always a glimmer of light, or as others would call it, hope.

My story starts in a middle school in San Francisco known as A. P. Giannini Middle School. All was going well in the year of 2013; I was in eighth grade with the goal of achieving promising grades to put myself in a successful high school career. I was always a high achiever at school, tending to use my time after school accomplishing my homework with friends knowing that at home there were many distractions. I was disgusted by the people around me because everyone only cared about their grades, and the thing we all call friends with benefits came into effect. As this prominent image of not having real friends around me lasted for the last three years of middle school, attending school and trying to find joy in life had gotten more challenging. As I grew older with experiences of emotional sadness and maturity, I began to understand that the meaning of life deals with a broader subject than just existing and having fun in the world. As normal as this was for someone my age, I noticed that most of my days were too repetitive with homework, study, and sleep. And cognizant of this, I knew I had to balance some aspects of fun and motivation to find meaningful connections in my life.

I always had affection toward my family members. They had a tradition of showing their love for me in the form of providing me happiness. While in the midst of middle school, a formidable day entered my life that would change the course of my future forever. The day started off in a mood of a dark gloom. Feeling bitterness and disappointed as a confused teen, I went on with my day going to school getting my free education; staying with the path of successful individuals. Although it was a normal day, long and tiring, I had noticed something out of the ordinary. My mother had not yet returned home at a late hour. Although she eventually came home, something was off. My mother in the past had a routine of making sure I was on track of finishing my work, but her return today was radically different. She did not question me at all and instead remained quiet. At the dinner table, my mother and I sat together silently. And then there it was, the reason behind her silence and sorrow all spelled out. "I have breast cancer." The words filled my emotions with horror and panic. I sat there at the dinner table frozen with the fear of losing my mother. My hands were ceased with no intent of picking up my utensils. And so, the dark gloomy day went on for weeks, and weeks turned into years, until middle school had transitioned into high school.

Going to school, I was overwhelmed with the fear of losing my mother at any given moment. I decided to diverge myself from these thoughts by staying happy with my friends attempting to feel the sentiment of "truly living." My sorrow and sadness had turned into a meteor-heavy depression. Despite my mental state, I didn't let it ruin my decisions. I had felt an immense sympathy for my mother and my usage of free time for electronics and friends had now transformed into spending quality time with her. I wanted to show her that I loved her, cared for her, and most importantly that the time she spent with me was precious and nothing can come close to its value. My mother and I exercised every morning together, cooked dinner, did dishes, and even watched television together. The time I was spending with my mother was when I truly experienced authentic happiness. Using my friends as a source of happiness was not the solution to my sadness, but it created a buffer between my mother and me. At the same time, all she had hoped for was to feel the sentiment of love, care, and that her very existence in the world was meaningful and fulfilling. Despite my efforts of being an empathizing son, my mother passed away one day during high school. The period in retrospect lasted about five years. As human beings, there is always room for growth through trial and error. But here and there, moments of regret are ubiquitous. My mother had raised me well in my adolescent years and I had shown her through my empathy and sincerity in the last moments I spent with her. There are going to be ups and downs in life no matter what type of person you are. Not everything in your path will go your way, some say the things we encounter are predetermined. Well, Burton, that is a whole other story. In my experience, time was an extremely valuable resource and it was enough for her to have given me the gift of wisdom and unconditional love.

Sincerely,
Burton (Spring 2017)

MY MONSTER

———◆———

DANICA ROSE G.

was born in San Francisco and is almost eighteen years old.
She loves to take Polaroid pictures. After high school, Danica
plans to go to L.A. and continue her studies, particularly
social justice. Danica plans to go into pediatric nursing.

Starting my day like every other day, waking up in my room, getting ready for school, I didn't expect anything to happen that would change my life forever.

I'm just an eighteen-year-old girl, a senior at Phillip and Sala Burton High School, and I'm going to tell you a story about what happened to me. I believe it will be a good lesson to learn from a high schooler.

I was just a carefree student, minding my own business, continuing my day as usual. The thing to know about me is that I tend to care too much about my loved ones, to the point where I put them first, before myself. For example, no matter what time of day or where, even when I have school the next day or homework to prioritize, I spend time with them when they need me, Seems bad right? I should be doing the opposite. But what can I say, I love seeing people around me happy.

Anyway, back to my story. I was a junior in high school. It was the best year of my life. Everything was going smoothly, and I was friends with everyone in my own low-key way. I had had this one friend for a long time, and this had been a special person to me throughout my time in high school. Out of all my friends, this one was the one that broke me the most. That's when I realized I had made a mistake letting someone in.

We were best friends. We would act silly and see each other 24/7. We had goals for each other, cared for each other, never had arguments, etc. We were basically seen as a "couple," but we knew it was nothing like that—we just had a very close bond. Everything was better than fine, it was great. One time, we went to the city and decided to just explore. We shared so much laughter, going to places we'd never been. There was never a single awkward silence.

Then a few months passed, heading toward fall, closing in on Halloween. I noticed how odd my friend was being—very distant, even MIA. I didn't really pay attention since we both had our own social lives, plus we were worrying about colleges and trying to get the most out of junior year. So, I just moved on with my life and stayed neutral, minding my own business. I knew nothing was wrong between us. We had the type of relationship where even when we didn't see each other for a while, nothing would change.

But then a few days turned into weeks and I started wondering what was up. I hit up my friend to see if everything was okay. Everything seemed fine when we talked, the same as it had been a few months before. So, I was oblivious, carrying on my day until one night, a few days before Halloween, I got a text from my friend saying, "I have to confess something to you." In my head, I was trying to dial it down. Had I done anything wrong? If so—what? I tracked down every single moment that would possibly trigger a text like that. Was it the time I hung out with a different friend and cancelled our plans? Could that have caused the problem? Then, there it was. Our friendship had ended. Everything turned around.

At that moment, I knew I had lost my friend, and a part of my heart left too. Finding out that it was all just a lie. The past months had been full of lies: "Nothing is wrong." "I'm always here for you." "I care about you." I looked like an idiot caring so much about someone who would hurt me in the end.

Now let me tell you how I coped with all of this happening. I was a wreck. My world was literally crumbling down. I gave my all to this friend and all I got back was a broken heart. I stopped going to school for about a week, and just isolated myself from everyone. I wanted to be alone and just wanted to cry, cry as much as I could. As if crying would take the pain away. My parents and friends gave me great advice and supportive gestures throughout the process. But at that time, I didn't want to listen because they didn't know what I was going through, they didn't know what it felt like to lose someone you gave everything to.

I was being way emotional as usual.

A few days passed and then, one morning, I realized that it was time for me to move on. It just hit me how being miserable wouldn't bring me anywhere in life, and you know what they say, "Your enemies hate to see you thrive." So that's what I did, I got back on my feet little by little, every day and just carried on. I had to build myself up and surround myself in positivity. Days passed, and I was a completely different person than I had been at the start. I became very cautious.

I eventually went back to school. I knew that I was going to see my ex-friend, but I didn't let it bother me anymore. It was as if I was just seeing a stranger I had made memories with. No matter how much it hurt, even just passing each other in the hallway, I knew my friend had changed me. This taught me how to put myself first, not be too open, be neutral, and to just build a wall around my heart to prevent myself getting hurt again. A bad friendship had turned me into a stronger person.

I'd say that I'm grateful that this happened sooner than later for me. Catching this conflict has prevented me from reaching this stage again. I understand that people come and go in your life, but how I involved myself with this person backfired for me. I just want my reader to know that no matter how awful something seems, it can change you for the better.

NOT AGAIN. . .

EMILY C.

is a San Francisco native. She is passionate about mathematics,
eager to attend UCLA after high school, and plans to pursue a
career in healthcare. In her spare time, Emily enjoys playing
volleyball and softball, and watching the TV show Friends.

"Your grades are slipping—you need to quit!" stated Mom. At that moment, I started to wonder if I wanted to change what I wanted to do based on what my mom believed was the best fit for me.

This was the second time this week she lectured me about how my involvement in a sport negatively impacted my grades. All I heard were noises and sounds surrounding me, telling me to listen and follow. She even tried to convince me to participate in an activity that wouldn't be as time-consuming as volleyball. I didn't agree with her. Sports are the one thing that helps me, they are my stress-reliever from school.

"You come home every day tired, with no energy to do any homework, and you end up falling behind in your classes, causing your grades to slip," said Mom.

"Me being in a sport is not the problem. I just need to learn how to better manage my time."

"Why don't you do something that is less time-consuming? Maybe developing a desire for a hobby, like ballet class? Try to do something that wouldn't require your full commitment. My friend's daughter is in a ballet class that is only a few times a week, not every day, and she knows how to keep her education together with no problem. Also, it is something that is more of a graceful fit for a girl."

I felt misunderstood.

"You always tell me to keep myself busy by finding something I like to do, but once I find something that I'm passionate about, you start complaining about how it's too boyish. I want to do something that makes me feel comfortable, and not be forced into doing something that I don't want to do."

There she went again with suggesting what I should do that would be more feminine. I believe that being female does not mean I need to follow certain expectations. Hearing my mom's opinion, I understand that she wants me to be more "girly," but I disagree that I should change just to fit her standards. Having many disagreements with my mom has given me time to think about what I want to do. Most times, I decide to do what makes me feel comfortable. I take her opinions into consideration, but I do things differently, my own way.

The day after the lecture, I went to practice and really started to think about the conversation I had with my mom. I stood in one place, listening to my teammates yelling for the ball. Looking around the court, I asked myself if this is what I am really passionate about. My involvement in sports is the one thing I can count on to be there when I'm in a stressful situation, when I need a break from my education. Just the feeling of being able to spring in the air and spike a ball helps lighten the weight on my shoulders. It gives me the energy to go back to what I was struggling with, this time with more motivation to get things done. That day, I realized that being a student athlete is something I am proud of and something I want to continue. I am my own person, and I know that I should do what makes me happy, and not what others want me to do.

When she was my age, my mom was influenced by her friends about how females are supposed to appear and act—such as wearing dresses, make-up, and being small. Witnessing her friends' ability to afford nice clothes made my mom feel inferior, because she couldn't. She followed in their footsteps, and got so used to the idea of being girly that she began to believe that all girls should be this way. She didn't have the opportunity to get far in her education, but hearing about the amount of people who have succeeded with an education has led her to believe that getting a quality education is one of the most important things in life. This is why she nags me about my grades and how I need to use more of my time to focus on my studies instead of extracurricular activities. She is not telling me to quit having extracurriculars; she wants me to find something that would be less time-consuming.

The more times my mom suggests new things for me to do, the more it is made clear to me that only sports bring me happiness. Being in sports has shaped who I am today, an independent individual.

THE PIRATE SHIP

ANTHONY A.

*was born and raised in San Francisco, California with his
two sisters, mom, dad, and his dog. He likes to listen to
rap while skateboarding. He plans to go to a community
college and hopes to transfer out to a better college.*

It is nighttime in the summer of 2012 and I have finished playing video games on my Xbox 360 and out of nowhere I get a phone call from one of my good friends, Daniel, whom I go to school with. I let my phone ring for five seconds and wonder to myself, *why is he calling me right now?* I pick up the phone and answer anxiously, "Hello?"

"Hey dude, want to come to Great America with me and Chris? We already bought our tickets earlier and they were cheap. Just letting you know, so give me a heads up if you want to come!" Daniel replies.

"Alright, I'm going to ask if I can go. I'll let you know." After that conversation, I hang up the phone and get excited because I was invited to go to Great America. As excited as I am, I rush to my parents' room, I open the door and ask my mom, "Can I go to Great America tomorrow with my friends? The tickets are cheap right now my friend said!" Usually my mom *never* agrees to let me out because she wants me to stay safe.

"How much is it?" she says. I am surprised at the fact that she said that, because usually my mom says no when I ask to go out with my friends. After that, I go on my laptop and my Mom helps me purchase the ticket, and then I go to bed. I wake up the next morning to a text message from Daniel that said, "Once you're done getting ready

"I look around at everyone and they are screaming for joy, while I am screaming for my life!"

let me know and you could meet at my house. Chris is coming over, too." After reading that, I went to take a shower, brush my teeth, and get dressed. Once I am done getting ready I text Daniel saying, "I just got done getting ready. My dad is going to drop me off at your house. See you soon!" I go to my parents' room and ask my Dad if I could get a ride to Daniel's house, and he says, "Yes, meet me in the car!"

I go to my room and grab my backpack with things that would be useful, such as a towel to dry off, extra clothes if the clothes that I am wearing get wet, chocolate chip granola bars for something to snack on, and a water bottle to keep myself hydrated. As I grab my stuff, I tell my mom that I am leaving and leave the house to get inside the car.

Now that I am on my way to Daniel's house, I look out the window and stare outside of the car. Typical of San Francisco weather, the sun is out while the wind is blowing. It is cloudy and foggy in one area, but if you drive or move to another area it will be sunny and have clear skies. There are cars honking at each other, always people on the sidewalk walking, and the smell of food in the air—such as tacos, burritos, noodles, pizza, and chicken.

The sidewalk is always full of buildings, like houses, fish markets, Walgreens, coffee shops, bus stops, and corner stores. Even though Daniel and I both live in the Mission District, it is a big place. The difference is that we are fifteen minutes apart. Finally reaching my destination, I see Daniel and Chris in a van waiting for me. I tell my dad thank you for the ride, and that I will see him later, as I open the door to exit the car. I shut the door then run toward the van. I am so excited at this point, because it will be my first time doing something fun in a long time. I open one of the doors and I see both Daniel and Chris sitting next to each other laughing and smiling as they turn their heads to look at me. I greet Daniel and Chris with a handshake and say hello to Daniel's mom and aunt who will be watching us at Great America.

Finally, on our way to Great America, we are driving on the freeway for a while, so Daniel, Chris, and I talk about video games, since that is a common interest we all have. We are on our phones. I listen to music and watch a lot of YouTube videos. Chris plays games on his phone, and Daniel plays games as well. Getting off the freeway, we start to drive onto the Bay Bridge. I look out the window and start to admire the environment, because of how beautiful everything looks. The water has the sun's reflection shining on it, and the sky is so clear. There are no clouds. Then I accidently fall asleep during the ride. I wake up and we are at Great America. That fast! I feel like we flew here!

Once we get to the parking lot, Daniel, Chris, and I get into a line to get into the park. We get our tickets, and run straight to one of the rides that is supposed to be "scary." Luckily there isn't a line there, so we get places right away in the ride. This is my first time riding a rollercoaster, so I don't know what to expect. This rollercoaster has us standing and strapped in tight. Once everyone is ready, the workers start the ride. The ride starts off at a normal speed then we go up. . . really, really, slowly. Now, I'm getting worried. Halfway up and not at the top yet, I look down and think to myself, *I am really high.* After that a *big* drop happens and the ride starts to turn left and then right at a high speed. I hear everyone on the ride screaming and I hear myself screaming as well.

We go to our last ride. Being on the Pirate Ship feels exciting. I first feel an adrenaline rush through my body, just like any other rollercoaster, until I realize that my harness iss loose. At this moment, I feel like screaming for help, but that won't work. We are all the way up in the sky hanging upside down. Instantly that adrenaline rush goes away, as the Pirate Ship moves in a downward motion toward the ground. It goes straight to my stomach, giving me the feeling of butterflies flying around. I catch myself looking straight down at the ground. My eyes turn big. I look around at everyone and they are screaming for joy, while I am screaming for my life! In my head, all I could think to myself is that everything will be okay. The ride goes on for another two minutes of swinging back and forward and doing full loops. I have to tough it out and stay on the ride until it is done, because I can't do anything about it. As the ride starts to slow down, I start to calm down. After all those loops that the Pirate Ship did, now I feel sick. Getting off the ride I run to the nearest seat to sit down. I find a nice bench to sit on and as I sit, I see Daniel and Chris walking toward me laughing because of what happened. I start to laugh as well.

"My harness was a little loose when we were on that ride, and when we were high up in the air I kept feeling butterflies in my stomach," I explain to them.

"I know. During the ride, I was looking at you and felt bad. That's how roller coasters feel the first time. You'll get used to it once you start to ride them more." Chris tries giving me advice.

"Dude, I'm not going to lie. It was scary for me watching you go through that, but it was also pretty funny," Daniel says and we all laugh about it.

REWRITING THE STORY: THE FAMILY LIFE

(based on characters in the 'Fast and Furious' movie series)

❖

DEREK H.

was born in San Francisco, California, in 1999. He lives in the Bayview with his parents and grandparents. Derek's sister goes to UC Davis. Derek's dream is to be an interior designer.

𝔇ear Brian,

Today you are happily married with seven kids and thinking about leaving Dom's street racing crew. Six years ago, Brian, you made the difficult decision to quit the police force and become a street racer.

Brian, you had just met Mia when you were assigned as an undercover agent to bust her brother Dom. You were in Honolulu watching Dom's crew follow big rigs to steal supplies from the trailer. Brian, you were driving a 1995 Supra and Dom was driving a 1969 Charger R/T. Dom's brother jumped from the car to the big rig and tried to stop the driver. The truck driver pulled a gun. Dom's brother didn't get shot, but you watched as he was injured badly when he was stuck in the door. You came to him and got him off the truck as fast as you could and got him to the ground and then you called the cops for help and blew your cover in front of your family.

Dom found out that you were a cop. "I can't believe that you betrayed us and you're a cop," Dom screamed at Brian. "He was mad because he trusted you, Brian."

When they left, you were regretting that you had been trying to bust them because you were falling in love with Mia. Later, you started to join 'the family' and started street racing with Dom. You explained that you should have come clean with Dom and his whole family and that you were sorry. Brian, you felt like a brother to Dom because he was so close to Mia; he wanted to be with his kids and with Mia all the time and be a part of Dom's crew, so he can street race and help them out all the time.

Brian, some people think you were wrong for blowing the undercover case. But for me, I agree with what you did. I understand that you wanted to be with Mia and your kid and to be with the street racing family and be a part of Dom's family. Most of all, you were right to blow your cover because you saved Dom's brother's life.

After you blew your cover, you decided to quit the police force. Some people think it was a good decision and some people think it's bad. It was wrong to quit the police force because it was your job to stop criminals and illegal street racing. On the other hand, it was a good idea to quit your job because you chose to be with your family. You chose love over your duty as an officer. You were falling in love with Mia and you were already thinking about your future together with Mia, getting married and having children. You were growing close with Dom, and wanted to be a street racer with Dom's crew. Your duty as a police officer was important, but not as important as having a family with Mia and meeting others in the family, including Dom's wife, Letty. You thought Dom's crimes weren't serious and didn't hurt anyone.

Fast forward seven years. Brian, you left street racing to be with Mia, who is now your wife, and mother of your children. Your kids' names are Ashlund Jade, Hailey, Sienna, Jack, Kylie, Sofia, and Kaylie. The two set of twins are Hailey and Sienna, and Kylie and Sofia.

Brian and Mia went to Aulani with their kids and have a nice vacation and travel with Dom's crew to street race everywhere they go. They went to a nice resort in Aulani for Hailey's and Sienna's birthday, celebrating it there with the whole family. Ashlund Jade was only three years old and helping her parents out by watching her little sisters and making sure they don't do anything bad. Two hours later everyone started to come for the party and all the kids hang out together and play in the kids' pool and Ashlund and her other cousins Meadow and Chrissy also help out watching the little ones. Madison is Brian's sister and she hasn't seen Brian for ten years so they also had a reunion party just to catch up and enjoy being together and reunited.

Two months later Brian decided to buy a 2018 Chevy Traverse premier package for Mia and the kids to enjoy and Brian bought himself a 2018 Nissan GTR Nismo package. Brian, you started a street race war right by the beach to have some fun and earn some money while Mia took the kids to the mall to shop around and watch a movie. Meadow went with her friends to a concert until her friend was kidnapped. When she called you, you came rushing down the road to help his niece Meadow because she was upset. Brian, you didn't give up looking for her friend. Three hours later, Mia took the kids to the pet store and ending up buying a little puppy. It's a Pomeranian and a Chihuahua mix.

Melissa is the sister of Meadow; they haven't seen each other for three years, so they decided to have a party with the whole family and Melissa invited her best friends, Isabella and Emily, to come over to their house to have fun and enjoy the party.

Two months later, they traveled to Miami for a nice family trip with Dom's crew. Mia and Brian didn't go because they wanted a whole two weeks to themselves without the kids at home.

Maddie is a country singer who met Dom's crew at the beach performing. She was only ten years old and decided to join Dom's crew to have more fun. Sienna and Ashley are sisters in Dom's street racing family. Sienna told Madison that she is pregnant with a baby girl and that was raped by her boyfriend, and that he dumped her because he lost interest in her. Sienna was bullied by four other guys until Ashley found her a new boyfriend, Jake. Sienna fell deeply in love with him because he was honest and caring. They had a lot in common. They went out to dinners and movies. After two months, Jake took Sienna to the beach for a picnic. He took out a ring and proposed to her.

"Yes," Sienna said. "You'll be the best father for my baby girl."

Mia met her friend, Natalie, at the mall alone and she ran into Kaylie, her little niece, with Mia's sister-in-law. Dom decided to plan a race war out in Hollywood and they met Jessa and Jill there and invited them to join their families. Two hours later, Brian, you got a phone call from Mia saying she was at the hospital with her friend Natalie because she was feeling so sick.

"Come quickly," she told you. But when you showed up at the hospital Mia started to cry because her friend Natalie passed away, and they haven't seen each other for ten years. Natalie had died from a severe illness. Mia cried even more.

Brian, you called Dom to rush over to meet in the parking lot of the hospital because Mia's best friend just passed away and he needed Dom's help. One hour later Dom showed up and they came upon Shaw and his gang of street racing rivals. Shaw told you and Dom and that they needed to leave town or else he would hurt their families.

Meadow and the rest of the family went to the hospital and started to plan what to do. Brian, you told Mia and the rest of the family to take a plane to Hawaii and stay in Aulani because you didn't want them to get harmed. Five hours later, you and Dom decided to call up all the street racing crew and Dom's crew to join in the fight to take down Shaw and his crew before he destroyed the rest of the city of Los Angeles. Hobbs came along and took you and Dom's side to help you take down the bad guys. Brian, you called Gisele and Han to come help them out to take down the bad guys and help out with the street racing business.

Mia finally landed in Aulani, Hawaii with the family to enjoy their time and have fun. Brian, you called Mia to check in on the family and to see how they are doing. You told Mia there is a street war going on, and that Dom and Han and Gisele are with them to help. Brian, you told Mia if she was home, Shaw might come after the family and the kids. Five hours later, Shaw's crew showed up and questioned you, Brian, about where your family was. You didn't answer. Dom stepped up and pointed a gun at Shaw and told him to back off and that he doesn't belong in this town, and that he belonged in prison.

Brian, after all that happened, you were thinking about quitting street racing, because you didn't want to harm your kids and wanted to have a positive influence on them. Mia didn't agree.

"Since you are part of Dom's family, you really can't quit street racing," she said. I agree with Mia that it isn't a good idea to quit racing because you're close to the street racing family. They'll be disappointed if you give up street racing.

"Brian, if you quit, your kids will be upset with you," Dom told you. "They want you to be strong and not a quitter."

Brian, you finally decided not to quit street racing, mainly because you want Mia to be happy. You did promise to watch out for your kids and spend more time with them, and keep them away from street racing.

You decided to throw a big giant neighborhood party for your friends and family to enjoy, and listen to country music back in Hollywood where they live. Two hours later, Brian, you invited your long lost friend to the party and have another reunion while Dom barbecued food for the friends and families.

Sincerely, your buddy,
Derek

A CURSE AND
A BLESSING?

CARMEN C.

*was born in San Francisco and is seventeen years old.
She loves figure skating and badminton and watching
movies. Her favorite movie is* Polar Express. *She lives with
her mom and dad and has a sister who attends university.
She plans to travel after high school and visit the
crocodile zoo. She is also the number one female
Ping-Pong champion in San Francisco!*

Dear Carmen,

Remember? It was a Friday night in October when we were fourteen years old. Mom, Dad, and Cally were rushing out the door, so we could make it on time for practice. I remember the tension was tight; everyone was so stressed because we were late. When we made it to South San Francisco, we rushed into the gym. Practice had already started.

Cally and I quickly put on our shoes and tried to catch up with our teammates who were doing footwork. With no warm up or stretching, I went on the court raw, cold, stiff, and tried to catch up with them. I shuffled toward the back of the court and jumped up. My ankle twisted and I landed on the side of my foot. When my ankle touched the cold ground, the pain was instant and it spread. I knew that was it. My badminton career would never be the same.

Sitting on the ground, holding my ankle, I was bawling too hard to call for help. My voice didn't make a sound. I couldn't feel my left foot.

No one saw me on the ground for the first two minutes because my coach was helping other kids. But my mom's friend, Rita, who was sitting on the empty bench, noticed me and ran over to my rescue.

"What happened? Are you okay?" She asked.

"I hurt my ankle."

When she came over, she attracted the attention of my parents and my coach. My teammates carried me to the bleachers. Everyone asked me how I felt. After much deliberation, I was brought to the nearest hospital. Getting out of the car, I was rolled through the sliding doors in a wheelchair. The lights shone brightly on me. I was in a spotlight. Everyone turned toward me. Yikes!

About twenty people tried to diagnose my situation just from looking at me. They saw a little girl just five feet tall in a wheelchair, crying, wearing shorts with T-shirt, grabbing onto her ankle. Her whole face was red. Rolling past the people, I felt like I was a new exhibit at the zoo. My mom had parked me next to her at the receptionist's desk, while she tried to get a room right away.

Within five minutes, a nurse called, "Carmen? Are you here?"

"Right here," I replied while raising my hand as discreetly as possible.

"Your room is ready for you; follow me," said the nurse.

I was placed in a room right in front of the door. How wonderful! I already hated being in the hospital and having all the people in the waiting room stare at me. Everyone who walked past the door could see me first.

My mom and I waited for about two hours until the doctor came. Off we went, to the x-ray/MRI room. It was a long night. I fell asleep and the rest of my x-ray experience was a blur. The next thing I knew, I woke up back in the hospital room. My mom informed me I had a very bad sprain and would be out of practice for six weeks. The doctor came back to teach me how to use crutches.

Being stuck at home and missing practice seemed like a curse for the first two weeks. Badminton was a sport I never had the intention to play or train for. The standards for badminton are being tall, and physically fit with a passion for the sport, but I was short my whole life, with no stamina, and no commitment.

However, since I came from a serious badminton family, I had no choice. My mother was a national competitor in Macau, where she was born. My father was born in Vietnam, where he was a competitor for the junior team and played tournaments internationally. They introduced me to the sport.

I started playing with my sister and parents at the age of five. I started to train with a real coach at nine and began to compete at age eleven. Badminton had been a major part of my life, but I never considered it to be a good thing. My parents had signed me up for practice, but personally, I hated the sport. I hated how it took up all my time away from my school friends and family parties. I hated the physical pain that came along with practice, being sore and muscles cramping up.

Ever since I was twelve years old, I constantly asked to quit badminton. Even though my parents said no, I felt like something else was preventing me from quitting badminton.

A couples of weeks into my injury, I realized the sport I once hated became something I missed. I wanted to give it another chance. During my injury, my sister still had training so I had to come along. When I was there watching my teammates and sister train, there was this strange feeling that I never correlated with badminton. Was it jealousy from not being able to play? Or regretting not putting in as much effort as I should've? Or could it have been that I missed being part of a team and all the traveling during competitions? It was all of the above.

The first day I went back to the courts, that familiar smell of sweat and warehouse came rushing back. Those feelings I had during my injury vanished. The clock hit 2:00. Practice time. Although I was excited to play, I was reluctant to start over—basic drills, that wouldn't hurt my ankle and wouldn't require me to move too much. Practice felt boring but this just pushed me to heal faster so I would be able to get back into the swing of things. As days went by, I was getting better and better. This competitive spirit took off, and the next step for my badminton career was to switch gyms and coaches.

My new badminton gym, Synergy Badminton Academy, was located in Menlo Park. The gym had a completely different vibe compared to my old gym. The coaches were Olympians, and they knew what it took to get to the top. Their expectations were high, and it took a while for me to adjust.

What made this gym different was the advice my coaches gave me. During one of the matches when I was struggling, my coach said to me, "Do this for yourself. Make yourself proud of your achievements."

I worked hard for two years through forty tournaments and eventually my points added up. Now I am ranked number one in the country at age sixteen.

Looking back, I realize I have missed out on a lot of my childhood experiences, but there was a reason for it. When I was younger I didn't understand that the attitude I had toward badminton could slow my progress of getting better. If I could rewind time, I would tell myself, "Badminton is in your life forever. Don't focus on the negative experiences, but create positive experiences to make it more enjoyable." Before, I was practicing for my parents to make them proud of me, but ever since I grew up and moved to the new gym, I was training hard for myself.

It took six years to finally hop over that hurdle, to finally realize badminton isn't a curse, but a blessing. I learned to enjoy it for myself and make the best of it. We have learned a lot about ourselves and how to turn a curse into a blessing.

Sincerely,
Carmen

THE RED CAR

RUTHMAE R.

was born at St. Luke's Hospital in San Francisco, California.
She is eighteen years old. She likes to sing and play volleyball.
She hopes to be a preschool teacher someday.

It was a cold, stormy night and my parents were at work. My brother was out with his friends. This was my first time being home alone. I was excited but also scared because I have always felt like someone is watching me and that they might pop out. Despite being scared, I like to watch suspenseful movies. I decided to watch *Taken* and throughout the movie I was at the edge of my seat. I couldn't sit still. I was picturing myself as the daughter and getting frustrated by her decisions because I would've done things differently.

I was getting anxious and I started to feel scared that someone was inside the house. I turned on all the lights, went to my room and locked the door, and hid myself in my warm, comfortable pink blanket. Silence. *Ding!* I jumped out of my bed and fell on the floor. I saw that I got a text from a blocked number.

"I'm watching you. . . ," it said. I immediately called my mom and we had a long conversation because I didn't want to feel alone.

"I'll be home in ten minutes," she said. I let out a huge breath knowing my mom would be home soon.

The next day at school I was looking around the crowded hallways, wondering who would've sent that text. I was suspicious of one of my closest friends, Emily, because she would always scare me. All of my friends know that I get scared so easily because I jump at the smallest things. As I was talking to Emily at the end of the day about the text I received, my other friend Dylan came up behind me and yelled, causing me to scream. I punched him in the arm. Everyone stopped and looked my way and I could feel the heat rush to my face. I turned to my friends and said, "Shut up! I don't have time for you guys, I have to go to work!"

As I was walking to work, I went to the back and out of nowhere my manager popped out. I screamed so loud that the customers jumped and one of them spilled their smoothie. My manager started dying of laughter and she had tears in her eyes. I spent the rest of my shift wondering who would've sent that text.

As I was on my way home, I was regretting not asking for a ride home from my brother. It was unusually dark because of daylight savings. The streets were narrow and I saw a family of raccoons scurrying across the street, their eyes glowing. I heard cars passing by, but there was one that was moving slowly right next me, like it was following me.

I started to walk faster and I looked to the left at the red beat-up car and there were two older Latino guys staring directly at me. One of them yelled, "Hey!" I looked away and just ignored them and kept walking. I sped up more and they kept trying to talk to me. They were saying inappropriate things. I looked at my surroundings: it was empty and dark. No one was around besides the car. I tried to call my parents and brother, but no one was answering. I was getting more nervous and I looked at the car again. They had their windows pulled down and they had their heads out and they were still trying to talk to me. One of the guys was about to get out of the car. They would not leave me alone and I felt so uncomfortable. My hands were shaking because I was scared that they might come up to me. My phone dropped. I picked it up and kept walking and in my head, I kept telling myself, *just three more blocks.*

The guys in the car were still beside me, slowly following me, still catcalling, and I was almost by my house. I just had to walk one more block. I could see my friendly neighbor across the street. He noticed the situation I was in and yelled, "Hey!" and he started to make conversation. I felt relieved that he saw me because once the guys in the red car saw my neighbor, they drove away. After my conversation with my friendly neighbor across the street, I went inside the house.

As I was walked in I could hear pots and pans. I could smell my mom's cooking while my dad was chopping some vegetables. I told them about what just happened. They both were worried and they were giving me advice like pretending to be on the phone, not talking to the strangers, and they wanted to buy me some pepper spray to carry so I could feel safer. The next day after school I went home and my mom told me that she talked with the neighbor and that he told her that he would look out for me. I felt safer that I knew somewhere in my neighborhood, someone was looking out for me. Later on, that day my brother admitted that he was the one that sent the creepy text. He was laughing at me because I was so paranoid about it so, I punched him.

SPARK
OF
COURAGE

◆

A Guide for Educators

A NOTE FROM OUR PROGRAM LEADERS

———◆———

By Ryan Young, 826 Valencia Program Manager, and
Eric Chow, Phillip and Sala Burton High School Teacher

𝔄s with most great things, the writing in this book developed from a simple idea. Eric Chow's seniors at Phillip and Sala Burton High School were about to embark on a journey through Mary Shelley's *Frankenstein*—learning about the romantic period, analyzing the gothic classic, and picking apart the themes therein—when we first sat down to meet. Mr. Chow had taught the novel for years, and in the past, his students explored it as critical readers through a number of critical lenses. In class, students grappled with important questions related to the themes of knowledge, creation, monsters, and nature vs. nurture. Students would engage in inquiry-based student discussions, or Socratic seminars; discuss the unique structure of the narrative and explore themes that Mary Shelley's novel commented on such as the hubris of man, xenophobia and bigotry, and representations of women.

But this time, we wondered, *how could we take things a step further?* Why not take some of these themes and have students write reflective pieces, thinking deeply about how they can relate to their own lives and experiences? Why not offer the opportunity of rewriting stories in ways that offer redemption? Why not give students the space to create their own worlds and write creatively?

By taking this approach, students were able to have choice, to step out of their comfort zones, and to extend their thinking. The culmination of this unit—the students' writing—represents a synthesis of themes across time and genre: past and present, fictional and personal.

THEME QUESTIONS

Students considered the following questions as they read *Frankenstein*.

KNOWLEDGE

Does the quest for knowledge (science, discovery, philosophy) lead to sorrow?

Why do people devote their lives to the pursuit of knowledge or search for the unknown?

What kinds of knowledge should be left unknown/undiscovered?

CREATION

What does it mean to be a creator? To be the created?

What are the responsibilities of each? What happens if those responsibilities are not met?

How much does the created one owe his or her creator?

MONSTERS

How does society react to monsters?

Does Shelley's monster show us what she and the Romantics feared?

Are there some universal qualities to monsters? (Are there basic fears that all humans share?)

How have our monsters changed since Shelley's time?

NATURE VS. NURTURE

Are human beings born good, evil, or a mixture of both?

How much of our behavior is due to our environment and how much is due to heredity?

Does society cause social deviance or would some people commit crimes even if they lived in a Utopia?

ESSAY PROMPTS

MISUNDERSTOOD MONSTERS: Write a personal narrative about a time when you were misunderstood or judged. Use techniques such as dialogue, pacing, description, reflection, and multiple plot lines to develop experiences, events and/or characters.

Guiding questions:

How do you see yourself? How do you wish to be seen?

How are you different inside than you appear to be on the surface?

How are stereotypes about your race, ethnicity, culture, gender, sexuality, religion, etc, different from how you really are, or how your culture really is?

How does this experience of being misunderstood inform who you are in the world?

FEARS AND HORRORS: Write a personal narrative about a fear you are working to overcome. Use techniques such as dialogue, pacing, description, reflection, and multiple plot lines to develop experiences, events and/or characters.

Guiding questions:

What is your fear? What is your relationship to your fear? How did the fear first develop? What steps did you take to overcome the fear? What changed in your life? What is the central conflict of your story? What series of events build toward a climax? What is the resolution?

A SCIENCE EXPERIMENT GONE WRONG: Write a fictional narrative about a scenario in the future where the growth of science and/or technology have unintended consequences. Use a variety of techniques to sequence events so that they build on one another to create a coherent whole and build toward a particular tone and outcome (e.g., a sense of mystery, suspense, growth, or resolution).

Guiding questions:

What aspects of science and/or technology are you curious about? Why?

Should we fear the power of science and/or technology? Why or why not?

When can the pursuit of knowledge become dangerous?

What responsibility do scientists have in relation to their creation/research? What responsibility do inventors have in relation to their technology?

REWRITING THE STORY: Pick a moment when things went wrong, a mistake was made, or someone did something they regret. Write a letter where you tell someone what they should do and/or what you want them to know with the perspective you have now. Use precise words and phrases, telling details, and sensory language to convey a vivid picture of the experiences, events, setting, and/or characters.

Guiding questions:

Identify your moment. Who are you writing to? Is it your past self, or someone else? What were you thinking before, during, and after the action took place? How did feelings change at each stage?

Do you assign blame to someone or something? Can you say who is at fault, or is it harder to determine?

How will your letter make things more right/just? Will the outcome of your letter be more right/just for one person than another?

How does someone's perspective impact his/her thoughts on whether something was a mistake/regret, or not?

INTERACTIVE ACTIVITIES TO PAIR WITH
WE ARE HERE, WALKING TOWARD THE UNKNOWN

MAKING CONNECTIONS: Choose a narrative to read together as a class. As they read, students will actively annotate the text with connections to themselves, other texts, and the world. What does this narrative remind you of? Can you relate to the narrator? What images come to mind as you read? How is it similar to other stories you have read, heard, or watched? What local and global issues are raised? How does the narrative connect to history, current events, and the future? Start with modeling and guided practice of the strategy, and then transition to independent work. Student responses can then be synthesized in a discussion or through writing.

SOCRATIC DIALOGUE: Read one of the following narratives together as a class and use that as a springboard to explore the theme questions listed above. Have students then identify textual evidence to support their stance on the selected theme question to prepare for the discussion. The dialogue can occur between a pair of students, as a fishbowl, or you can split the class to present and defend opposing views. The teacher or students can act as facilitators. Establish norms for participation. Consider the following open-ended questions to start, or create your own that are specific to the text: What is the narrative saying about the selected theme? How does the narrative's outcome support your claim? How could the chain of events have played out differently? What are other points of view? **Pair with:** *Lifeless, Geno-Mare, The Bluebird, Logs of Dock Torr, The Material Men, John Doe, The Child with the Power, Wish, Selhani, Human Sensation, The Child, Scientist's Regret, Not Again, Heaven, Toxicity Now, Karma, Hope, The Earths, Prosthetic, The Switch, Blue Eyes, Solitario, Spectrum.*

DRAMATIZE IT: Assign a group of students to a scene or scenes, and ask them to write a play based on the narrative. Ask students to create additional text, like character and scene descriptions, stage directions, and design. Invite students to act out their plays, or film their dramatization and share it with others.

WRITE WHAT HAPPENS NEXT: Starting with a piece of writing that ends unresolved, allow students to adopt and extend the narrative. Invite them to pick up where the author left off, and write what might happen next, based on what they know about the characters and plot. Students are welcome to write multiple possible endings, and reflect on the strengths and limitations of each.

CREATE A GRAPHIC REPRESENTATION: Incorporating a visual element is helpful to both plan and process. In developing the pieces in this book, many students utilized plot maps in order to flesh out their ideas and to stay on track. For this activity, have students choose a narrative to interpret visually—in graphic novel form, via photography, or through another visual medium—in order to see the piece from a fresh perspective and bring it to life in a new way.

FORCED CHOICE: Place a sign in each corner of the room: strongly disagree, somewhat disagree, somewhat agree, strongly agree. Read the following statements aloud and direct students to move to the corner representing their opinion about the statement. "I can't get anywhere in life without my computer." (from *The Day the Internet Went Black*). "I feel like I'm living in a city that is forcing me to change." (from *Forced to Change*). "We should not be limiting kids to what they can and cannot do. We should be teaching them they can do whatever they desire." (from *That's Not for Girls*). "I honestly couldn't care less of what people think of me." (from *Misunderstood Teen*). "When you have experienced your fear, it won't be as bad as you think." (from *The Biggest Fear Is Fear Itself*). "Not all cops are bad." (from *Extremely Uncomfortable*). "As human beings, there is always room for growth through trial and error. But here and there, moments of regret are ubiquitous." (from *The Silver Lining*). Call on students with different views to explain their stance. Students will then select a statement that they had a strong reaction to (positive or negative) and read the narrative it came from. As an extension, students can write a note to the author. What is your reaction? Why? What is or isn't effective about their narrative? What questions do you have?

CONTENT STANDARDS

This project-based unit was designed to address a broad array of standards in English Language Arts. The following are key standards:

READING

CCSS.ELA-LITERACY.RL.11-12.1: Cite strong and thorough textual evidence to support analysis of what the text says explicitly as well as inferences drawn from the text, including determining where the text leaves matters uncertain.

CCSS.ELA-LITERACY.RL.11-12.2: Determine two or more themes or central ideas of a text and analyze their development over the course of the text, including how they interact and build on one another to produce a complex account; provide an objective summary of the text.

CCSS.ELA-LITERACY.RL.11-12.3: Analyze the impact of the author's choices regarding how to develop and relate elements of a story or drama (e.g., where a story is set, how the action is ordered, how the characters are introduced and developed).

CCSS.ELA-LITERACY.RL.11-12.4: Determine the meaning of words and phrases as they are used in the text, including figurative and connotative meanings; analyze the impact of specific word choices on meaning and tone, including words with multiple meanings or language that is particularly fresh, engaging, or beautiful. (Include Shakespeare as well as other authors.)

CCSS.ELA-LITERACY.RL.11-12.5: Analyze how an author's choices concerning how to structure specific parts of a text (e.g., the choice of where to begin or end a story, the choice to provide a comedic or tragic resolution) contribute to its overall structure and meaning as well as its aesthetic impact.

CCSS.ELA-LITERACY.RL.11-12.6: Analyze a case in which grasping a point of view requires distinguishing what is directly stated in a text from what is really meant (e.g., satire, sarcasm, irony, or understatement).

WRITING

CCSS.ELA-LITERACY.W.11-12.3: Write narratives to develop real or imagined experiences or events using effective technique, well-chosen details, and well-structured event sequences.

CCSS.ELA-LITERACY.W.11-12.4: Produce clear and coherent writing in which the development, organization, and style are appropriate to task, purpose, and audience. (Grade-specific expectations for writing types are defined in standards 1-3 above.)

CCSS.ELA-LITERACY.W.11-12.5: Develop and strengthen writing as needed by planning, revising, editing, rewriting, or trying a new approach, focusing on addressing what is most significant for a specific purpose and audience.

CCSS.ELA-LITERACY.W.11-12.6: Use technology, including the Internet, to produce, publish, and update individual or shared writing products in response to ongoing feedback, including new arguments or information.

CCSS.ELA-LITERACY.W.11-12.10: Write routinely over extended time frames (time for research, reflection, and revision) and shorter time frames (a single sitting or a day or two) for a range of tasks, purposes, and audiences.

SPEAKING AND LISTENING

CCSS.ELA-LITERACY.SL.11-12.1: Initiate and participate effectively in a range of collaborative discussions (one-on-one, in groups, and teacher-led) with diverse partners on grades 11-12 topics, texts, and issues, building on others' ideas and expressing their own clearly and persuasively.

CCSS.ELA-LITERACY.SL.11-12.2: Integrate multiple sources of information presented in diverse formats and media (e.g., visually, quantitatively, orally) in order to make informed decisions and solve problems, evaluating the credibility and accuracy of each source and noting any discrepancies among the data.

CCSS.ELA-LITERACY.SL.11-12.3: Evaluate a speaker's point of view, reasoning, and use of evidence and rhetoric, assessing the stance, premises, links among ideas, word choice, points of emphasis, and tone used.

CCSS.ELA-LITERACY.SL.11-12.4: Present information, findings, and supporting evidence, conveying a clear and distinct perspective, such that listeners can follow the line of reasoning, alternative or opposing perspectives are addressed, and the organization, development, substance, and style are appropriate to purpose, audience, and a range of formal and informal tasks.

MORE BOOKS AND RESOURCES FOR EDUCATORS

826 Valencia produces a variety of publications of student writing. Check out these previous Young Authors' Book Project publications and other resources for educators and writers, all of which are available for sale on our website and at bookstores nationwide.

Walk the Earth in Our Shoes & Plant Some Seeds behind You (2016) is a collection of essays from the ninth- and tenth-grade authors from John O'Connell High School. The students, who participate in an integrated English/Language Arts and Science class, answered many questions, such as *What would we learn if we could interview a whale? Is diversity as advantageous in a social community as it is in a coral reef?* and *How does our environment affect us, and how do we affect our environment?* These young authors share their views and experiences as they investigate the way ecosystems work—and their answers hold insights everyone should read.

If the World Only Knew: What Fifty-Five Young Authors Believe (2015) contains reflections from ninth graders at Mission High School on their beliefs and where they came from—the people who imparted them, the times when they are most necessary, and the ways in which the world has tested them. It speaks to the power of personal conviction, and why young peoples' voices should be both heard and believed. With a foreword by Glynn Washington, host of *Snap Judgment*.

Uncharted Places: An Atlas of Being Here (2014) is a collection of stories about place: searching for one's place in the world, places of origin, places of comfort. Be it metaphorical or explicit, these young men and women write about places that make them feel safe, that make them feel whole. They write about wishing to be seen for who they are, for more than who they are. They write about the pain of not being heard, and the triumph of finding their voice. With a foreword by Rabih Alameddine.

The Enter Question (2013) is a collection of essays about, in the words of the 11th grade authors from San Francisco International High School, "What it is like to start over in a new place." SFIHS is a high school specially designed for students who have recently immigrated to the United States, and the essays in *The Enter Question* cover a wide variety of topics including the challenges of communicating in a new language, the courage it takes to ask for help, and the joy in meeting new people from all over the world.

Arrive, Breathe, and Be Still (2012) is a collection of monologues and plays exploring the themes of resistance and resilience written by thirty-five students at Downtown High School in San Francisco, with a foreword by playwright Octavio Solis. After a semester of working intensely with actors at American Conservatory Theater and writing tutors from 826 Valencia, the students produced this powerful look into the realities of high school life, the pressures surrounding young people, and the strength it takes to keep going.

Beyond: Stolen Flames, Forbidden Fruit, and Telephone Booths (2011) is a collection of essays and short stories, written by fifty-three juniors and seniors at June Jordan School for Equity, in which young writers explore the role of myth in our world today. Students wrote pieces of fiction and nonfiction, retelling old myths, creating new ones, celebrating everyday heroes, and recognizing the tales that their families have told over and over. With a foreword by Khaled Hosseini, the result is a collection with a powerful message about the stories that have shaped students' perspectives and the world they know.

A Time to Eat Cake (2011) is a collection of short pieces from the students in 826 Valencia's after-school tutoring program. In collaboration with San Francisco pastry shop Miette, students spent a month exploring memories, imagining their ideal treats, and spinning amazing tales of cake adventures. With a foreword by Miette founder Meg Ray, this book shows that you don't have to be Proust to know the power of sweets.

We the Dreamers (2010) is a collection of essays by fifty-one juniors at John O'Connell High School reflecting on what the American Dream means to them. The students recount stories about family, home, immigration, hardship, and the hopes of their generation—as well as those of the generation that raised them. The result is a firsthand account of these essayists' often-complicated relationship with our national ethos that is insightful, impassioned, surprising, and of utmost importance to our understanding of what the American Dream means for their generation.

Show of Hands (2009) is a collection of stories and essays written by fifty-four juniors and seniors at Mission High School. It amplifies the students' voices as they reflect on one of humanity's most revered guides for moral behavior: the Golden Rule, which tells us that we should act toward others as we would want them to act toward us. Whether speaking about global issues, street violence, or the way to behave among friends and family, the voices of these young essayists are brilliant, thoughtful, and, most of all, urgent.

Thanks, and Have Fun Running the Country (2009) is a collection of letters penned by our after-school tutoring students to newly elected President Obama. In this collection, which arrived at inauguration time, there's loads of advice for the president, often hilarious, sometimes heartfelt, and occasionally downright practical. The letters have been featured in *The New York Times*, *The San Francisco Chronicle*, and on *This American Life*.

Seeing through the Fog (2008) is a guidebook written by seniors from Gateway High School that explores San Francisco from tourist, local, and personal perspectives. Both whimsical and factually accurate, the pieces in this collection take the reader to the places that teenagers know best, from *taquerias* to skate spots to fashionable shops that won't break your budget.

Exactly (2007) is a hardbound book of colorful stories for children ages nine to eleven. This collection of fifty-six narratives by students at Raoul Wallenberg Traditional High School is illustrated by forty-three professional artists. It passes on lessons that teenagers want the next generation to know.

Home Wasn't Built in a Day (2006) is a collection of short stories based on family myths and legends by students at Galileo Academy of Science and Technology. With a foreword by actor and comedian Robin Williams, the book comes alive through powerful student voices that explore just what it is that makes a house a home.

I Might Get Somewhere: Oral Histories of Immigration and Migration (2005) exhibits an array of student-recorded oral narratives about moving to San Francisco from other parts of the United States and all over the world. Acclaimed author Amy Tan wrote the foreword to this compelling collection of personal stories by Balboa High School students. All these narratives shed light on the problems and pleasures of finding one's life in new surroundings.

Don't Forget to Write (2005) contains fifty-four of the best lesson plans used in workshops taught at 826 Valencia, 826NYC, and 826LA, giving away all of our secrets for making writing fun. Each lesson plan was written by its original workshop teacher, including Jonathan Ames, Aimee Bender, Dave Eggers, Erika Lopez, Julie Orringer, Jon Scieszka, Sarah Vowell, and many others. If you are a parent or a teacher, this book is meant to make your life easier, as it contains enthralling and effective ideas to get your students writing. It can also be used as a resource for the aspiring writer. In 2011, 826 National published a two-volume second edition of *Don't Forget to Write*, also available in our Pirate Supply Store.

Waiting to Be Heard: Youth Speak Out about Inheriting a Violent World (2004) addresses violence and peace on a personal, local, and global scale. Written by thirty-nine students at Thurgood Marshall Academic High School and with a foreword by Isabel Allende, the book combines essays, fiction, poetry, and experimental writing to create a passionate collection of student expression.

Talking Back: What Students Know about Teaching (2003) is a book that delivers the voices of the class of 2004 from Leadership High School. In reading the book—previously a required-reading textbook at San Francisco State University and Mills College—you will understand the relationships students want with their teachers, how students view classroom life, and how the world affects students.

ACKNOWLEDGEMENTS

———◆———

A THANK YOU LETTER
FROM THE EDITOR

The Young Authors' Book Project (YABP) is an annual labor of love that relies heavily on the generosity and dedication of an incredible number of people. This year was no exception. Our 2017 YABP by the numbers: one school, five weeks, ten sessions, four editorial board meetings, a record sixty volunteers, eighty students, and countless hours of editing, book design, and illustration. It's been a whirlwind and we are deeply grateful for all of the support.

We'd first like to thank the school community at Phillip and Sala Burton High School for being such a welcoming and inclusive collaborator for this project. We'd especially like to thank Burton High Principal Samuel Bass for welcoming 826 Valencia and other great resources for students into their school. Thank you also to the staff, administrators, and students who make Burton such a great place to be.

We are honored to have worked with an incredible partner teacher on this project, Eric Chow. Mr. Chow is an outstanding educator in every way; he knows his students well and celebrates them as he pushes them to succeed, works tirelessly to ensure that everyone has access to the greatest support and most authentic opportunities possible, and inspires confidence and enthusiasm amongst all who set foot in his classroom. For these reasons and more, Mr. Chow was a dream collaborator for this project. We look forward to seeing the many ways in which his students will carry the skills and confidence they've gained in his classes with them as they move through the world.

A small group of students and volunteer tutors took their dedication to this book above and beyond by continuing to manually copyedit each of the narratives collected here, and to develop the editorial direction for the book. The editorial board showed great professionalism and growth over the course of this process. In just four weeks, these students went from authors to co-editors, and in doing so they gained confidence in their writing skills and became empowered to make the big decisions that made this book a reality. Their hard work shines on these pages. As such, we'd like to extend a special thanks to students Trevor S., Derrick W., and Holly Y., and volunteers Courtney Aldor, Randie Bencannan, Tehan Carey, Megan Cliff, Emily Downey, Lucie Duffort, Shanika Badoya-Mulkerin, Jake Murphy, Sean Nishi, David Rosen, Karen Sabine, and Kaci Vargas.

Enormous thanks to Laura Bagnato, the designer of this book, for honoring the young authors' words by giving them such a beautiful home! We owe so much to Matt Leunig, our brilliant illustrator who brought the cover and icon art to life. To Meghan Ryan, our Design Director, and Amy Popovich, our Production Manager, thank you both for your invaluable work on this publication, for amplifying the students' voices with your design expertise and for keeping us all on deadline. Huge thanks to Helaine Lasky Schweitzer, our copy editor whose super-human eyes catch every single extra space and misplaced comma, for lending your time to helping our young authors' words shine, and to our production artist Terri Bogaards for your meticulous attention to detail.

Finally, we are so proud of the young writers collected here. Writers, for sharing your unique and poignant perspectives with us, for your courage in offering your stories and voices to the world, and for never giving up on the writing process, we commend and profoundly thank you.

Ryan Young
826 Valencia Programs Manager

SUPPORTERS

We couldn't do this work without all of our donors, including our 2015–16 Shipmates Society leadership supporters, whose generosity makes this annual project possible.

CAPTAIN

826 National
Anonymous (4)
Kirsten & Michael Beckwith
Art Berliner & Marian Lever
The Brin Wojcicki Foundation
City Arts & Lectures
Dolby Laboratories
Lee & Russ Flynn, Teachers Housing
    Cooperative
GGS Foundation
Horace W. Goldsmith Foundation
Google.org
Walter & Elise Haas Fund
Daniel Handler & Lisa Brown
Hellman Foundation
Frances Hellman & Warren Breslau
The Kimball Foundation
Kochi Foundation
Lampert/Byrd Family Fund
Levi Strauss & Co.
Coltrane & Christopher Lord
Maverick Capital Foundation
Matt Middlebrook & Lisa Presta
Mosser Companies, Inc.
Panta Rhea Foundation
Dave & Gina Pell
Pincus Family Fund of Silicon Valley
    Community Foundation
Arthur & Toni Rembe Rock
Saint Francis Foundation

San Francisco Arts Commission
San Francisco Department of Children,
    Youth, and Their Families
Tom Savignano
Severns Family Foundation
Brad & Ali Singer
Michael & Shauna Stark
Andrew Strickman & Michal Ettinger
Laurie & Jeff Ubben
Advisors of the Walnut Fund

FIRST MATE

50 Fund
The Isabel Allende Foundation
The Amster Family Fund
Anonymous (3)
AT&T Foundation
John Baldessari Family Foundation
Joya Banerjee & Harris Cohen
Burnett Fund
CISCO Systems Foundation
Cleo Foundation
The Comis Foundation
craigslist Charitable Fund
Rose and David Dortort Foundation
ExCEL After School Programs
Fleishhacker Foundation
The Futures Project
The Hosono/Axelrod Family & Sundri Alim
Vy & Matthew Hyman
Kimberly & Zachary Hyman

Philip Jackson
Diana Kapp & David Singer
David L. Klein, Jr. Fund
Stanley S. Langendorf Foundation
George C. Lee
Jim & Tricia Lesser
Michael Moritz & Harriet Heyman
The Bernard Osher Foundation
Remick Family Foundation
Robin Renfrew & family in honor of
    Taylor Renfrew Ingham
Sakana Foundation
Santel McGinnis Family Charitable Fund
Scandling Family Foundation
Cameron Schrier Family Fund
Stanford Center on Philanthropy and
    Civil Society
Twitter
Gene & Suzanne Valla
Kyle & Tracy Vogt
Karen & Jim Wagstaffe
The Walther Foundation

SHIP'S MASTER
Anonymous
Annikka Berridge
Brickyard Family Fund
Sam & Susie Britton
Arlene Buechert
Sylvia & Barry Bunshoft in honor of
    Jennifer Bunshoft Pergher
The Campodonico Family
Cole Haan
Jill Cowan & Stephen Davis
EMIKA Fund
Abhas Gupta

Jen Hamilton & Seth Boro
Reece Hirsch & Kathy Taylor
June P. Jackson Charitable Fund
Jeri & Jeffrey Johnson
Jordan & Theo Kurland
Alexander M. & June L. Maisin
    Foundation of the Jewish Community
    Federation and Endowment Fund
The Joseph & Mercedes McMicking
    Foundation
Mark Risher & Deborah Yeh
Lee & Perry Smith Fund
TPG Global, LLC
Mike Wilkins & Sheila Duignan
Kevin & Rachel Swain Yeaman

BOATSWAIN
Bill Graham Supporting Foundation of
    the Jewish Community Federation and
    Endowment Fund
The Donald & Carole Chaiken
    Foundation
Nathaniel de Rothschild in honor of
    Zoe Luhtala
John Eidinger
Shepard & Melissa Harris
Hellman & Friedman LLC
Derek G. Howard
Christina Hurvis & Steve Malloy
Melind John
Meg Krehbiel
Lesbians for Good, a fund of the
    Horizons Foundation
Olivia Morgan in honor of
    Nínive Calegari
David & Katy Orr
Delsa & Jay Rendon

Joe Vasquez

Valerie Veronin & Robert Porter

Molly West & Chuck Slaughter

Write & Raise: Hosted by Nicole, Arun, Sarah, Ani, Seif & Andy

Yelp Foundation

HELMSPERSON

Anonymous (2)

Michael S. & Sigrid Anderson-Kwun

Blakely & John Atherton

The Awesome Foundation

Bateman Group

The Baughman Co., Inc.

Meryl & James Bennan

Bien-Kahn Philanthropic Fund

Bluestone Family Fund

Scott & Jacqueline Botterman

Adriene Bowles

Kathy & Greg Calegari

Celia Sack & Omnivore Books on Food

Chambers & Chambers Wine Merchants

Melissa Clarke

Christine Comaford

Con-Volution 2015

Steven & Alexi Conine

The Conway Frankel Family Fund

Coulter 2006 Management Trust on behalf of Natalie J. Guo, Sanjay Banker, Nick Marncini, and Rob Snook

John Couch

David & Carla Crane Philanthropic Fund

David Foster Wallace Literary Trust

Disney VoluntEARS Community Fund

Holly Elfman

Nasseam Elkarra

Arline Epstein & the Quadra Foundation

Francis-Chapman Charitable Fund

Alison & Mark Garrett

Daniel Gelfand & Nicole Avril

Kristin & Jeremy Ginsberg

Andrew & Emma Gray

Green Bicycle Fund

Natalie Guo, Margaret Kirchner, Ashley Rape, & Gloria Herbert on behalf of Baking Event

Joe & Barbara Gurkoff Philanthropic Fund

Hammarskjold Family Fund

Jessica Hemerly & Jonathan Koshi

Paul Herman

Jonn & Max Herschend-Schroder

The Justin and Michelle Hughes Foundation

Kevin Hunt

Hyun Chin Charitable Fund

James Irvine Foundation

Jason Family Foundation

Nate Johnson

Amanda Kelso

Krummel Family Fund

Lisa Laukkanen

Gloria Lenhart

Angus MacLane

Joshua J. Mahoney

John & Lynda Marren

Donna Maynard

Coline McConnel

Paul Menage in honor of Vivienne Pustell

Steven Miller & Jennifer Durand

Amir Najmi & Linda Woo

Jennifer Noland

The Odell/Kemp Fund

Ginger & Dan Oros

Sruti Patel

Zachary Patton & Janel Thysen

PECO Foundation

Andrew & Emily Perito

Matthew Pirkowski

Jessica Powell

Alexandra Quinn & Mark Spoylar
as a gift for Daphne Spoylar

Rabine Family Fund

Marcia Rodgers & Garrett Loube

R. Rolfe

Brooke & David Rusenko

Joan Scott

Will Scullin

Irene S. Scully Fund

Silicon Valley Bank

Lisa Sison as a gift for Alyssa Aninag

The Stephen and Paula Smith Family
Foundation

Squire Patton Boggs in honor of
Nate Lane's retirement

Tamara Mellon Brand, Inc.

William Terrell

Tides Foundation in honor of the work of
Hollie Smiley

Samantha Tripodi in honor of Dan &
Geri Rolandson

Ellen & Rob Valletta

April & Cameron Walters

Warby Parker

Annie Ward

Gina Warren

Dan Welch

Tim Wirth & Anne Stuhldreher

Kirsten Wolfe in honor of Holden &
Dashiel Brown

Steven Nathaniel Wolkoff Foundation

Woodward Family Foundation

Maxine and Jack Zarrow Family
Foundation

SAILOR

Erika & Jordan Alperin

Kimberly Beverett

Robin Bot-Miller

Nicole Boyer

Robert K. Brown

Kim Connor

Michael Duckworth

Isabel Duffy-Pinner & Dickon Pinner

Kopal & Malcolm Goonetileke

Allyson Halpern & Dan Cohen

Marc Henrich

Lisa Kessler

James Kim

Marcia & Lawrence Lusk

Lutes & Abrons Family Fund

Thomas McVey

Sejal Patel & Sanjay Banker

Amber Reed & Dan Newman

Matthew Sonefeldt in honor of Gabe &
Jen Escovar

Mark Thomas

Rachel & Stephen Tracy

VanCheng Fund

Diane Zagerman & Donald Golder

826 VALENCIA

WHO WE ARE
AND WHAT WE DO

PROGRAMS

826 Valencia is a nonprofit organization dedicated to supporting students ages six to eighteen with their creative and expository writing skills and to helping teachers inspire their students to write. Our services are structured around the understanding that great leaps in learning can happen with one-on-one attention and that strong writing skills are fundamental to future success.

826 Valencia comprises two writing centers—our flagship location in the Mission District and a new center in the Tenderloin neighborhood—and three satellite classrooms at nearby schools. Both of our centers are fronted by kid-friendly, weird, and whimsical stores, which serve as portals to learning and gateways for the community. All of our programs are offered free of charge. Since we first opened our doors in 2002, thousands of volunteers have dedicated their time to working with tens of thousands of students.

FIELD TRIPS

Classes from public schools around San Francisco visit our writing centers for a morning of high-energy learning about the craft of storytelling. Four days a week, our Field Trips produce bound, illustrated books and professional-quality podcasts, infusing creativity, collaboration, and the arts into students' regular school day.

IN-SCHOOLS

We bring teams of volunteers into local high-need schools around the city to support teachers and provide assistance to students as they tackle various writing projects, including newspapers, research papers, oral histories, and more. We have a special presence at Buena Vista Horace Mann K–8, Everett Middle School, and Mission High School, where we staff dedicated Writers' Rooms throughout the school year.

AFTER-SCHOOL TUTORING

During the school year, 826 Valencia's centers are packed five days a week with neighborhood students who come in after school and in the evenings for tutoring in all subject areas, with a special emphasis on creative writing and publishing. During the summer, these students participate in our five-week Exploring Words Summer Camp, where we explore science and creative writing through projects, outings, and activities in a super-fun educational environment.

WORKSHOPS

826 Valencia offers workshops designed to foster creativity and strengthen writing skills in a wide variety of areas, from playwriting to personal essays to starting a 'zine. All workshops, from the playful to the practical, are project-based and are taught by experienced, accomplished professionals. Over the summer, our Young Authors Workshop provides an intensive writing experience for teenage students.

COLLEGE AND CAREER READINESS

We offer a roster of programs designed to help students get to college and be successful there. Every year we provide six $15,000 scholarships to college-bound seniors, provide one-on-one support to 200 students via the Great San Francisco Personal Statement Weekend, and partner with ScholarMatch to offer college access workshops to the middle- and high-school students in our tutoring programs. We also offer internships, peer tutoring stipends, and career workshops to our youth leaders.

PUBLISHING

Students in all of 826's programs have the ability to explore, experience, and celebrate themselves as writers in part because of our professional-quality publishing. In addition to the book you're holding, 826 Valencia publishes newspapers, magazines, chapbooks, podcasts, and blogs—all written by students.

TEACHER OF THE MONTH

From the beginning, 826 Valencia's goal has been to support teachers. We aim to both provide the classroom support that helps our hardworking teachers meet the needs of all our students and to celebrate their important work. Every month, we receive letters from students, parents, and educators nominating outstanding teachers for our Teacher of the Month award, which comes with a $1,500 honorarium. Know a SFSUD teacher you want to nominate? Guidelines can be found at *826valencia.org/our-programs/teacher-of-the-month/*

826 VALENCIA STAFF

Bita Nazarian
Executive Director

Alyssa Aninag
Volunteer Coordinator

Dana Belott
Programs Coordinator

Elaina Bruna
Development Coordinator

Bianca Catalan
Programs Associate

Lizzie Jean Coyle
Individual Philanthropy Officer

Ricardo Cruz Chong
Programs Associate

Lauren Hall
Grants and Evaluations Director

Allyson Halpern
Development Director

Caroline Kangas
Stores Manager

Kona Lai
Programs Coordinator

Kiley McLaughlin
Programs and Volunteer Coordinator

Molly Parent
Programs and Communications Manager

Christina Villaseñor Perry
Director of Education

Amy Popovich
Production Manager

Kathleen Rodriguez
Programs Manager

Meghan Ryan
Design Director

Susan de Saint Salvy
Operations Assistant

Anton Timms
Director of Volunteer Engagement

Ashley Varady
Programs Manager

Jillian Wasick
Programs Manager

Byron Weiss
Assistant Store Manager

Ryan Young
Programs Manager

AMERICORPS SUPPORT THROUGH SUMMER 2017

Sophia Cross
Programs Associate

Maggie Dapogny
Development Associate

Shelby Dale DeWeese
Programs Associate

Vera Lopez
Volunteer Associate

Genesis Montalvo
Programs Associate

Hisa Tome
Programs Associate

IT'S ALWAYS A GOOD TIME TO GIVE

WE NEED YOUR HELP

We could not do what we do without the volunteers who make our programs possible. It's easy to become a volunteer and a bunch of fun to actually do it.

Please fill out our online application to let us know you'd like to lend your time:
826valencia.org/get-involved/volunteer

OTHER WAYS TO GIVE

Whether it's loose change or heaps of cash, a donation of any size will help 826 Valencia continue to offer a variety of free writing, tutoring, and publishing programs to Bay Area youth. We would greatly appreciate your financial support.

Please make a donation at:
826valencia.org/get-involved/donate

You can also mail your contribution to:
826 Valencia Street, San Francisco, CA 94110

Your donation is tax-deductible. What a plus! Thank you!

SUBSCRIBE!

The 826 Quarterly Subscription

The 826 Quarterly Subscription delivers brilliant student writing
to your doorstep four times a year.

4 TIMES A YEAR!

Too easy, we know.

FOR ONLY $75, YOU'LL RECEIVE

The Spring Quarterly

Filled with the best student writing from the semester.

Our latest Young Authors' Book Project

The Fall Quarterly

A Surprise Gift

Including some wisdom and whimsy from our students and our store.

TO SUBSCRIBE, PLEASE VISIT

826valencia.org/subscribe